José Maria da Silva Paranhos Júnior

Statement Submitted by the United States of Brazil

to the President of the United States of America as arbitrator, under the provisions

of the treaty concluded September 7, 1889, between Brazil and the Argentine

republic. Vol. 1

José Maria da Silva Paranhos Júnior

Statement Submitted by the United States of Brazil
to the President of the United States of America as arbitrator, under the provisions of the treaty concluded September 7, 1889, between Brazil and the Argentine republic. Vol. 1

ISBN/EAN: 9783337380304

Printed in Europe, USA, Canada, Australia, Japan

Cover: Foto ©ninafisch / pixelio.de

More available books at **www.hansebooks.com**

STATEMENT

SUBMITTED BY THE

UNITED STATES OF BRAZIL

TO THE

PRESIDENT OF THE UNITED STATES OF AMERICA

AS ARBITRATOR

UNDER THE PROVISIONS OF THE TREATY CONCLUDED
SEPTEMBER 7, 1889, BETWEEN BRAZIL AND
THE ARGENTINE REPUBLIC

VOL. I

THE STATEMENT

(ENGLISH TRANSLATION)

NEW YORK

1894

The Knickerbocker Press
New York

BOUNDARY QUESTION

BETWEEN

BRAZIL AND THE ARGENTINE REPUBLIC,

SUBMITTED TO THE DECISION OF PRESIDENT CLEVELAND, OF THE UNITED STATES OF AMERICA, AS ARBITRATOR, 1894.

INTRODUCTORY.

This Statement and appended documents form six Volumes:

I. The Statement translated into English;

II. The original Statement, in Portuguese;

III. Appendix of documents translated into English;

IV. The original texts of documents, in Portuguese or Spanish, translated in Vol. III.;

V. Thirty-four maps preceded by a Notice;

VI. Twenty-nine larger maps.

Three other maps are inserted in this Vol. I.

Each Volume has its special Table of Contents, and at the end of this there is an abridged Table of all the documents in the other Volumes, to facilitate comparison between the original texts and their translation.

Nearly all the fac-similes of maps collected in Volume V. are sections of the larger maps in Volume VI. The list at the end of this Volume I. gives the two different numbers of each map in the two sets.

WASHINGTON, February 8, 1894.

CONTENTS.

VOLUME I.

Introductory   iii

I.

Subject of the controversy	1
The present divisional line	2
Disagreement as to the frontier between the Iguaçú and the Uruguay	2
The boundary defended by Brazil	2
The boundary claimed by the Argentine Republic	2
Boundaries of the contested territory	2
Area. Population.	3
Treaty of Arbitration, September 7, 1889	3
How the frontier shall be constituted according to the Treaty of Arbitration	4

II.

Treaty of Madrid, January 13, 1750	4
1st Demarcation (1759–1760)	5
Treaty of El Pardo, February 12, 1761	5
Treaty of San Ildefonso, October 1, 1777	5
2^d Demarcation (1788–1791)	6
The war of 1801. Peace of Badajoz	7
The Treaty of 1777 void	7
Rules adopted by the Brazilian Government: *uti possidetis* of the period of the Independence and such provisions of the Treaty of 1777 as do not conflict with that *uti possidetis*	7

v

	PAGE
Argentine Independence, 1810	12
Brazilian Independence, 1822	13
The question of the nullity or validity of the Treaty of 1777 is of no practical importance in the present controversy	13
The right of Brazil based upon the colonial *uti possidetis*	13
But Brazil accepts all the historical documents upon which the Argentine Republic seeks to found its claim	14

III.

First line of demarcation agreed upon at Tordesillas (1494). Its location	15
Both the Spaniards and Portuguese overstepped the line of Tordesillas	17
Unfounded accusations	18
How Brazil as it is now was formed	19
Occupation of the left bank of the River Plate by the Portuguese (1680)	21
Disputes and hostilities	21
Treaty of Utrecht (1715)	22
New disputes and hostilities. Armistice of 1737	22

IV.

Portugal and Spain recognize the necessity for a Treaty of Limits	23
Treaty of Madrid, January 13, 1750	23
Natural boundaries and *uti possidetis*. Mutual cessions	24
The divisional line of 1750	32
Between the Uruguay and the Iguaçú	33
Examination of Article V. of the Treaty	33
The Pepiry was already the boundary of Brazil since the XVIIth century	37
The Seven Oriental Missions	39

CONTENTS. vii

PAGE

The manuscript Map of 1749, made in duplicate at Lisbon, and called "Map of the Courts"; the three copies made at Lisbon in 1751, and the three made at Madrid. Declarations written by the Plenipotentiaries on the two originals and on the six copies 40

V.

General Instructions to the Demarcating Commissioners, signed at Madrid, January 17, 1751 . 54
The Commissioners 59
Opposition to the Treaty 60
Insurrection of the Guaranys and war of the Missions. 61
The Joint Commission which made the demarcation in 1759-1760 62
An invention of 1789 63
Transformations through which the invention of 1789 passed 64
The invention of 1789 destroyed by the production of the Special Instruction of July 27, 1758, now found at Simancas 66
One of the documents quoted in support of the Argentine pretension never existed . . . 75
The demarcation of 1759. Ascent of the Uruguay in search of the Pepiry 76
River Mbororé, the limit of the Spanish occupation . 76
River Itacaray, the extreme point of the fluvial journeys of the Guaranys of Misiones . . . 77
Ancient look-out to watch the movements of the Brazilians of S. Paulo 78
The guide Arirapy. His previous journey to the Pepiry 78
Jaboty-Guaçû or Pepiry-Mini 79
Great Falls of the Uruguay 79
River Pepiry or Pequiry 80
Doubts of the Spanish Commissioner . . 80

	PAGE
Journey up the Uruguay to ascertain the positions of the Apitereby and Uruguay-Pitã	81
Rivers Apitereby and Uruguay-Pitã (the second river to which this name was given)	82
Map of the Brazilian-Argentine Joint Commission. Two historical errors to be corrected	83
Signs of the old Brazilian rule	84
Small Falls of Fortaleza	85
Conference of March 7, 1759. Statement made by the 1. Spanish Commissioner	86
All agree that the river pointed out by the guide is the Pepiry of the Treaty. They return to the mouth of the Pepiry	88
Act of identification of the Pepiry (March 8, 1759)	88
Inscription: "R. F. Anno de 1759"	93
Latitude of the mouth of the Pepiry	94
The Longitude could not be determined in 1759. Determination of 1788, of 1887 and 1889	94
Survey of the course of the Pepiry in 1759 by the geographers of Portugal and Spain	95
Affluent Pepiry-Mini	96
The geographers, unable to reach the principal headwater, return	96
Section of the Pepiry explored	98
Section of the Pepiry unexplored	98
The Commissioners determine to come down the Uruguay in accordance with Art. 6 of the Special Instruction	99
Journey to the Paraná	100
Arrival at the Iguaçú	101
Great Falls of the Iguaçú	101
Discovery of the River S. Antonio	102
It is determined to explore the S. Antonio	103
Survey of the S. Antonio	104
Affluent S. Antonio-Mini	104
Supposed source of the Pepiry	105
Source of the S. Antonio	106

CONTENTS. ix

	PAGE
Declaration signed by the Commissioners (January 3, 1760)	107
Report by the Principal Spanish Commissioner	108
Map of 1760, signed April 8, at S. Nicolas de Misiones	109
The Map of 1760, a document of the greatest importance, because it already presents the Pepiry under the name of Pepiry-Guaçû	109
The adjectives *guaçû* and *mirim* or *miní*	110
Maps in which the Pepiry surveyed in 1759 appears under the name of Pepiry-Guaçû, and maps in which it appears under that of Pequiry	110

VI.

Examination of the Argentine allegations against the demarcation of 1759 and 1760	111
An error in the demarcation, but of no importance	112
Extent surveyed in 1759	112
The survey of the source of the Pepiry in 1759 was not indispensable. The essential thing was to survey the mouth of the Pepiri and that of the affluent of the Iguaçû	113
The affluent of the Iguaçû was to be approximately on the meridian of the Pepiry. The S. Antonio satisfies this condition	115
Another Argentine allegation :—characteristic features of the Pepiry	118
A full-flowing river	119
An island in front of the mouth	120
The supposed island in the Map of 1749 is the Great Falls of the Uruguay	121
A reef within or without the mouth	122
The only true information the Commissioners of 1759 had concerning the Pepiry :—the reef and the proximity of the Great Falls	123
The Chapecó (Pequiri-Guazú of the Argentines) is very far from the Great Falls	124

VII.

	PAGE
Examination of maps anterior to that of 1749	124
A declaration of the Argentine Government	124
First Map of Paraguay by the Jesuits of that Province, drawn between the years 1637 and 1641, and presented to the R. F. Vincenzo Caraffa, VIIth General Prefect of the Society of Jesus (1645-1649)	126
This Map cannot benefit either one cause or the other.	127
Maps of Paraguay, by G. Sanson (1668) and by G. De l'Isle (1703). They are not maps of the Jesuits, as has been stated. They in no way favor the Argentine cause	128
Map of Paraguay by Nicolas de Fer	133
Second Map of Paraguay by the Jesuits of that Province, drawn in 1722, presented to R. F. Michelangelo Tamburini, XIVth General Prefect, and engraved in 1726 by J. Petroschi. It is the first map in which the positions of the rivers Pepiry and Uruguay-Pitá of the Jesuits can be examined	133
Edition of Augsburg (1730), engraved by Matthew Scutter	134
Third Map of Paraguay by the Jesuits of that Province, presented to R. F. Franciscus Retz, XVth General Prefect, engraved in 1732 by J. Petroschi	134
Map of Paraguay by d'Anville (1733) made in view of the maps of the Jesuits, and appended to Vol. XXI of the *Lettres Édifiantes*	135
Map of South America by d'Anville (1748)	136
Examination of the maps of 1722, 1732, 1733, and 1748, and refutation of Argentine allegations. All these maps are of Spanish origin	136
In all the maps of Spanish origin anterior to 1749, the Pepiry and the Uruguay-Pitá are below the Great Falls. The Pepiry of the Jesuits was a river in the present Argentine territory of Misiones to the West of the Pequiry or Pepiry of the Paulistas	139

CONTENTS. xi

                                                                 PAGE

F: Lozano's description of the Upper Uruguay (1745).
He also locates the Pepiry and the Uruguay-Pitã
below the Great Falls 140
Examination of the maps of 1733 and 1748 by d'An-
ville, and refutation of Argentine allegations . 144
Conclusions 147
The Brazilian Pequiry or Pepiry in the Map of 1749:—
first river above the Great Falls 148
Examination of the Portuguese Map of 1749, called
" "Map of the Courts" 148
Superpositions made under the direction of M. Emile
Levasseur 148
How the Portuguese Map of 1749 was composed . 149
Praised by Walckenaer 151
Latitude of the upper course of the Uruguay . . 151
Relative positions of the Pepiry and Uruguay-Pitã in
this map. Explanation 152
Transfer of names. The first Uruguay-Pitã, named
Paricay in 1759, afterwards Piray or Cebollaty,
and lately Turvo 153
The Uruguay-Pitã in the "Map of the Courts" is the
first river of that name—that is to say, the Uru-
guay-Pitã of the Jesuits, below the Great Falls
and below the point where the Uruguay, turning
to the South, changes its first direction . . 156
The Treaty of 1750 and the Instructions of 1751 and
1758 do not mention the Uruguay-Pitã . . 157
The Uruguay-Pitã was a river of unknown course . 158
The important point is to ascertain whether the Pequiry or Pepiry of the Map of 1749 was the Pepiry
demarcated in 1759, or whether it is the Chapecó,
the limit of the Argentine pretension . . . 158
Comparison of Latitudes 158
Comparison of Longitudes 160
Distance from the Great Falls 161
Distance from the sea-coast 161
The question is solved as proposed by the Argentine

xii CONTENTS.

PAGE

Memorandum of 1883:—the river of the boundary in the "Map of the Courts" is the Pepiry-Guaçú of the Brazilians, and not the Pequirí-Guazú of the Argentines 161

This is so evident that even the author of the Argentine pamphlet *Misiones* indirectly acknowledged it when he analyzed the Map of Paraguay by Bellin. Demonstration 162

VIII.

Treaty of 1761 annulling that of 1750. Reason of the annulment 166
War of 1762-1763, and Peace of Paris 170
Violation of the Treaty of Peace by the Spaniards . 171
Renewed hostilities in Brazil 171
Negotiations for a Treaty of Limits 172
Spanish Consulting Junta (1776) and Map of South America by Olmedilla given to the Junta for the examination of the boundary question . . . 172
Treaty of San Ildefonso, Oct. 1, 1777 174
Examination of Article 8 of the Treaty . . . 175
Treaties of 1750 and 1777 compared 178
Differences 180
Question of names. Refutation of the Report of 1892 of the Argentine Foreign Office (180-191) . . 180
Official maps giving to the Pepiry since 1760 the names of Pepiry-Guaçú and Pequiry 182
Examination of the Spanish Maps of 1768 and 1770 by Millau, Cosmographer to the King of Spain. . 183
Map of Paraguay by Azara, 1787 184
The most important of the Spanish Maps is that of South America, dated 1775, by Olmedilla, Geographer to the King of Spain, and afterwards Chief Cosmographer of the Kingdom . . . 185
This Map was used by the Spanish Plenipotentiary in the negotiation of the Treaty of 1777 . . . 185

CONTENTS. xiii

	PAGE
Defence of Olmedilla and reply to the pamphlet *Misiones*	186
Olmedilla's Map and the Brazilian cause . . .	190
Olmedilla corrects Millau's mistake concerning the headwaters of the Pepiry	191
The demarcating Commissioners received limited powers	192
Spanish Instructions of 1778 and 1779	193
The Spanish Instructions were drawn up in view of Olmedilla's Map and of the Diary of the Demarcation of 1759	198
Comparison of the Spanish Instructions of 1779 with the Spanish Diary of 1759	198
The Uruguay-Pitã of the Spanish Instructions . .	207
The Commissioners in 1788 mistook the Trigoty or Picada River (now da Varzea) for the Uruguay-Pitã of 1759	208
This error produced another on the occasion of the first journey on the Uruguay in search of the Pepiry-Guaçû (May, 1788)	208
The error was promptly corrected	208
Second journey on the Uruguay (July, August, 1788). Demarcation of the mouth of the true Pepiry-Guaçû of the Treaty, and discovery by the Spaniards of the River Caudaloso, farther to the East (now the Chapecó)	209
Inscriptions set up by the Portuguese and Spaniards at the mouth of the Pepiry-Guaçû . . .	210
The First Spanish Commissioner alleges since 1789 that the River Caudaloso (Chapecó) was the Pepiry or Pequiry of the Treaty of 1750, and that in the demarcation of 1759 there was an error, because the Pepiry should be above the Uruguay-Pitã	210
Surveys made jointly, and the reason why the Portuguese allowed the survey of the River Caudaloso to be made. Oyárvide discovers the sources of a river which he names S. Antonio Guazú . .	211

	PAGE
The Spanish Instructions disregarded	213
The Spanish Government never took into consideration the change of the boundary line proposed by its Commissioners	214

IX.

The contested territory was never a part of Misiones	215
Missions of the Spanish Jesuits in the XVIIth century. Province of Guayra	215
Conquest of Guayra by the Paulistas (1630–1633)	217
Missions of the Spanish Jesuits to the East of the Uruguay, in Rio Grande do Sul	219
Conquest of Rio Grande do Sul by the Paulistas (1636–1638)	219
The Paulistas in the territory now contested	220
Seven new missions established by the Jesuits to the East of the Uruguay (1687–1706)	225
Limits of the Spanish occupation on the Uruguay and Paraná	225
The Spaniards and their Jesuit Missionaries never occupied the territory now contested	229
Cabeza de Vaca was not the discoverer of the territory now contested, and never saw it	230
The territory now contested was discovered by the Brazilians	234

X.

First negotiation for a Treaty of Limits, on the initiative of the Brazilian Government	234
Treaty of December 14, 1857	235
Approved by the Argentine Congress	236
Why the ratifications were not exchanged	238
Importance of the Treaty of 1857, although it did not become effective	240

Examination of the law of the Argentine Congress
approving the Treaty of 1857 241
Alliance between Brazil and the Argentine Republic
against the Dictator of Paraguay. The Paraguayan War ended 1870 245
Evacuation of the territory of Misiones by the Paraguayans 245
Treaty of Limits between the Argentine Republic and
Paraguay (1876). The territory of Misiones between the Uruguay and Paraná definitively belonging to the Argentine Republic . . . 246
To this Brazil contributed 246
Second negotiation for a Treaty of Limits with the
Argentine Republic, initiated by Brazil . . 247
Without result 251
The Argentine pretension to the Brazilian territory of
Palmas manifested for the first time in 1881 . 251
The occupation of the territory of Palmas by the Brazilians since 1836 and 1838. The Argentine Government could not be ignorant of it since 1841,
and for forty years it did not protest against it . 253
Seventy years without a protest against the Brazilian
maps 259
The Argentine official maps admitted the Pepiry-Guaçú and S. Antonio as boundaries of Brazil . 260
Creation of the Argentine Gobernacion of Misiones,
1882 265
Third negotiation initiated by Brazil in 1882 . . 266
Treaty of September 28, 1885, for the survey of the
rivers Pepiry-Guaçú and S. Antonio, the boundary
defended by Brazil, and the Chapecó (Pequiri-Guazú) and Chopim, the boundary of the Argentine claim since 1881 271
The Brazilian-Argentine Joint Commission ascertain
that the Jangada, and not the Chopim, is the S.
Antonio Guazú of Oyárvide 271
This increased the extent of the contested territory . 271

	PAGE
Argentine proposal for the division of the contested territory (1889). Rejected by Brazil	274
Treaty of Arbitration of Sept. 7, 1889 .	275
Brazilian Revolution	275
The Provisional Government of Brazil agrees to the Argentine proposal for the division of the territory of Palmas. Treaty of January 25, 1890	275
Rejected by the Brazilian Congress (August 10, 1891)	276
Recourse to Arbitration, in accordance with the Treaty of 1889 .	276

APPENDIX.

List of Documents in Vols. III. and IV.	279
List of Maps in Vols. I., V., and VI. .	282

ERRATA.

PAGE.	LINE.	ERROR.	CORRECTION.
61	26	contubare	conturbare
131	6	FRANCESCO	FRANCISCUS
133	3 of the note.par.		by
134	6 of the note.1726./Joannes		1722./Joannes
137	7	Great Falls of Uru- guay	Great Falls of the Uruguay
"	"	the affluents of the	the affluents
146	7	Gaucû	Guaçû
"	14	of D'ANVILLE	by D'ANVILLE
163	4 of the note.1892		1893
186	12 of the note. Dictionario		Dicionario
194	3	navigation,	navigation, such as are
211	28	to explore and survey	to survey and draw up the Plan of
"	29	Pepiry-Guaçû	Pepiri-Guazú
242	15	that Treaty	the Treaty
246	23	definitely	definitively
273	26	Report	Memoir
274	18	geometical	geometrical

ADDITIONAL ERRATA.

VOL. I.:

PAGE.	LINE.	ERROR.	CORRECTION.
20	21	Rio Real to the	Rio Real to
125	16	of the XVIth	from the XVIth
"	17	and XVIIth centuries	to the XVIIIth century
148	21	conditions.	additions
154	2nd note	Piray ou	Piray or
161	12	$\frac{1}{2}$	$\frac{2}{3}$
168	4	right bank	left bank
185	1st marginal note	1777	1775
"	2nd marginal note	1775	1777
186	21	BOUGER	BOUGUER
208	1 of the note.witness		witness (in CALVO, X, 92)
225	14	South	South of the Uruguay
229	30 and 31	momenarily	momentarily
244	1	An examination	The examination
250	24	in a letter	in the letter
251	31	2052	2502
259	5	the first of the notice	the first notice of the
265	27	five	four
275	10	1881 and 1889	1889
"	11	The project of 1881	The first project of 1889
"	13	that of 1889	the second project

VOL. III:

69	19	*month*	*mouth*

VOL. V:

Map N.º 5		W. from Ferro I. .E. from Ferro I.

BOUNDARY QUESTION BETWEEN BRAZIL AND THE ARGENTINE REPUBLIC.

STATEMENT OF THE RIGHTS OF BRAZIL.

I.

THE controversy submitted by the United States of Brazil and the Argentine Republic to the arbitration of the President of the United States of America has reference to the dominion over a territory, now in possession of Brazil, between the rivers Iguaçú and Uruguay.[1]

Subject of the controversy.

The present divisional line between the two countries begins, in the North, at the river Paraná, opposite

---

[1] The present boundaries of Brazil and the location of the territory claimed by the Argentine Republic can be studied on three Maps drawn up by the Brazilian Special Mission at Washington, and appended to this Statement.

The title of the first is: "*Brazil, its contested territory, and the bordering countries.*"

The second: "*Map of Southern Brazil.*"

The third: "*Map of the Judicial Division (Comarca) of Palmas in the Brazilian State of Paraná; of the Argentine Government (Gobernacion) of Misiones; and of a part of the Brazilian State of Rio Grande do Sul.*" This Map is Nº 29A, in Vol. VI. In it are given the present and the former names of the rivers of that region.

Two other Maps, drawn on a larger scale, show only the contested territory. One, Nº 25A, is a reduced fac-simile of the Map constructed by the Brazilian-Argentine Joint Commission, which, under the Treaty of 28th September, 1885, surveyed this territory. The other, Nº 26A, is a fac-simile of the authenticated copy of the same Map, drawn by the Argentine Commission.

the confluence of the Iguaçù; it follows the course of the latter from its mouth in the Paraná to the point where it is joined by the Santo Antonio; it then turns to the South, going up-stream by the S. Antonio to its principal headwater; thence it passes from the basin of the Iguaçù to that of the Uruguay, continuing along the highest ground to the principal source of the Pepiry-Guaçù; it then follows in a **Southerly** direction the course of the Pepiry-Guaçù to its confluence with the Uruguay, and afterwards proceeds down this river to the mouth of the Quarahim.

This boundary line is thus composed of three distinct sections: the Iguaçù, the Uruguay, and the line which connects these two rivers, forming the boundary of the intermediate territory.

The Brazilian and Argentine Governments agree as to the two boundary lines of the Iguaçù and the Uruguay, but they disagree touching the definition of the two rivers, which, flowing into them in opposite directions, must definitively constitute the international boundary of the intermediate territory.

Brazil maintains that this boundary must be formed by the Pepiry-Guaçù and the S. Antonio.

The Argentine Republic has claimed, since 1881, two rivers more to the East. Until 1888, they were the Chapecó and the Chopim. In 1888 it transferred its claim from the Chopim to the Jangada.

The contested territory thus came to have the following boundaries: to the North, the Iguaçù; to the South, the Uruguay; to the West, the S. **Boundaries of the contested territory.** Antonio and the Pepiry-Guaçù; and to the East, the Jangada and the Chapecó.

The Argentine Government gives to the

BOUNDARY QUESTION. 3

Chapecó the name of Pequirí-Guazú, and to the Jangada that of San Antonio-Guazú.[1]

This territory forms the greater part of the Comarca (Judicial Division) of Palmas, in the State of Paraná, one of the United States of Brazil, and is bounded on the West by the Argentine territory of Misiones, and on the South by the Brazilian State of Rio Grande do Sul.

The disputed area is more than 30,621 square kilometres, or 11,823 English square miles, or 1,313,6 English square leagues, which equal nearly 1,000 geographical square leagues, or exactly, 991.3.   *Area.*

On December 31, 1890, the date of the last census taken in Brazil, the population of the Comarca of Palmas was 9,601 inhabitants, of whom 9,470 were Brazilians and 131 aliens.   *Population.*

The contested part of the Comarca then had 5,793 inhabitants, 5,763 being Brazilians, and 30 aliens. Among the latter there was not a single Argentine citizen.

The number of urban and rural houses was 1,004.[2]

It was by the Treaty of September 7, 1889, that

---

[1] The names *Pepiry* and *Pequiry* are written indifferently with the termination *y* or *i*.

Guaçú, in the language of the Guarany or Tupy Indians, means great, and *mirim*, or *mirín*, small. The Portuguese wrote *guaçú*, or *guassú*. The Brazilians also spell it either way. The Spaniards and their Argentine descendants write *guazú*. The adjective *mirim*, or *mirín*, so written by the Portuguese and Spaniards from the early times of the conquest until the XVIIIth century, was at last transformed by the Spaniards, Argentines, and Paraguayans into *minin* and *mini*.

Santo Antonio in Portuguese, and *San Antonio* in Spanish, are one and the same name.

[2] Statistical tables containing other information are given at the end of the two volumes of documents (English translation, Vol. III., Portuguese text, Vol. IV.).

Treaty of Arbitration. Brazil and the Argentine Republic agreed to submit their controversies regarding boundaries to the Arbitration of the President of the United States of America.

Article V. of the Treaty is as follows:

"The frontier shall be constituted by the rivers which Brazil or the Argentine Republic have designated, and the Arbitrator shall be invited to pronounce in favor of one or the other of the Parties as he may consider just after due investigation of the reasons and documents produced."

No division of the contested territory.

Thus, in accordance with this provision, Brazil and the Argentine Republic have invited the President of the United States of America as Arbitrator to give his award for one of these two boundary lines:

1) That of the rivers Pepiry-Guaçú and S. Antonio, the present boundary of Brazil; or

2) That of the rivers Jangada (S. Antonio Guazú) and Chapecó (Pequiri-Guazú), the boundary claimed by the Argentine Republic.

II.

The Pepiry-Guaçú was known under the names of Pepiry or Pequiry when Portugal and Spain, by the Treaty of Madrid, of the 13th of January, 1750, determined the limits of their possessions in South America. The affluent of the Iguaçú which was to complete the divisional line in this region, was at that time unnamed.

Treaty of 1750.

Pepiry or Pequiry.

The Portuguese and Spanish Commissioners charged

with the demarcation, fulfilling exactly the instructions they had received, surveyed (1759) the greater part of the course of the Pepiry or Pequiry, and discovered and surveyed the affluent of the Iguaçú which completed the line of demarcation, necessarily a meridian line in this place, since its object was to connect two initial points situated, the one to the South, on the Uruguay, and the other to the North, on the Iguaçú. *1st demarcation.*

The river by means of which the boundary was thus completed they called the S. Antonio, and they declared that they preserved for the Pepiry or Pequiry the first of its former names. *S. Antonio.*

But from 1760 the Pepiry began to appear in the Portuguese maps under that of Pepiry-Guaçú, and in the official Spanish maps now under this name and now under the old name of Pequiry. *Pepiry-Guaçú or Pequiry.*

By the Treaty of El Pardo of the 12th of February, 1761, Portugal and Spain annulled that of 1750, not because they disagreed as to this part of the boundary, but for reasons that will be stated in the proper place. *Treaty of 1761.*

Then came the Preliminary Treaty of San Ildefonso, of the 1st of October, 1777, the last agreement concluded between the Crowns of Portugal and Spain as to the limits of their possessions in South America. *Treaty of 1777.*

In this Treaty, the two affluents of the Uruguay and of the Iguaçú were designated and determined, one by the name of Pepiry-Guaçú or Pequiry, the other by that of S. Antonio under which they appeared in the printed and manuscript maps used in defining the divisional line. The instructions given by the Spanish Government to its Commissioners stated most minutely and clearly that the boundary line was to be traced along the same rivers Pepiry-Guaçù and S. Antonio, as defined by common accord in 1759 and 1760.

2d demarcation.

But in 1788,—eleven years after the Treaty of San Ildefonso,—the Spanish Commissioners discovered on the right bank of the Uruguay, above the confluence of the Pepiry-Guaçù, and, therefore, more to the East and within the Portuguese territory, the mouth of another river, which had already appeared, although without a name, on the maps of the beginning of that century. Then, on the basis of alleged errors of the Commissioners of the previous demarcation, they attempted to carry the boundary, not along the Pepiry-Guaçù and the S. Antonio, as defined in the Treaty of 1777 and in the Instructions of the two Governments, but by the river which they discovered in 1788, and along that which, rising on the opposite slope of the watershed line between the basins of the Uruguay and the Iguaçù, should empty itself into the last named. The sources of the tributary of the Iguaçù, proposed by the Spanish Commissioners as a substitute for the S. Antonio, were not found till 1791,—fourteen years after the conclusion of the Treaty.

River discovered in 1788.

Pretension of Spanish Commissioners.

River discovered in 1791.

The Spanish Commissioners gave the name of Pequiry-Guazú to the river discovered in 1788, and the other, whose head-waters were found in 1791, they called the San Antonio Guazú. The former appeared in the Portuguese and Brazilian maps of the end

Pequiry-Guazú or Chapecó.

S. Antonio Guazú.

of last century and of the beginning of this under the name of Rio Caudaloso, but that of Chapecó, which the Indian natives of that country had given it, prevailed. The course of the second river, which the Spaniards had been unable to survey, was arbitrarily represented by them as following now a northerly, and now a northwesterly direction. Until 1888 the Brazilian and Argentine Governments supposed that this river was the one which is locally known as the Chopim, and flows in the direction of the Northwest, emptying itself into the Iguaçú above the mouth of the Santo Antonio. The survey made in 1888 proved that the head-waters of the S. Antonio Guazú of 1791 form the river Jangada which discharges itself into the Iguaçú much more to the East. Supposed to be the Chopim. The Jangada is the S. Antonio-Guazú.

The demarcation of the extensive boundary line between Brazil and the Spanish possessions was not completed, nor had the two interested Governments solved the doubts raised by their Demarcating Commissioners, when, in 1801, the King of Spain, by the Manifesto dated at Aranjuez, on the 28th February of that year, declared war against the Queen of Portugal, Her Kingdoms and dominions, and immediately afterwards issued instructions to the Spanish Viceroys and Governors in South America to begin hostilities against Brazil. *The War of 1801.*

Thus was violated and broken the Treaty of Amity and Guarantee between the two Crowns of Portugal and Spain, signed at El Pardo on the 11th of March, 1778, and the Preliminary Treaty of Limits of 1777 was broken and annulled, because there was a conquest of territories in America, and the Treaty of Peace concluded at Badajoz on the 6th of *The Treaty of 1777 void.*

June, 1801, did not provide for the *status quo ante bellum* nor restore the Treaty of Limits of 1777.

Portugal retained the territories it had conquered in Rio Grande do Sul, and they were thus definitively incorporated into Brazil.

The nullity or validity of the Treaty of 1777, and the definition of the boundary between the rivers Uruguay and Iguaçú are the two principal questions upon which Brazil and the Argentine Republic disagree in the discussion of their boundaries.

<small>Another point of disagreement.</small>

The Brazilian Government has always maintained that the *uti possidetis* of the period of the independence of the South American nations, and such provisions of the Treaty of 1777 as do not conflict with that *uti possidetis*, are the only bases upon which agreements as to limits between Brazil and the adjoining States of Spanish origin are to be founded.

<small>Rules adopted by the Brazilian Government.</small>

At the conference of the 12th of March, 1856, the Brazilian Minister for Foreign Affairs,[1] in a discussion with the Plenipotentiary of Paraguay, expressed himself as follows:

<small>Declarations in 1856.</small>

"The Imperial Government recognizes, as does that of the Republic (of Paraguay), that the Treaties of Limits concluded between the two mother-countries, Portugal and Spain, are to be considered as broken and of no value, because they were never carried into effect on account of the doubts and embarrassments which arose on both sides pending the demarcation, and in consequence of the wars which broke out between the said mother-countries.

"So that the Treaty of 1750 was revoked by that of

---

[1] Councillor PARANHOS, afterwards VISCOUNT DE RIO-BRANCO.

the 12th February, 1761, and after these conventions came the war of 1762 ended by the Treaty of Paris of 1763, things remaining in the state in which they were before.

"Then followed the Preliminary Treaty of the 1st October, 1777, which had the same fate as that of 1750, which it had in great part ratified. The doubts raised in the demarcation prevented the full effect of this last survey of the frontiers of the two countries; and, finally, the war of 1801 annulled it forever, seeing that the Treaty of Peace signed at Badajoz on the 6th of June of the same year did not restore it, or provide that things should return to the state *ante bellum*.

"But if the Imperial Government concurs upon this point with that of the Republic, it understands also that it is necessary to refer to the provisions of those Treaties, as an auxiliary basis in order to ascertain what constituted Portuguese territory and what Spanish territory, as well as the modifications undergone by the domain of either nation in the course of years and events. In places where one of the two States contests the domain of the other, and the latter is not established by effective occupation, or by material monuments of possession, that auxiliary basis throws light upon the doubt, and may peremptorily remove it.

"To Brazil indisputably belongs the territory which in South America formerly belonged to Portugal, with the losses and acquisitions which occurred after the Treaties of 1750 and 1777; and, reciprocally, to the adjoining States which were colonies of Spain belongs that which formed part of the dominion of this nation, saving the changes indicated by its *uti possidetis.*"[1]

---

[1] *Protocols of the Conferences held in the City of Rio de Janeiro between the Plenipotentiaries of Brazil and the Republic of Paraguay*, pp. 22. (Appended to the Report of the Department for Foreign Affairs of Brazil, 1857.)

The Memorandum delivered by the Brazilian Plenipotentiary on the 26th of November, 1857, to the Argentine Government, began by affirming these very principles:

Declarations in 1857.

"The boundaries between the Empire of Brazil and the adjacent Republics," this document says, "cannot be determined by the Treaties concluded between Portugal and Spain, their ancient mother-countries, unless both the contracting parties are willing to adopt them as a basis for the demarcation of their respective frontiers.

"The conventions by which the two Crowns of Portugal and Spain sought to divide among themselves lands not yet discovered or conquered in America and to define their possessions already established on that continent, never produced the desired effect.

"The doubts and uncertainties of such stipulations, the difficulties arising from one side or the other, and, finally, war, successively nullified all agreements, and established the right of *uti possidetis* as the only title and the only barrier against the encroachments of either nation and of their colonies in South America.

"The last stipulations made and concluded between the two Crowns for the demarcation of their dominions in the New World are those of the Preliminary Treaty of the 1st October, 1777, whose provisions were in great part copied from the Treaty of the 13th January, 1750, which the former was intended to modify and explain.

"The Treaty of 1777 was broken and annulled by the war which supervened in 1801, between Portugal and Spain, and remained so for ever, not having been restored by the Treaty of Peace signed at Badajoz on the 16th June of the same year. Spain kept the fortified town of Olivença, which it had conquered by right of war, and Portugal all the territory belonging to Spain, which, by virtue of the same right, it had occupied in America.

"It is, therefore, incontestable that neither even Spain or Portugal could to-day appeal to the Treaty of 1777, because the principles of International Law would be opposed to any such pretension.

"The Government of His Majesty the Emperor of Brazil, recognizing the absence of any written definition of its borders with the neighboring States, has adopted and proposed as the only reasonable and equitable basis that can be appealed to: the *uti possidetis*, where this exists, and the stipulations of the Treaty of 1777, where they are in conformity with, or do not oppose, the actual possessions of either of the contracting parties.

"These principles are supported by reason and justice and are sanctioned by Universal Public Law. If they be rejected, the only regulating principle would be the convenience and strength of each nation."

The Argentine Government holds that the principle of the colonial *uti possidetis* can only be invoked in the transactions concerning boundaries between the Spanish-American Republics, considering the Treaty of 1777 to be in full vigor, and binding on Brazil and the Argentine Republic.

<small>Argentine Government considers Treaty of 1777 in full force.</small>

This question of 1801 can be decided only in accordance with the principles prevailing at that time, and with the rule uniformly observed in peace negotiations between Portugal and Spain.

<small>Treaties of peace between Portugal and Spain prior to 1810.</small>

An examination of the Treaties of Peace between these two Crowns since the independence of Portugal will show that the express restoration of all conventions *ante bellum*, and most particularly of those relating to limits, was an indispensable condition to their re-acquiring the force they previously possessed. It was for this reason that Article 13 of the Treaty of Utrecht, of February 6, 1715, restored the Treaties of 13th February, 1668, and 18th June, 1701; that Article 2 of the Treaty of Paris, of 10th February, 1763, restored the Treaties of 1668 and 1715, and that of 12th February, 1761; and that Article 1 of the Treaty of San Ildefonso, in 1777, revived the Treaties of 13th February, 1668, 6th February, 1715, and 10th February, 1763, in all that was not incompatible with the provisions of the new Treaty.

In the Treaty of Peace of Badajoz that customary clause was omitted, because both Governments hoped to secure great territorial conquests in South America.[1]

Peace of Badajóz, 1801.

If, in 1801, the Treaty of San Ildefonso ceased to be binding on Portugal and Spain, it could not be binding on Brazil or the Spanish Colonies, which proclaimed themselves independent.

In 1810 the provinces of the Viceroyalty of Rio de la Plata, seceding from the mother-country, dismem-

---

[1] The following passage of a letter written from Buenos-Aires on the 1st of March, 1802, by D. FELIX DE AZARA, Spanish Commissioner for the demarcation of limits, shows the current opinion in Spain and in its possessions at that time:

"On the other hand I doubt whether the Treaty of limits should be the basis of my remarks, because it appears to me that that of 1777, according to which I was charged to make the demarcation, should be held to have been annulled and broken at the time of the declaration of the last war, and I do not know whether, on the conclusion of the present peace, this has been agreed upon in other terms, because I have not seen that Treaty of Peace."

This document is in the Archives of Alcala de Henares, in Spain.

bered themselves. The greater number of them formed as early as 1816 the Republic of the United Provinces of Rio de la Plata, later the Argentine Confederation, and, lastly, the Argentine Republic.

Argentine Independence, 1810.

In 1821 the United Kingdom of Portugal, Brazil, and the Algarves recognized the independence of the new Republic.

In 1822 the Kingdom of Brazil proclaimed its independence and continued to be, until 1889, the Constitutional Empire of Brazil. The two new nations certainly inherited, as to territorial limits, the rights and obligations of their respective mother-countries, but the only principle in force at the time of the proclamation of independence, inasmuch as there was then no Treaty of Limits, was that of *uti possidetis*, already recognized by Portugal and Spain since 1750 as the only reasonable and safe rule by which their boundaries in South America were to be determined.

Brazilian Independence, 1822.

But the Brazilian and Argentine Governments having agreed, as has been said already, that the principal boundaries of the two countries are to continue to be formed by the two fluvial lines of the Uruguay and the Iguaçú, the question of the nullity or validity of the Treaty of 1777 is of no practical importance in the present controversy, inasmuch as the war of 1801 in no way modified the extent of the domain of Portugal or Spain in the zone comprised between those two rivers.

Brazil bases its rights upon the fact that, as early as the XVIIth century, the territory to the East of the river Pequiry or

The right of Brazil.

Pepiry, afterwards Pepiry-Guaçú—discovered by the Brazilians of S. Paulo, called Paulistas, and not by CABEZA DE VACA, as has been recently alleged, by modifying the known itinerary of that Spanish Governor,—was under the sway of the Paulistas and formed an integral part of Brazil. It bases its right upon the *uti possidetis* of the period of the Independence, which was the same as was recognized by the Spanish Missionaries when, from the XVIIth until the middle of the XVIIIth century, they maintained to the West of the Brazilian Pequiry a post of observation to give warning of the movements of the Paulistas: a possession equally recognized by Spain in the Treaty of 1750, and admitted by the Argentine Government itself, since during the long period of seventy years which elapsed between 1810 and 1881, it never set up any pretension whatever to a more Easterly boundary than this, and in the period of forty years which elapsed from the effective and permanent occupation of that territory by Brazilian citizens and authorities in 1838 and 1840, to 1881, it made neither claim nor protest against the Brazilian occupation. It bases its right, besides, on the special position of that territory, which is indispensable to it for its security and defence, and for the preservation of inland communications between Rio Grande do Sul and the other States of the Brazilian Union. It accepts, however, all the historical documents upon which the Argentine Republic seeks to found its claim. Those documents are the Treaties of 1750 and 1777, the Instructions issued to the demarcating Commissioners, and an official Map of 1749.

The Treaties, with the events that preceded them,

BOUNDARY QUESTION.   15

and the subsequent surveys, will now be examined, and, at the same time, the allegations of the Spanish Commissioners of 1789, and the arguments which the Argentine Government has sought to deduce from them, will be refuted.

III.

Brazil has been represented as the heir to Portuguese usurpations by some of the defenders of the Argentine cause, who, taking up the old and heated discussions of the colonial period, speak, even now, of the celebrated meridian "line of demarcation."

It is known that, in the XVIth century, when Portugal and Spain began to colonize South America, the only boundary of their dominions beyond the seas was the famous but never respected line of demarcation designated by Pope ALEXANDER VI, on May 4, 1493, and modified by the Treaty of Tordesillas, of June 7, 1494, between D. João II of Portugal, and FERDINAND and ISABELLA of Castile.

<small>First line of demarcation agreed upon at Tordesillas, 1494.</small>

ALEXANDER VI had divided the world by a meridian traced a hundred leagues to the West of the Azores and Cape Verde Islands. The lands discovered to the East of that meridian were to belong to Portugal, and to the West to Spain. The Treaty of Tordesillas, approved by Pope JULIUS II (Bull of January 24, 1506), placed the meridian of demarcation 370 leagues to the West of the Cape Verde Islands.

The determination of that imaginary line gave rise until the XVIIIth century to many doubts and con-

Position of that line which could only be determined in the middle of the XVIIIth. century. troversies which it would be useless to refer to here. It suffices to say that, according to the knowledge we have at the present day, the terminal point of the 370 leagues, counted from the most Western extremity of the island of Santo Antão of Cape Verde, is in Longitude 48° 35′ 25″ West of Greenwich, on the hypothesis, little favorable to Brazil, as VARNHAGEN says,[1] that those leagues were of $16\frac{2}{3}$ to the degree,[2] and not of 15, as COLUMBUS, AMERIGO VESPUCCI, and other navigators, Spanish or in the service of Spain, reckoned them at the time of the discovery of the New World.[3] In the opposite hemisphere, this line of demarcation, therefore, corresponded to 131° 24′ 35″ of Longitude East of Greenwich.

These leagues being counted at the rate of $17\frac{1}{2}$ to the degree, as the Spaniards afterwards wished them to be,—which is an anachronism, since such a rule of computation did not exist when the Treaty of Tordesillas was concluded,[4]—the terminal point would be 47° 29′ 05″ West of Greenwich.[5]

---

[1] VISCOUNT DE PORTO-SEGURO (VARNHAGEN), *Historia Geral do Brazil*, 2d ed., p. 69.

[2] ENCISO, *Suma de Geographia que trata de todas las partidas y provincias del mundo*, 1519; and FRANCISCO FALERO (FALLEIRO), *Del tratado de la esphera y del arte del marear*, . . . 1535.

Concerning ENCISO and his work HARRISSE says: "A great hydrographer and explorer, his work is invaluable for the early geographical history of this continent."

[3] *De orbe novo* PETRI MARTYRIS AB ANGLERIA, Alcala, 1530, fol. lxxviij., verso: " . . . Si computationem leucarum sumpserimus *nautarum hispanorum more, 15 continet quisque gradus leucas:* ipsi vero contra omnium opinionem aiunt gradum continere leucas 17 cum $\frac{1}{2}$."

[4] VARNHAGEN, *Examen de quelques points de l' Histoire Géographique du Brésil*, Paris, 1858, p. 36.

[5] These calculations were made starting from the Western point of the Island of Santo Antão, 17° 5′ 30″ N. Lat. and 27° 42′ 30″ of Longitude W. from Paris (Greenwich West of Paris 2° 20′ 14″). A league of $16\frac{2}{3}$ to the equatorial

There is no doubt that the Portuguese in Brazil occupied a great extent of land to the West of that line, but that occupation was effected in good faith during the XVIIth and the beginning of the XVIIIth century, when the reckonings of longitude could not be made with the accuracy of the present day, and the exact measure of an equatorial degree was not known. The old maps of South America located that continent much more to the East than it is. In the last volume just published of the *Histoire de la Géographie de Madagascar*, M. GRANDIDIER compares the positions indicated in the maps of the XVIth and XVIIIth centuries and finds differences of more than 32° of longitude. Both Governments overstepped the line of Tordesillas before the XVIIIth century.

Spain also overstepped her allotted hemisphere.

The first controversy to which the Treaty of Tordesillas gave rise related to the ownership of the Moluccas, Spain maintaining that those islands, occupied by the Portuguese, were within the Spanish hemisphere. The agreement signed at Saragoça on April 22, 1529, settled the question, Portugal paying to Spain the price asked for the Moluccas and for the transfer of the line of demarcation in Oceania 17° to the East of those islands. The new boundary in the East passed through the Velas, now the Marianne or Ladrone Islands, in Polynesia.

Later on, Spain violated the agreements of Saragoça and Tordesillas by occupying the Philippine Islands, which, as well as the Moluccas, were within the Portuguese limits.

It is, therefore, unjust to attribute usurpations to

---

degree = 6.678^m, 396. The 370 leagues in Latitude 17° 05′ 30″ give 23° 13′ 09″. The league of 17½ to the degree = 6.360^m, 377. In the same Lat. they give 22° 06′ 48″.

one side while keeping silence regarding those of the other, and to accuse the Portuguese of falsifying, in their geographical maps of the XVIth and XVIIth centuries, the position of Brazil. No one having any acquaintance with geographical history can take such an accusation seriously. It is more loyal and dignified and truthful to admit that both Portuguese and Spaniards were then acting in good faith, and to forget errors and contradictions which have no connection with the present controversy. Astronomical and geographical knowledge was then very incomplete, and it should be remembered that the good faith of the Spaniards was also suspected, as may be seen from the following passage of D'Anville:

Unfounded accusations.

"Herrera had his own motive for thus reducing the extent of the South Sea; it was to enclose the Philippines and the Moluccas within the limits of the concession made to the King of Castile by Alexander VI: for this Pope, having divided the circumference of the Earth into two portions of 180 degrees of longitude each, between the Kings of Castile and Portugal, had attributed to the former the Western part, reckoning it at a certain distance from the Azores towards the West. By narrowing the South Sea, the Castilian writer found means of pushing the meridian or line of *demarcacion*, according to the Spanish term, as far as the Strait of Sunda, between Java and Sumatra; otherwise the islands in question would have appeared to be comprised in the concession made to Portugal: but geography could not lend itself, if such an expression may be used, to this political arrangement."[1]

---

[1] D'Anville, *Mesure conjecturale de la terre sur l'équateur*, Paris, 1736, in 12.

If the line of demarcation passed between Java and Sumatra, as the Spaniards pretended in the XVIth century, nearly the whole of South America would be within the 180 degrees of longitude attributed to Portugal.

One of the most renowned Ministers of State that Spain ever had, COUNT DE FLORIDABLANCA, recognized the inadvertence of those who in the XVIIth century thought it possible to restore the line of Tordesillas. In 1781 he said : " . . . To extend our possessions in Brazil, as some appear to desire, by virtue of the famous division made by ALEXANDER VI., is a project impossible of execution, and, what is more, contrary to anterior agreements. Moreover, admitting the principle, we should have to surrender to the Portuguese the Philippine Islands, which, according to the demarcation made by that Pontiff, belong to them." [1]

From 1580 to 1640 the two Crowns of Portugal and Spain were united and, therefore, both Brazil and the Spanish possessions in America were under the same sceptre.

How Brazil as it is now was formed.

It was during the time of this union that the frontiers of Brazil, even then undefined, because the true position of the line of Tordesillas was not known with certainty, began to be enlarged.

1580-1640.

In 1637 (14th June), PHILIP IV of Spain, at the same time King of Portugal under the name of PHILIP III, created the Captaincy of Cabo do Norte and annexed it to Brazil, giving it as its Northern boundary the

---

[1] *Memorandum presented to Carlos III., of Spain* (10 Oct., 1788), *by Count de Floridablanca* (Vol. 59 of the *Biblioteca de Autores Españoles*). Transcribed Vol. IV. of this Statement of Brazil, pp. 129-133, and translated in Vol. III., pp. 137-141.

river Vicente Pinçon, a name which the Oyapock also had at the time.

On August 16, 1639, PEDRO TEIXEIRA, obeying the instructions of the same King, took possession of the left bank of the Napo, establishing there the Western boundary of the lands of the Portuguese Crown on the North of the Amazonas.

At the same time, the Brazilians of S. Paulo, called Paulistas, continuing their expeditions into the interior, drove out the Spaniards and their Jesuit missionaries from the positions they occupied in territories considered to be within the Portuguese demarcation: on the Upper Paraguay; to the East of the Paraná, between the Paranapanema and the Iguaçù; and, more to the South, to the East of the Uruguay.

The revolution of the Independence of Portugal in 1640 found Brazil increased in the North by the territories that were annexed to it by the King of Spain, to the West and South by those which had been conquered by the Paulistas, but deprived of all the seaboard from the Rio Real to the Maranhão, then occupied by the Dutch. That part of Brazil only returned to the Portuguese dominion in 1654.

1640-1668.

The war with Spain ended with the recognition of the independence of Portugal. In the Treaty of Peace signed at Lisbon on February 13, 1668, nothing was stipulated as to boundaries in America. Article 2 provided for a mutual restoration of the strongholds conquered "during the war," the two Kingdoms to keep the "boundaries and frontiers they had before the war."

Treaty of 1668.

In 1680, the Governor of Rio de Janeiro, D. MANOEL LOBO, in fulfilment of instructions received from Lisbon, occupied the left bank of the River Plate, which was reputed by the Portuguese the Southern boundary of Brazil, and there founded, almost in front of Buenos Aires, Colonia do Sacramento. In the same year, and by order of the Governor of Buenos-Aires, the new settlement was invested and taken by storm by a numerous army of Spaniards and Guarany Indians. *Disputes and hostilities.* *Colonia do Sacramento.* *Taken by the Spaniards, 1680.*

As soon as he was informed of this occurrence, CARLOS II of Spain sent to Lisbon, as his Ambassador Extraordinary, the DUKE of GIOVENAZZO, charged to give the fullest satisfaction to the Prince Regent of Portugal, afterwards King D. PEDRO II. The Provisional Treaty of May 7, 1681, was then signed in that city, by which Colonia returned to the Portuguese dominion, it being agreed that the question of right should be examined by Commissioners appointed by the two Governments. *Restored to Portugal, 1681.*

The old discussion as to the true position of the meridian of Tordesillas and its points of intersection with the littoral of South America, was then renewed, but it was not possible to come to any agreement.

During the war of Succession, the Spaniards besieged and attacked Colonia (1704-1705), which was defended by General VEIGA CABRAL. By order of the King, D. PEDRO II., who was unable to relieve it, the fortress was evacuated and fell for the second time into the possession of the Spaniards. *Evacuated by the Portuguese, 1705.*

The Treaty of February 6, 1715, signed at Utrecht,[1] restored it "with its territory" to Portugal, the King of Spain renouncing all his rights and claims (Arts. 5 and 6), with only the condition that he might offer, within the period of one year and a half, an equivalent, which the King of Portugal might or might not accept, for the said "territory and Colónia" (Art. 7).

Returns to the Portuguese dominion by the Treaty of Utrecht, 1715.

The Governor of Buenos-Aires, however, restored only Colonia and the land within cannon-shot of the fortress. The Portuguese Government protested, maintaining that what was understood at Utrecht by the "territory and Colonia" was all the left bank of the River Plate, but the Court of Madrid would not admit that interpretation of the text which really was not very clear.

New disputes.

From 1735 to 1737, the fortress of Colonia, then commanded by General VASCONCELLOS, was again attacked and besieged by the Spaniards. An expedition which came out from Colonia under the command of General SILVA PAES, occupied (February 19, 1737) and fortified the bar of the Rio Grande do Sul and established the military posts of Tahim, Chuy, and S. Miguel.

Third siege of Colonia.

Occupation of Rio Grande do Sul by the Portuguese.

In the territory of Rio Grande do Sul there were already, to the North of the Jacuhy, several Portuguese settlements founded by Brazilians of Laguna, Curityba, and S. Paulo.

By the Armistice signed at Paris on March 16, 1737, the Portuguese and Spanish Governments agreed

---

[1] BORGES DE CASTRO, *Collecção de Tratados*; C. CALVO, *Recueil de Traités*.

Armistice of to issue orders for the cessation of hostili-
1737. ties in America, to preserve matters in the
state in which they might be at the moment of the
arrival of those orders, until a definitive settlement of
the pending claims.

IV.

These continual disputes and hostilities at length
convinced the two Governments that it
was expedient to determine clearly and Portugal and Spain recog-
permanently the limits of their dominions nize the neces-
in America and in the East Indies, re- sity for a Trea-
nouncing claims which the progress of ty of Limits.
geographical knowledge had made it impossible to
sustain.

Negotiations were entered upon which proceeded
with greater activity after Spain, by the peace of Aix-la
Chapelle (18th October, 1748), freed herself from other
cares abroad. From these negotiations resulted the
Treaty of Madrid of the 13th January, 1750,[1] Treaty of Ma-
the first agreement on limits between the drid, 13 Jan^y
two Crowns in which appears the Pepiry 1750.
or Pequiry, the subject of the controversy raised in
1789 by the Spanish Commissioners and lately revived
by the Argentine Government.

The apparent negotiator of the Treaty on the part of
Portugal was Major-General THOMAZ DA SILVA TELLES,
VISCOUNT DE VILLA NOVA DE CERVEIRA, Ambassador
Extraordinary at Madrid, and, on the part Alexandre de
of Spain, the Minister of State D. JOSEPH Gusmão.

---

[1] Portuguese text in Vol. IV., translation into English in Vol. III., first document.

DE CARVAJAL Y LANCASTER; but the actual exponent of the cause of Portugal and Brazil and of the true interests of America in that discussion was the celebrated Brazilian statesman and diplomatist ALEXANDRE DE GUSMÃO.[1]

In the conferences that preceded the signing of the Treaty it was resolved that the laying down of imaginary lines of demarcation should be entirely renounced, that boundaries should be determined by the most notable and best known rivers and mountains, and that each one of the Contracting Parties *should remain in possession of what it held at that date*, excepting such mutual cessions as might be made.

Natural boundaries instead of imaginary lines.

Uti possidetis.

Portugal agreed to surrender Colonia do Sacramento and the left bank of the Amazonas to the West of the Westernmost mouth of the Japurá, to renounce its rights over the Philippines, and to give up its claim to the restitution of the price unduly paid for the Moluccas under the agreement of Saragoça. Spain agreed to recognize all the Portuguese possessions in America and to surrender the territory on the left bank of the Uruguay to the North of the Ibicuhy in exchange for Colonia do Sacramento and of the territory contested on the left bank of the River Plate.

Mutual cessions.

The study of the Treaty of 1750 leaves the most keen and gratifying impression of the good faith, loyalty, and breadth of view which inspired that amica-

---

[1] He was then private Secretary to King D. João V., a member of the Colonial Council (Ministro do Conselho Ultramarino), and a member of the Royal Academy of History. He had been Secretary to the Portuguese Embassy at Paris, and Envoy Extraordinary at Rome. On that occasion he refused the title of Prince offered to him by the Pope. He was born at Santos in 1695, and died at Lisbon in 1753.

ble settlement of old and petty quarrels by consulting only the superior principles of reason and justice and the requirements of peace and civilization in America. At that moment, as the English historian, ROBERT SOUTHEY says, the contracting Sovereigns, D. João V. of Portugal and FERDINAND VI. of Spain, knew how to show themselves far in advance of their century.[1]

The Preamble of the Treaty summarizes the allegations presented by both parties, the conclusions at which they arrived, and the principles and rules they adopted. <small>Preamble of the Treaty of 1750.</small>

This Preamble, drawn up, as was nearly the whole of the Treaty, by ALEXANDRE DE GUSMÃO, says :

"The Most Serene Kings of Portugal and Spain, wishing effectively to consolidate and make closer the sincere and cordial friendship they profess for each other, have considered that the means most conducive to the attainment of so salutary a purpose are to remove all pretexts and clear away all impediments that may in future impair it, and particularly *such as may arise with reference to the Boundaries in America of the two Crowns, whose Conquests have advanced with uncertainty and doubt, because, until now, the true Boundaries of those Dominions, or the position in which must be imagined the Divisional Line, which was to be the unalterable principle of the demarcation for both Crowns, have not been ascertained.* <small>The imaginary divisional line.</small>

---

[1] " The language and the whole tenor of this memorable Treaty bear witness to the sincerity and good intentions of the two Courts ; the two contracting Sovereigns seem indeed to have advanced beyond their age. They proceeded with an uprightness which might almost be considered new to diplomacy ; and in attempting to establish a perpetual peace in their colonies, whatever disputes might occur between them in Europe, they set an example worthy of being held in remembrance as a practicable means of lessening the calamities of war." (ROBERT SOUTHEY, *History of Brazil*, London, 1817-1819, III. vol., page 448.)

And considering the invincible difficulties which would arise if this Line had to be marked with the requisite practical knowledge, they have resolved to examine the reasons and uncertainties that may be urged by both parties, and, in view of them, to conclude an agreement to their mutual satisfaction and convenience.

"*On the part of the Crown of Portugal it was alleged* that, inasmuch as it was to reckon the one hundred and eighty degrees of its demarcation from the line to the East, the other one hundred and eighty to the West remaining for Spain ; and while each one of the Nations was to make its discoveries and establish its Colonies within the one hundred and eighty degrees of its demarcation ; nevertheless it is found that, according to the most exact and recent observations of Astronomers and Geographers, beginning to count the degrees to the West of the said Line, the Spanish Dominion at the Asiatic extremity of the South Sea extends to many more degrees than the one hundred and eighty of its demarcation ; and that consequently it has occupied a much larger space than any excess attributed to the Portuguese can amount to in that which perhaps they may have occupied in South America to the West of the same Line, and at the beginning of the Spanish demarcation.

"It was also alleged that by the Deed of Sale with an agreement as to repurchase (com pacto *de retrovendendo*) entered into by the Attorneys of the two Crowns at Saragossa on the 22d of April, 1529, the Crown of Spain sold to the Crown of Portugal all that by whatsoever means or right appertained to it to the West of another imaginary Meridian Line,

[margin: Portuguese claims.]

through the Velas Islands,[1] situated on the South Sea, at a distance of 17° from Maluco,[2] with the declaration that if Spain allowed and did not prevent its subjects from navigating to the Westward of the said Line, then the agreement as to repurchase should at once be rescinded and become void; and that when any Spanish subjects, through ignorance or through necessity, should pass within the Line, and discover any islands or lands, whatever might be so discovered should belong to Portugal. That notwithstanding this convention, the Spaniards subsequently proceeded to discover the Philippines and, in fact, settled therein shortly before the union of the two Crowns, which took place in the year 1580, and on account of which the controversies between the two Nations caused by this contravention ceased; but when they had again separated, the conditions of the Deed of Saragossa gave rise to a new title by which Portugal may claim restitution of or equivalent for all that the Spaniards had occupied to the West of said Line, in violation of that which had been capitulated in the aforesaid Deed.

"As to the Territory of the Northern bank of the River Plate, it was alleged that, because of the foundation of the Colonia do Sacramento, a controversy arose between the two Crowns, relative to Boundaries: that is to say, as to whether the lands upon which that fortress was built, were to the East or to the West of the Boundary Line agreed upon in Tordesillas; and, while this question was being decided, a provisional Treaty was concluded at Lisbon on the 7th of May, 1681, by which it was agreed that the aforesaid fortress should remain in the possession of the Portuguese; and that

[1] Now Marianne or Ladrones Islands.
[2] Moluccas Islands.

they should have in common with the Spaniards the use and benefit of the lands in dispute. That by Article VI. of the Treaty of Peace, concluded at Utrecht between the two Crowns, on the 6th of February, 1715, His Catholic Majesty ceded all action and right he may have had to Colonia and its Territory, the Provisional Treaty being abolished by virtue of cession. That whereas by virtue of the same cession the whole of the disputed Territory was to be delivered to the Crown of Portugal, the Governor of Buenos-Ayres intended to surrender only the fortress, saying that by Territory he only understood what was within cannon-shot of it, reserving to the Crown of Spain all the other lands in dispute, on which was afterwards founded the Fortress of Montevideo and other establishments: That this interpretation of the Governor of Buenos-Ayres was manifestly opposed to what had been agreed, it being evidence that the Crown of Spain, by means of its own cession, could not be placed in a better position than that in which it was before, in regard to the same thing that it had ceded; and that both Nations, having by the Provisional Treaty been left in common possession and enjoyment of those Plains, there is no more violent interpretation than to suppose that, by means of the cession of His Catholic Majesty, they were vested exclusively in his Crown.

"That inasmuch as that Territory belongs to Portugal by a title different from that of the Boundary Line defined at Tordesillas (that is to say, by the agreement made in the Treaty of Utrecht, in which His Catholic Majesty ceded his right under the old demarcation), such Territory ought, independently of questions concerning that Line, to be entirely surrendered to Portugal, together with everything which might newly have been built upon it, as having been erected upon foreign soil. Lastly that, assuming that His Catholic Majesty had reserved the right of offering an equivalent, to the satisfaction of His Most Faithful Majesty, for the said Colonia and its Territory, nevertheless as many years had elapsed since the expiration of the terms fixed for this offer, every pretext or motive, even apparent, for delaying the cession of the same Territory has ceased to exist.

"*On the Part of the Crown of Spain it was alleged* that as a Line from North to South was to be imagined three hundred and seventy leagues West of the Cape Verde Islands, in accordance with the Treaty concluded at Tordesillas on the 7th of June, 1494, all the land that might lie within the three hundred and seventy leagues from the said islands to the place where the Line ought to be laid down, belongs to Portugal, and nothing more in this direction; because the one hundred and eighty degrees of the demarcation of Spain must be counted thence Westward: and, although, because it is not stated from which of the Cape Verde Islands the three hundred and seventy leagues are to be reckoned, a doubt has arisen, and this point is of great interest, seeing that they are all situated East and West with a difference of four and a half degrees; it is certain also that, even if Spain yielded, and consented that the counting should begin from the most Westerly, which is named Santo Antão, the three hundred and seventy leagues would scarcely extend as far as the City of Pará, and other Colonies, or Portuguese Captaincies founded formerly on the coasts of Brazil; and as the

<small>Spanish claims.</small>

Crown of Portugal has occupied the two banks of the River Amazonas, or Marañon, up as far as the mouth of the River Javari, which flows into it by the Southern bank, it clearly follows that it has encroached upon the territory of the Spanish demarcation to the extent of the distance of the said City from the mouth of the said river,[1] the same being the case in the interior of Brazil with regard to the advance inward made by this Crown to Cuyabá and Matto-Grosso.

"With regard to Colonia do Sacramento, it was alleged that, according to the most accurate Maps, the place at which the Line ought to be imagined does not reach by a long distance the mouth of the River Plate; and, consequently, the said Colonia with all its Territory lies to the West of it, and within the boundary of Spain, without prejudice to the new right under which the Crown of Portugal retains it by virtue of the Treaty of Utrecht, since restitution by an equivalent was stipulated therein; and although the Court of Spain offered the equivalent within the period prescribed by Article VII., that of Portugal did not accept it; on which account the period was extended, the equivalent being, as it was, proportionate; and the not having admitted it was more through the fault of Portugal than that of Spain.

"*These reasons having been seen and examined by the two Most Serene Monarchs* with the replications that were made on both sides, proceeding with that good faith and sincerity which is so becoming in Princes so just, so friendly, and who are related, wishing to maintain their

<small>Impossibility of maintaining the imaginary boundary line.</small>

---

[1] It has already been said that by a decision of the King of Spain, at the same time King of Portugal, all the right bank of the Amazonas as far as the Napo had been annexed to the dominions of the Portuguese Crown in 1639.

Subjects in peace and quietness, and recognizing the difficulties and doubts which in all time would complicate this controversy, if it had to be decided by means of the demarcation adjusted in Tordesillas, both because it was not stated from which of the Cape Verde Islands the three hundred and seventy leagues was to be reckoned, and on account of the difficulty of determining on the coasts of South America the two points on the South and North from which the Line was to begin; on account, also, of the moral impossibility of establishing accurately through the centre of the same America a Meridian Line; *and, lastly, on account of many other almost insurmountable difficulties which would occur in the way of preserving without controversy or encroachment a demarcation regulated by Meridian Lines;* and considering at the same time that the said difficulties were perhaps in the past the chief cause of the encroachments set out by both parties, and of the numerous conflicts which disturbed the peace of their Dominions; they have resolved to put an end to past and future disputes, and to forget and desist from all actions and rights that they may have by virtue of the said Treaties of Tordesillas, Lisbon, Utrecht, and the Deed of Saragossa, or of any other grounds whatever which may influence them in the division of their Dominions by a Meridian Line; *and it is their will that for the future the same shall not be further considered, the Boundaries of the two Monarchies being reduced to those which are specified in the present Treaty, it being* their desire that two purposes shall be carefully secured by it: *The first, and principal one is that the Boundaries of the two Dominions shall be defined, taking as*

<small>Natural boundaries and uti possidetis to be adopted.</small>

landmarks the best known spots, so that they may never be mistaken or give rise to disputes, such as the sources and courses of rivers, and the most remarkable mountains: The second, that each party shall remain in possession of that which it holds at the present time, with the exception of mutual cessions, which shall be mentioned in the proper place; which cessions shall be carried out for mutual convenience, and in order that the Borders may be as little subject to controversy as possible."

Article 21 clearly shows that the mind of a superior man and true American presided over the making of this Treaty. It is sufficient to reproduce here the beginning of that article:

"War being the principal occasion of abuses and the principal reason for disturbing the best concerted rules, Their Most Faithful and Catholic Majesties desire that if a rupture between the two Crowns should occur (which God forbid), all the Subjects of both who are established throughout South America may remain at peace, each living as if there were no such war between their Sovereigns, and without displaying the least hostility, either for themselves alone, or jointly with their Allies. And the promoters and leaders of any invasion, however slight it may be, shall be irremissibly punished with the penalty of death; and any seizure which they may effect shall be restored in good faith and in its entirety."

Peace in America, even when the two Crowns may be at war.

In Articles 4 and 9 the boundaries of Brazil are determined from Castillos Grandes near the entrance to the River Plate, as far as the North of the Amazonas and of the equinoctial line. From the sea coast, at Castillos Grandes, the divisional line followed along the high ground

The Divisional Line of 1750.

which separates the waters flowing to Lake Mirim and Rio Grande from those which flow to the River Plate and Rio Negro; it reached thus the principal source of the Ibicuhy, and then went down along this river as far as its confluence on the left and Eastern bank of the Uruguay.

Article V. describes the frontier from the mouth of the Ibicuhy as far as that of the Igurey in the Paraná. In it are comprised the Western boundaries of the territory now disputed, that is to say, the present boundaries of Brazil between the Uruguay and the Iguaçû.

Article V. says:

"From the mouth of the Ibicuí, the Line shall run up *the course of the Uruguay until reaching the River Pepirí, or Pequirí, which empties itself by the Western Bank of the Uruguay; and it shall continue up the bed of the Pepirí as far as the principal source thereof; from which it shall follow along the highest ground to the principal head of the nearest river that may flow into the Rio Grande de Curituba, otherwise named Iguaçû.* The Boundary shall continue along the bed of the said River nearest to the source of the Pepirí, and afterwards, along that of the Iguaçû, or Rio Grande de Curituba, until the point where the same Iguaçû empties itself by the Eastern bank of the Paraná; and from that mouth it shall go up the course of the Paraná, to the point where the Igurey joins it on its Western bank."[1]

Article V. of the Treaty of 1750.

Between the Uruguay and the Iguaçû.

Pepiry, or Pequiry, an affluent of the Uruguay.

An affluent of the Iguaçû.

---

[1] Portuguese text of Article V.: " " Subirá " (a linha divisoria) " desde a bocca do Ibicuí *pelo alveo do Uruguay, até encontrar o do rio Pepirí ou Pequirí, que desagua na margem Occidental do Uruguay; e continuará pelo alveo do Pepirí acima, até a sua origem principal; desde a qual proseguirá pelo mais alto do ter-*

The position of the Pepiry or Pequiry was not described in the Treaty, neither was that of the other rivers and mountains mentioned therein, because the Map used by the Plenipotentiaries, and of which copies were about to be given to the Demarcating Commissioners, indicated it with all possible clearness and according to the most recent and reliable information.

Examination of Article V.

From Article V it is merely seen that the Pepiry or Pequiry is an affluent of the right bank of the Uruguay, a bank which the Treaty calls Western, using a local and common expression arising from the circumstance that this river flows in the general direction of North to South from its Great Falls (Salto Grande), until it enters the estuary of the River Plate. As in this lower part of the course of the Uruguay, the only settlements then existing were situated, the custom began, in the XVII century, which still prevails to-day, of calling the right bank—occidental side (banda occiden-

---

reno att a cabeceira principal do rio mais visinho, que desemboque no Rio Grande de Curituba, por outro nome chamado Iguaçú. Pelo alveo do dito rio mais visinho da origem do Pepiri, e depois pelo do Iguaçú, ou Rio Grande de Curituba, continuará a Raya até onde o mesmo Iguaçú desembocca na margem Oriental do Paraná; e desde esta bocca proseguirá pelo alveo do Paraná acima, até onde se lhe ajunta o rio Igurey pela sua margem Ocidental."

Spanish text: "Subirá" (a linha divisoria) "desde la boca del Ybicui por las aguas del Uruguay hasta encontrar la del rio Pepiri ó Pequiri que desagua en el Uruguay por su rivera occidental, y continuará aguas arriva del Pepiri hasta su origen principal, desde el qual seguira por lo mas alto del terreno hasta la cabecera principal del Rio mas vecino del Origen del Pepiri, y despues por las del Yguazú, ó Rio Grande de Curituba continuará la Raya hasta donde el mismo Yguazú desemboca en el Paraná por su rivera oriental, y desde esta boca seguira aguas arriva del Paraná hasta donde se le junta el Rio Ygurey por su rivera occidental."

The translation of the two texts into English gives, and could not but give, the same result, but the small differences will be noted with which the Portuguese and Spaniards, and their Brazilian and Spanish-American descendants, write the geographical and native names.

tal), and the left—oriental side (banda oriental). If the expression had to be taken in its literal and rigorous sense, the Pepiry or Pequiry of the Treaty would be a river more to the West, and below the Great Falls, because the Upper Uruguay, from its headwaters to those Falls, follows the general direction of East to West, and so, in that section, its right side is the Northern and the left the Southern side.

Faithful to the idea of choosing perfectly visible and indisputable landmarks, the two Governments designated the Pepiry or Pequiry, among other reasons, because it was the first important affluent of the right bank of the Uruguay immediately above its Great Falls (Salto Grande). They preferred the tributary of the Iguaçù nearest to the Pepiry, not only because it was necessary to seek in that region a natural line in a Northerly direction, but also because this affluent would certainly have its mouth a little above the Great Falls of the Iguaçù (Salto Grande do Iguaçù). And in the Paraná, when the line had to incline to the West, seeking the basin of the Paraguay, they chose the Igurey, the first affluent below the Great Falls of the Paraná (Salto Grande do Paraná), or Salto das Sete Quédas (Cataract of the Seven Falls). *Natural landmarks. Great Falls. Great Falls of the Iguaçù. Great Falls of the Paraná.*

In this manner, the three Great Falls of the Uruguay, Iguaçù, and Paraná, would become so many natural and indestructible landmarks, signalizing the proximity of the confines of the two dominions in three of the most important knots of the extensive and winding divisional line. The distance between the mouths of each one of these rivers and the neighboring cataract being determined, the situation of three out of the four points at which in that region the frontier line changed its direction could not leave room for doubts or controversies. The fourth of the points of deflection was also well indicated by the mouth of the Iguaçû.

In respect to the Pepiry there was, moreover, the circumstance that this river emptied itself, not only very near the Great Falls (Salto Grande), but also at the place where the Uruguay, coming from its headwaters in a Westerly direction, bends rapidly to the South. As, starting from that river, the divisional line went towards the North seeking the course of the Paraná, the choosing of affluents that should speedily connect the two great fluvial boundaries was naturally suggested. To follow beyond the Great Falls and the Pepiry, continuing up the course of the Uruguay, would be to change the direction entirely to the East, as the Argentines now wish to do, and therefore to turn more and more away from the objective, which was the North and the Paraná.

Moreover, in an official Letter dated February 8, 1749, addressed to the Ambassador in Madrid, the Secretary of State for Foreign Affairs of Portugal, MARCO ANTONIO DE AZEREDO COUTINHO, thus explains, with perfect clearness and in the following terms, the proposal of the Pepiry or Pequiry as a boundary:

"If there be any scruple regarding the name of the river Pequirí, along which the Draft" (the project of the Treaty) "leads the boundary to reach the Iguaçû, it may be said, *that it may continue along the river which, discharging into the Uruguai, shall form with the course of the same Uruguai the line nearest to the North direction,* and that from the headwaters of such river, those of the nearest river that discharges into the

Iguaçû shall be sought, and that along it the boundary shall run."[1]

In the Treaty of 1750 the Pepiry or Pequiry,—since 1760 Pepiry, Pequiry, or Pepiry-Guaçú,—was thus designated:

Pepiri or *Pequiri*, and afterwards, twice *Pepiri*, in Article V; *River Pepiri*, in Article XIV; and *Pequiri* in XVI.

In Article XIV it may be read that the King of Spain "also cedes all and whatsoever settlements and establishments may have been founded by Spain in the angle of land included between the Northern bank of the River Ibicuí and the Eastern bank of the Uruguay, *and such as may have been founded on the Eastern bank of the River Pepiri.*" <small>The Pepiry was already the boundary of Brazil since the XVII. century.</small>

And in Article XVI: "Those settlements which are ceded by Their Most Faithful and Catholic Majesties on the banks of the rivers Pequiri, Guaporé, and Amazonas, shall be surrendered under the same circumstances as Colonia do Sacramento, according to the provisions of Article XIV."

Those clauses relating to the settlements that might have been founded by Spain on the Eastern or left bank of the Pepiry or Pequiry were written as a simple precaution, because the Jesuits who ruled the Missions[2] of the Uruguay and Paraná with complete independence of the civil authority, formed in the dominion of the King of Spain a true *imperium in imperio*, and could, without the knowledge of the two

---

[1] Document in the Department of Foreign Affairs at Lisbon.
[2] In Portuguese—Missões (singular, Missão); in Spanish—Misiones (singular, Mision).

Courts, have recently advanced their possessions in that direction.

But, that such possible occupation of the Pepiry had not taken place, was ascertained by the Commissioners of the two Crowns who went to make the demarcation in 1759 and 1760.

When, further on, the territory now contested, its special history, and the expeditions of the Paulistas or natives of S. Paulo, in Brazil, are treated of, it will be proved that there never was to the East of the Pepiry any settlement, not even a temporary one, of the Spaniards and the Jesuit Missionaries, and that after the XVIIth century that river was always considered by them as the boundary of Brazil.

To enter now upon these matters would involve an interruption of the examination of the Treaty of 1750 and of the subsequent demarcation. It is sufficient to say here that, as early as 1636, it was in the Campos (Plains) of Ibituruna, or land of the Biturunas, now Campos de Palmas, that the Paulistas concentrated when they went to the attack of the Missions of the Uruguay ; that there, near the Pepiry, they had a fort or entrenched camp; that even in the middle of the XVIIIth century, the Jesuits of the Missions maintained to the West of the same Pepiry, on the Yaboty or Pepiry-Miní,[1] a post of observation called Espia, to give notice of the movements of the Paulistas ; that from 1636 to 1638 these Brazilians destroyed all the settlements which the Jesuits of Paraguay had just formed to the South and East of the Uruguay ; and that only in 1687 did those missionaries, who had concentrated all their Guarany Indians in the mesopo-

---

[1] F 10 in Map No. 29 A.

tamia formed by the drawing together of the courses of the Paraná and Uruguay, venture to return to the left bank of this last river, laying the foundations of seven villages, all far distant from the Great Falls of the Uruguay and the Pepiry.

In 1687 they removed to the West bank of the Uruguay the missions of S. Nicolas and S. Miguel, placing them between the Ijuhy, to the North, and the Piratiny, to the South, and they established between these two the new mission of S. Luis Gonzaga. Afterwards, in 1690, they founded S. Borja, more to the South, near the left bank of the Uruguay ; in the following year, S. Lorenzo, and in 1698 S. Juan Bautista, to the South of the Ijuhy: lastly, in 1706, S. Anjel, the most advanced on the Northern side of the same Ijuhy.

These were called the Seven Eastern Missions, or "Siete Pueblos Orientales de Misiones" (Seven Oriental Towns of the Missions, or, as the Portuguese commonly called them, "Sete Povos de Missões") between the Ibicuhy and the Uruguay, surrendered by Spain to Portugal in exchange for the fortified city of Colonia do Sacramento and its territory. The seven oriental missions had then 29,052 inhabitants, and the others, between the Uruguay and the Paraná and on the right bank of this last river, 66,833. The total population subject to the Jesuits, and composed entirely of Guarany Indians, was, therefore, 95,885 inhabitants. In 1755 it rose to 106,392.

The Seven Oriental Missions.

At first Spain showed herself disposed to surrender, in exchange for Colonia do Sacramento, all the territory to the North of the Rio Negro, an affluent of the left bank of the Uruguay. Afterwards she thought this concession too great, and offered, in place of it, the line of the Ibicuhy, much more to the North.

When the Spanish counter-proposal was accepted by Portugal the manuscript Map which was used in the final discussions between the Pleni- potentiaries had been completed, and for that reason the divisional line as seen upon it is represented as passing along the Rio Negro.

The manuscript Map of 1749.

This manuscript Map, commonly called "Mappa das Cortes" ("Map issued by the Courts"),[1] bears the date of 1749, the year before the signing of the Treaty. It shows not only the boundaries between the two Crowns, but also the territories effectively occupied by each Nation, and those which at that date were still unoccupied.

The best Map of South America published previously was that of D'ANVILLE (1748); but it lacked the whole course of the Guaporé along which the frontier ran; the Upper Uruguay was represented in accordance with information furnished anterior to 1733 by the Jesuits of Paraguay, who were not acquainted with it; and lakes Mirim and dos Patos, with the adjacent territories, as well as the Southern littoral, from Cape Sta Maria to Sta Catharina, were represented according to a sketch hastily made in 1737 by General SILVA PAES.

The manuscript Map of 1749 was made at Lisbon, under the supervision of the Portuguese Government, by a Portuguese engineer or geographer, and not by

---

[1] It began to be so called from the demarcation by the Portuguese and Spanish Commissioners. The former wrote " Mappa das Cortes " ; the latter, " Mapa de las Cortes."

engineers and geographers of the two nations, as was written many years afterwards.[1] It seems that, next to the part taken by ALEXANDRE DE GUSMÃO in the preparation of this Map, the largest part was performed by General SILVA PAES, who, about that time, arrived from Brazil where he had spent fourteen years, in Rio de Janeiro, S. Catharina, Rio Grande do Sul,

---

[1] In the *Memoria del Ministerio de Relaciones Exteriores* of the Argentine Republic, presented to Congress in 1892, a quotation may be read (p. 6) which begins as follows: "That, in fact, the said map had been drawn by engineers and geographers, and by skilled and well-informed persons of both nations . . . ." The same passage is transcribed in the new edition of that *Memoria*, published by its author, Dr ESTANISLÃO S. ZEBALLOS, under the title —*Cuestiones de Limites entre las Republicas Argentina, El Brasil y Chile*, Buenos-Aires, 1893, in 12.

DR. ZEBALLOS was misinformed when he wrote (p. 6 of the *Memoria* and 7 of the *Cuestiones*) that the Plenipotentiaries drew up that "document" upon the geographical map (" a geographical map upon which the Plenipotentiaries drew up the following act "), and when he gives to the passage quoted the name of " Protocol " :"—in the Protocol transcribed in the preceding Chapter " (p. 12 of the *Report* and 15 of the *Cuestiones*).

The passage quoted by DR. ZEBALLOS is not, as he supposes, a Protocol signed in 1751, but a translation of a note in Vol. III., p. 114, of the *Collecção de Tratados* by BORGES DE CASTRO. The note is simply a copy of a passage in the *Portuguese Memorandum of 2d April, 1776*, delivered on that date (far removed from 1751) by the Secretary of State for Foreign Affairs, the MARQUIS DE POMBAL, to the Portuguese Ambassador at London. The title of the Memorandum is: " *Analytical and Demonstrative Compendium of the notorious errors of fact by which the Governors of Buenos Ayres have attempted to excuse at the Court of Madrid the violence, hostilities, and, lastly, the war which General D. JOÃO JOSEPH DE VERTIZ declared against the Portuguese Governors of Southern Brazil by the Manifesto issued by him on the 5th January, 1774*."

The title is quoted by BORGES DE CASTRO, and the Brazilian Special Mission possess an authentic copy of this document, duly legalized by SR. JOSÉ DE HORTA MACHADO DA FRANCA, Assistant Director in the Portuguese Foreign Office.

As to the error of the Memorandum in attributing the Map of 1749 to Portuguese and Spanish geographers, when this Map was made at Lisbon by *a Portuguese geographer* according to documents existing there and others sent from Madrid, it cannot cause surprise considering that POMBAL wrote 27 years after this fact, and was not at Lisbon in 1749 when this occurred.

and Colonia do Sacramento. It will perhaps never be possible to settle this point, because in the great earthquake at Lisbon many important documents were lost, and also because at that time such matters were not always entered into in official correspondence.[1]

The important point to know is that the manuscript Map of 1749 is a Portuguese Map, made in duplicate and on the 8th of February of that year sent by the Secretary of State for Foreign Affairs, AZEREDO COUTINHO, to Madrid, where it was used by the Plenipotentiaries in the final discussion and definitive drawing up of the Treaty.[2]

To these two identical reproductions the Plenipotentiaries gave the name of "Mappas Primitivos" (First Maps), because later, in 1751, three copies were made at Lisbon and the same number at Madrid to be exchanged and given to the Commissioners of the different Parties charged with the demarcation of the extensive frontier line.

Map No. 7 A (Vol. VI.) is a faithful reproduction of one of the two first copies of the Manuscript Map of 1749, kept in the Geographical Depot of the French Foreign Office. The fac-simile No. 7 A is the same in size and coloring as the original.[3]

The original of the Map of 1749 at Paris.

---

[1] In a despatch of 24th June, 1751, the Portuguese Ambassador does not state the name of the geographer who made the three Spanish copies of the first Map. Referring to this geographer he says: "the man who made them." This man, however, must have had a certain importance, as, farther in the same despatch, the Ambassador says he was one of the Spanish Commissioners appointed to carry out the demarcation in Northern Brazil.

[2] Official Letter of the 8th February, 1749, from the Secretary of State for Foreign Affairs, MARCO ANTONIO DE AZEREDO COUTINHO.

[3] The copy presented by the Brazilian Special Mission is made from the original numbered 2,582 in the Geographical Depot of the French Foreign Of-

The geographer of that Department, M. E. Desbuissons, certifies that this copy is an exact copy of the "original reproduction," and on the back there is the following declaration under No. 43, written when the French Government acquired this Map: ". . . It is a correct copy of the original. It comes from the archives of Lisbon."

The document in the possession of the French Foreign Office is not an authenticated reproduction as these two notes state, but *one of the two originals* of 1749, as may be seen from the correspondence of the Portuguese Ambassador, VISCOUNT THOMAZ DA SILVA TELLES.

The following letter of the 24th June, 1751, addressed by the Ambassador to the new Secretary of State for Foreign Affairs, CARVALHO E MELLO, afterwards MARQUIS DE POMBAL, speaks of the three copies which came from Lisbon that year, of the three made at Madrid, and of the divergence regarding the frontier line in the South, represented in the Lisbon copies by the Rio Negro, as in the two first Maps, and in those of Madrid by the Ibicuhy, as had been agreed [1]:

"As the Maps which D. JOZÉ DE CARVAJAL had ordered to be copied from the first that came from

fice and is signed on the back by the Plenipotentiaries of Portugal and Spain (date 12th July, 1751). The copy is authenticated by MM. E. DESBUISSONS, geographer to the same Department; GIRARD DE RIALLE, Minister Plenipotentiary, Director of the Division of Archives (date, 11th Feb., 1893); and HENRY VIGNAUD, Secretary of the Legation of the United States of America at Paris (date, 13th February, 1893).

[1] It is to be remarked that ALEXANDRE DE GUSMÃO was at Madrid only as the adviser of the Embassy to discuss the question of limits. When this was settled, he returned to Lisbon where, in 1751, he defended the Treaty against the attacks of General VASCONCELLOS. If in 1751 GUSMÃO had been at Madrid, the form of this and the following document would be very different.

that Court (Lisbon) before the Treaty of Limits was
made were at Madrid, and as there was a delay of
some days in the coming with them of the man by
whom they were made, and afterwards some more
days were spent in the comparison of the said Maps
with the three Your Excellency sent to me lately, it was
not until now that a difference could be found which,
although it could easily have been corrected by a declaration, I do not venture to make without orders and
without informing Your Excellency of the said declaration, so that if the King our Master approves it, all
the geographical Maps which have been ordered to be
made by either side and are necessary for the execution
of the said Treaty may be signed.

"The difference consists in the fact that in the first
two Maps that came for our guidance, one which D.
José de Carvajal had with the copy of the Draft, and
another which I hold with a copy of the same Draft,
a red line is drawn which beginning at Castilhos Grandes
seeks the headwaters of the Rio Negro, and proceeds
along it to the Uruguay, marking and touching all the
points of the demarcation. But under the Treaty, the
demarcation does not follow the Rio Negro, but from
its headwaters it proceeds to the source of the river
Ibicuí, as is seen in Article 4 of the said Treaty.

"In the three copies your Excellency sends me the
original was followed by putting in the red line as it
was there, without regard to the alteration that was
made in the Treaty.

"In the three copies which this Minister ordered to
be made, the same red line appears, but it is drawn in
conformity with the alteration that has been made in
the Treaty with regard to the first Map.

"In order to show what I mean I send Your Excellency by this same messenger one of the geographical Maps which Your Excellency sent me, and another which D. Jozé de Carvajal lent me in order that I might compare it at greater leisure with those I have in my possession . . . . .

"The declarations which are to be placed, as well on the first Map, as on the copies Your Excellency has now sent me, Your Excellency will see on the enclosed paper, which has already been compared by me and by D. Jozé de Carvajal . . ."

In a letter of the 12th of July of the same year the Ambassador said:

" . . . The difficulty which occurred was that, in the exchange of the said Maps, the custom which prevails in the exchange of the copies of any Treaty could not be followed. Your Excellency knows very well that they are always written in duplicate on each side, either in its own language, or in that in which it is customary to draw up such documents, and that although all on each side are signed, only one is exchanged, so that at the Court of each one of the respective Ministers they may be preserved, and may be compared and collated at any time, and also that similarity in the order of signature may be observed, a very important and delicate point.

"As there are *three Maps on one part and three on the other*, this rule cannot be observed; to this difficulty another and more delicate one was added which was that the Portuguese Commissioners would have to take the Maps made in Madrid, and the Spanish Commissioners the Maps drawn in Lisbon, and in connection with this I considered some circumstances on our side which in my opinion deserved attention. As, however, Your Excellency in your letter makes use of the following words: " But as to the other point regarding the signature, that which has been previously and is now still understood is that all three of the Maps which I sent to your Excellency must be signed and exchanged in authenticated form; this Court remaining in possession of the Maps which your Excellency will receive from D. JOSEPH DE CARVAJAL, and D. JOSEPH DE CARVAJAL of those he will receive from Your Excellency,"—I have no alternative but to obey and carry out the orders conveyed to me by Your Excellency.

"I spoke to D. JOSEPH DE CARVAJAL and informed him of the contents of the letter of Your Excellency; and he agreed to everything, yielding with regard to the doubt that had occurred to him.

"*We accordingly signed first the two original Maps by which we were guided in drawing up the Treaty of the demarcation of limits.*[1]

"*In both I had the declarations of Minute A written in the Portuguese language*, and I signed in the best place: of these I handed one to D. JOSEPH DE CARVAJAL, to be kept in the Archives of Spain, and the other I send to Your Excellency that you might order it to be placed in suitable keeping.

The two Maps of 1749.

"*We immediately signed the three which your Excellency lately sent to me*,[2] *and the three which* D. JOSEPH DE CARVAJAL *had ordered to be drawn;*[3] and

---

[1] That is the Map of 1749, drawn in duplicate, at Lisbon.

[2] The three copies made at Lisbon in 1751 and under that date.

[3] The three modified copies made at Madrid in 1751, and bearing the date of 1749.

I handed him mine and he delivered his to
me. *On those which I gave him, I ordered* The three Portuguese and
Declaration B to be written in the Portu- the three Spanish copies of
guese language, and I signed in the best 1751.
place. *On those which he gave me he
ordered Declaration C to be written in the Spanish
language,* and these he signed in the best place.

"Of these I send Your Excellency two and keep the
third, until the conclusion and drawing up of the Instructions which are to be taken by the Commissioners
who are to proceed to the North of South America;
but it will be better that Your Excellency should send
me a newly made copy which I can use and keep with
the original Map which I am sending."

This was "Declaration A" written on the two
original Maps,[1] according to the quoted despatch of
July 12, 1751:

"This Geographical Chart which is to remain in the
Royal Archives of Portugal, as well as the other
similar Chart which is to remain in the Declaration written on the
Royal Archives of Spain, is that which was two originals
used by the Minister Plenipotentiary of of 1749.
His Most Faithful Majesty for the drafting
of the Treaty on the division of Limits in South
America, signed on the 13th of January, 1750. And
because in the said Chart there is a red line which

---

[1] Title and reference of the two original Maps made at Lisbon in 1749 :

"MAPA DOS CONFINS DO BRAZIL COM AS TER- / RAS DA COROA DE ESPᴬ NA AMERICA MERIDᴬᴸ / O q˜ está de Amarelo he o q˜ se acha occupado pelos Portuguezes. / O q˜ está de Cor de Roza he o q˜ tem occupado os Espanhoes. / O q˜ fica em branco não está até o prezente occupado. / Feito no anno de 1749."
("MAP OF THE CONFINES OF BRAZIL WITH THE LANDS OF THE CROWN OF SPAIN IN SOUTH AMERICA. What is yellow is occupied by the Portuguese ; pink is occupied by the Spaniards. The space left in white is not yet occupied. Done in the year 1749.")

points out and passes through the places where the demarcation is to be made, which line, being anterior to the Treaty of Limits which was concluded afterwards, does not agree with it in passing from the foot of the Hill of Castilhos Grandes to the headwaters of the River Negro, and thence down the latter until it enters the River Uruguay, whereas, in accordance with the said Treaty, it should run to the principal source of the River Ibicui; it is hereby declared that the said line shall serve only so far as it is in conformity with the aforesaid Treaty, and in order that this may remain at all times proved, We, the undersigned Ministers Plenipotentiary of His Most Faithful Majesty and of His Catholic Majesty, have hereto placed our signatures and the Seals of our Arms. Madrid, the 12th of July, 1751."

In the three copies from Lisbon, made in 1751, was written the following "Declaration B" appended to the same despatch of the Ambassador:

"This Geographical Chart is a faithful and exact copy of the first upon which the Treaty of Limits, signed on the 13th of January, 1750, was drafted and concluded. And because in the said Chart there is a red line which points out and passes through the places where the demarcation is to be made, which line, being anterior to the Treaty of Limits which was concluded afterwards, does not agree with it in passing from the foot of the Hill of Castilhos Grandes to the headwaters of the River Negro, and thence down the latter until it enters the River Uruguay, whereas, in accordance with the said Treaty, it should run to the principal

Declaration on the three Portuguese copies of 1751.

source of the River Ibicui; it is hereby declared that the said line shall serve only so far as it is in conformity with the aforesaid Treaty, and in order that this may remain at all times proved, We, the undersigned Ministers Plenipotentiary of His Most Faithful Majesty and of His Catholic Majesty, have hereto placed our signatures and the Seals of our Arms. Madrid, the 12th day of July, 1751."

Map No. 9A (Vol. VI.) is a reduced reproduction of one of those three Portuguese copies of 1751, in the Archives of the Department of State at Madrid. It agrees perfectly with Map No. 7A.[1]

"Declaration C" in the three Spanish copies of 1751 was conceived as follows:

"This Geographical Chart is a faithful and exact copy of the first upon which the Treaty of Limits, signed on the 13th of January, 1750, was drafted and concluded. And because in the said Chart there is a red line which points out and passes through the places where the demarcation is to be made; it is hereby declared that the said line shall serve only so far as it is in conformity with the aforesaid Treaty, and in order

Declaration on the three Spanish copies of 1751.

---

[1] The copy in the possession of the Brazilian Special Mission is a photograph legalized by Sr. MANUEL DEL PALACIO, Director of the Archives and Library in the Department of State, Madrid. Date: 2d March, 1893.

The title and reference are as follows:

"Mapa dos confins do Brazil com as ter- , ras da Coroa de Esp? na America Meridion! / O que esta de cor Amarela he o que se acha ocupado pelos Portug.^s / O que está de cor de Roza he o que tem ocupado os Espanhoes. / O que fica em Branco está athé ao presente por ocupar. / Feita no anno de 1751." ("Map of the Confines of Brazil with the lands of the Crown of Spain in South America. What is yellow is occupied by the Portuguese; pink is occupied by the Spaniards. The space left in white is not yet occupied. Done in the year 1751."

that this may remain at all times proved, We, the Ministers Plenipotentiary of their Catholic and Most Faithful Majesties, have signed it and sealed it with the Seal of our Arms. At Madrid, the 12th of July, 1751."

The Spanish copies. It has been impossible to find at Lisbon a single one of the three Spanish copies which must be lost there in some of the Archives, unless they have been mislaid, as happened with one of the two original Maps, fortunately preserved since 1824 in the French Foreign Office.

From the despatches of the Portuguese Ambassador above quoted, it is seen that the Spanish copies differ from those made at Lisbon and from the two original Maps, inasmuch as they show the corrected boundary line along the Ibicuhy, as it was finally determined in the Treaty, and not along the Rio Negro, as in the first draft. In the *Collecção de Tratados* (Collection of Treaties) of BORGES DE CASTRO (Vol. III., 1856), there is a lithographed reproduction which must have been made from one of the three Spanish copies delivered in 1751 to the Portuguese Government, or from a copy of one of them. It has seemed unnecessary now to reproduce that copy fully, because the Department of State has in its Library the compilation of BORGES DE CASTRO. Nevertheless, in Vol. V., under N° 11ter that part of the Map is presented which may be of use in the study of the present controversy. In the same Vol. will be found under N° 11, of the size of the original, a part of another contemporaneous Spanish Map, which much resembles BORGES DE CASTRO's copy, and was drawn by PALOMARES. Under N° 11bis the latter, which belongs to the Department of State at Madrid, is presented on the same scale as the first Maps collected in Vol. V.[1]

The trustworthiness of VISCOUNT BORGES DE CASTRO cannot be doubted. Neither he, nor the Portuguese Government which published the *Collecção de Tratados*, had, in 1856, any interest whatever in the old question which was revived by the Argentine Republic only in 1881; nor could they in any case have had recourse to the sorry and ingenuous expedient of tampering with a document of which there were various authentic copies. Moreover, BORGES DE CASTRO was merely a compiler and collector of Treaties which he published without commentaries or explanations. When he gave this Vol. III. to the press, he was Secretary of

---

[1] Of this Spanish Map the Brazilian Special Mission has a traced copy of the small section between the Uruguay, the Iguaçú, and the Paraná. It is legalized by SR. MANUEL DEL PALACIO, Director of the Archive and Library of the Department of State at Madrid, on the 2d of December, 1893. Besides this copy the Special Mission has another, legalized on the 12th of December, 1842, by the Director of the Archive, GARAZA, and by COUNT DE ALMODOVAR, Secretary of State, but the copyist made a mistake which was corrected in the copy now received.

The document has not the signatures of the Plenipotentiaries. This is the title and explanation:

"MAPA / *de los Confines del Brasil con las / Tierras de la Corona de España / en la America Meridional, / Lo que está de color de Rosa es lo que tienen los Españoles. / Lo de Amarillo, es lo ocupado por los Portugueses. / Lo que está de color Leonado aun no está ocupado. / Palomares del!.*" Translation:—"Map of the Confines of Brazil with the lands of the Crown of Spain in South America. What is Pink belongs to the Spaniards. Yellow is occupied by the Portuguese. Brown is not yet occupied." PALOMARES del!.

The Spanish copy which BORGES DE CASTRO caused to be reproduced, and is appended to Vol. III. of his *Collection of Treaties*, has this title and explanation :—"MAPPA (sic) / *de los confines del Brasil con las tierras de la Corona de España en / la America Meridional : lo que está de amarillo se halla ocupado / por los Portugueses : lo que está de color de rosa tienen ocupado los Españoles ; lo que queda en blanco no está todavia al presente* (sic) *ocupado. 1749.*" Lithographed at the National Printing House at Lisbon by J. M. C. CALHEIROS. Translation :—"Map of the Confines of Brazil, with the lands of the Crown of Spain in South America : What is Yellow is occupied by the

Legation at Madrid, and probably had no knowledge of the controversy between the Portuguese and Spanish Commissioners who made the demarcation under the Treaty of 1777, a question upon which nothing had been said since the end of the last century.

In 1776 the MARQUIS DE POMBAL examined and described in his Memorandum of 2d April, both the Portuguese original of 1749, which was at Lisbon and is now at Paris, and one of the three Spanish copies received from Madrid in 1751.[1] The description agrees perfectly with the copy of BORGES DE CASTRO. It is sufficient to transcribe this passage: " . . . under the yellow color is described as belonging to Portugal, that is to say: By the sea-coast and adjacent land, all that lies to the North and West from Castillos Grandes as far as the Rio Grande de S. Pedro, from which forward the coast of Brazil continues. And in the interior of the country, all that lies from

Portuguese; Pink by the Spaniards; what is left in White is not until now occupied. 1749."

At the top is to be read the following title, placed there by BORGES DE CASTRO: "CARTA GEOGRAPHICA / DE QUE SE SERVIU O MINISTRO PLENIPOTENCIARIO DE S. MAGESTADE FIDELISSIMA PARA AJUSTAR O TRATADO DE LIMITES NA AMERICA MERIDIONAL, ASSIGNADO EM 13 DE JANEIRO DE 1750./ (Tirada de copia authentica.)" Translation :—"Geographical Map used by the Minister Plenipotentiary of His Most Faithful Majesty in making the Treaty of Limits in South America, signed on the 13th of January, 1750. (Taken from an authenticated copy)."

On the back is transcribed Declaration C, in Spanish, signed by the Plenipotentiaries.

BORGES DE CASTRO, not having studied the negotiations of the Treaties he published, was mistaken in supposing that this was the copy used by the Portuguese Plenipotentiary. The document he caused to be reproduced is one of the Spanish copies subsequent to the Treaty, and not the original Map of 1749.

[1] The title and explanation of the three Spanish copies of 1751 were drawn up thus, as is seen in § 10 of the Portuguese Memorandum dated the 2d April, 1776, written by the MARQUIS DE POMBAL, who on that occasion examined them:

"MAPA / de los confines del Brasil con las tierras de la Corona de España en la America Meridional. Lo que está de Amarillo es lo que se halla ocupado por los Portugueses. / Lo que está de color de Rosa es lo que tienen ocupado los Españoles. / Lo que queda de Blanco no está todavia ocupado. / En el año de 1749."

the first red line on the North as far as the rivers Pequiry[1] and Uruguay-pitá.[2]"

Indeed, in the copy of BORGES DE CASTRO, and in that of PALOMARES,[3] the yellow extends as far as the Uruguay-pitá, because that affluent of the left bank of the Uruguay is represented as above the Great Falls (Salto Grande) and above the Pepiry, while in the original and in the Portuguese copies it is, as in the old maps of the Jesuits, below those Falls.

It seems certain, therefore, that the three Spanish copies departed from the Portuguese original, giving, as in BORGES DE CASTRO and PALOMARES, the names of the rivers Ñucorá, S. Juan, and Yriboba, which were not in the original, and transferring more to the East the Uruguay-Pitá, which in all the previous maps appeared to the East of the former Pepiry of the Jesuits. It is not possible to affirm this with absolute security, because the only indisputable proof would be the production of one of the Spanish copies with the signatures and seals of the Plenipotentiaries. But these considerations will serve here as a defence of the ever-honored name of BORGES DE CASTRO, against whom the accusation has been recently cast of having published "a contemptible document." If he published that copy it was because he held it to be authentic. Moreover, the Map of PALOMARES, preserved in the Department of State at Madrid, is there to show that no importance whatever was attached at that time to the position of the affluents of

---

[1] An affluent of the Paraná, not to be confounded with the Pepiry, or Pequiry, an affluent of the Uruguay.

[2] An affluent of the left bank of the Uruguay.

[3] Map of PALOMARES, N? 11 and N? 11bis in Vol. V.; copy of BORGES DE CASTRO, N? 11ter in the same Vol.

the left bank of the Uruguay, rivers whose courses were unknown and which were not mentioned in the Treaty.

It may be as well to say at once that Brazil does not need the Map of BORGES DE CASTRO in order to prove her right. That Map is a Spanish copy whose author, in points that were of no importance in the demarcation, thought fit to depart from the Portuguese original which was given him to copy.

The Map used for the final discussion of the Treaty of 1750 is the duplicate Portuguese Map made in 1749. One of the originals was lately found, and is now presented to the Arbitrator in a perfectly authenticated fac-simile.

An examination of this Map, which will be made further on, will show that the River Pequiry, or Pepiry, is represented in it as *the first above the Salto Grande of the Uruguay*, and, therefore, is the same river that the Brazilians are defending as a boundary of the territory now disputed.

V.

On the 17th of January, 1751, the following agreements were signed at Madrid by VISCOUNT THOMAS DA SILVA TELLES, the Portuguese Ambassador, and by the Minister of State CARVAJAL Y LANCASTER, the Spanish Plenipotentiary :

1st) A Treaty of Instructions for the Commissioners charged with the demarcation of Limits from the extreme South of Brazil to Matto-Grosso;[1]

General Instructions to the Demarcating Commissioners, 17th Jan., 1751.

---

[1] "*Treaty by which were defined the Instructions to the Commissioners who are to proceed to South America, signed at Madrid on the 17th of January of this present year 1751.*" The Portuguese text is in Vol. IV. of this Statement, pp. 25-42, and the English translation in Vol. III., pp. 27-47.

The Portuguese transcription is in accordance with the "*Chave da Demar-*

2d) Separate Articles of this Treaty, relating to the possible resistance that the Indians of the Jesuit Missions in Uruguay might offer to the execution of the Treaty of Limits[1];

3d) A Protocol or Declaration, which was styled Treaty, extending for one year the period for the surrender of the territories ceded[2];

4th) Another Protocol which was also styled Treaty, warning the Demarcating Commissioners against the possible inaccuracies of the Map used in the discussion and agreement regarding the question of Limits.[3]

Afterwards, on the 17th of April, the same Plenipotentiaries signed a "Supplement and Declaration" to the Treaty of Instructions to the Demarcators.[4] The new agreement modified and explained some of the Articles of the Instructions.

Of these five documents, only the first and the Protocol relating to the Map of 1749 can be of use in the examination of the present case. Nevertheless, all five accompany this Statement, transcribed in full from authenticated copies, and translated into English, with the sole and important object of showing that in these Instructions *there is no reference whatever to the Pepiry nor to the Uruguay-Pitã*, as was asserted afterwards

---

cagão" a collection of official authenticated copies of the last century, now in the keeping of the Brazilian Special Mission at Washington. The same Mission has also a copy of the Spanish original, legalized on the 10th of October, 1893, by the Director of the General Archives of Simancas, and on the 12th of the same month by the Secretary of the American Legation at Madrid.

[1] The Portuguese text, Vol. IV., pp. 47-49; English translation, Vol. III., pp. 52-54.
[2] Portuguese text, IV., 50; English translation, III., 55.
[3] English translation, Vol. III., 57; Portuguese text, IV., 53.
[4] English translation, III., 48; Portuguese text, IV., 43.

by the Spanish Commissioners of the survey made under the Treaty of 1777, and as has been affirmed by the supporters of the Argentine pretension.

The Instructions only gave explanations regarding the Igurey,[1] an affluent of the Paraná, and the Corientes,[2] a tributary of the Paraguay, the two Governments thus showing that they were not well assured as to the true situation of these two rivers designated to serve as boundaries.

Neither in the *Secret Instruction* given to the Principal Spanish Commissioner is there anything concerning the Pepiry or the Uruguay-Pitá.

Two Articles of the General Instructions of January 17, 1751, deserve special attention.

The First lays down the following rule which the Principal Commissioners were to impress upon their subordinates:

"Article 31: That the Commissioners shall avoid contentions regarding the demarcation, especially

Commissioners shall avoid contentions.

on matters of little importance, and that they should rather settle at once among themselves any differences that may arise, because it is not the intention of Their Majesties that any part of the work shall be left incomplete without very weighty reasons *nor shall the Commissioners take into consideration any small portion of territory, provided the Line is located by the most visible and lasting natural Boundaries.* But whenever they may be absolutely unable to agree, on account of the great importance of the matter in controversy, separate Maps

---

[1] Articles X. and XI. (Portuguese text, Vol. IV., 31 ; English translation, III., 34).

[2] Article XII. (Portuguese. Vol. IV., 32 ; translation, III., 34).

shall be constructed of the point contested, which shall be accompanied by documents signed by the Commissioners, Astronomers, and Geographers of both parties, in which they shall explain the reasons for their divergence of opinion, and which shall be remitted to the two Courts for the amicable settlement of the question. And, notwithstanding this, the Party shall proceed with the demarcation of the remaining portion of the Boundary."[1]

In Article 37 there is this final declaration:

"It is hereby declared that if the aforesaid Commissioners find any difficulty in any of the points of this Instruction, or if they discover a manner of carrying them out with greater facility, or if they find any inconvenience in the execution of any one or more of them, in all and in each of these cases *they shall decide on and carry out what may seem to them to be best*, provided they attain the principal object, which is the execution of the Treaty with sincerity and good faith, without forced interpretation, nor excuse, and in a manner becoming to the service of Their Majesties."[2] Ample power to the Commissioners.

The Protocol or Declaration, to which was given the name of a "*Treaty on the Interpretation of the Geographical Maps which are to guide the Commissioners who are to demarcate the Boundaries of Brazil*," is, as has been said already, a document of great value in the study of this question.   Declaration relating to the Map of 1749 of the Plenipotentiaries.

It says:

"We the undersigned Ministers Plenipotentiary of

---

[1] Portuguese text in Vol. IV., p. 39; English translation, III., 43.
[2] Vol. III., 46; IV., 42.

Their Most Faithful and Catholic Majesties, by virtue of the Full Powers which we have communicated to each other, and recognized to our reciprocal satisfaction: *Declare that whereas we have been governed by a manuscript geographical Map in drawing up this Treaty and the Instructions for its execution; for this reason a copy of the said Map is to be supplied to each Party of Commissioners of each Sovereign, for their guidance, all signed by us, inasmuch as by it, and in accordance with it, all the expressions are explained. We likewise declare that although according to the information of both Courts we hold all things noted in the said Map as very probable; admitting also that some of the territories demarcated have not been visited by persons now living, and that others have been taken from the Maps of trustworthy persons who have travelled through them, though, perhaps, with little skill to represent them by sketch, on which account there may be some notable variations upon the ground, both in the situations of mountains, and in the origins and courses of rivers, and even in the names of some of them, because it is customary for each Nation in America to give them different names, or for other reasons: It is the Will of the Contracting Sovereigns, and they have agreed, that any variation there may be shall not stay the course of the execution, but that it shall proceed as, in accordance with the Treaty, the mind and intention of THEIR MAJESTIES is manifested in the whole of it, and more particularly in Articles VII., IX., XI., and XXII., according to which the whole shall be punctually executed.* And We, the said Ministers Plenipotentiary, so declare it, in the names of our Sovereigns and by virtue of their Orders and Full Powers, and sign it. This declaration shall be ratified within the same time and period as that of the Extension of the Term, and the Instructions, and a copy of it shall be given to the Commissioners of both Sovereigns. Done at Madrid, on the seventeenth of January one thousand seven hundred and fifty-one."

In 1751 the Commissioners charged with the demarcation by the two Governments were appointed. The long boundary line was divided into two parts; the Southern part, from Castillos Grandes to the Jaurú and the Northern from this river to the North of the Equator.

<small>Appointment of Commissioners.</small>

The two Joint Commissions were subdivided into Sections or Parties and to each one of these a section of the boundary line was allotted. The South Commission thus formed three Parties according to the provision of the following Article of the General Instructions:

"Article 9.—The *First Party* shall survey from Castilhos Grandes to the entrance of the River Ibicuy[1] into the Uruguay, as provided in Art. IV. of the Treaty. To the *Second Party* are allotted the Borders which run from the mouth of the Ibicuy to the point which on the Eastern bank of the Paraná lies in front of the mouth of the River Igurei, in accordance with Art. V. And to the *Third Party*, the remaining borders from the mouth of the Igurei to the River Jaurú, as laid down by Art. VI."

It therefore fell to the share of the *Second Party*, or Subdivision, to make the survey and demarcation between the Uruguay and Iguaçú, and, thus, its work is the only one that need be examined.

---

[1] Also written Ibicuhy.

The Portuguese Government appointed as Principal or First Commissioner in the South Division, General GOMES FREIRE DE ANDRADA, afterwards COUNT DE BOBADELLA, and the Spanish Government the MARQUIS DE VAL DE LIRIOS.

Opposition to the Treaty in Spain and Portugal.

Meanwhile, great opposition to the Treaty of Limits had arisen. The Jesuits of Paraguay addressed representations to the King of Spain and to the Viceroy of Peru complaining of the cession of the Seven Missions to the East of the Uruguay, and petitioning the King to reconsider his action. These documents, as is known to-day, were drawn up by Father PEDRO LOZANO. In the Spanish Archives other representations are to be found, from Fathers JOSEPH QUIROGA, LUIZ ALTAMIRANO, and CARLOS GERVASONI, from the Bishop of Tucuman and from the Governors of this province and of that of Paraguay.

The Jesuits.

On the other hand, the Jesuits in Portugal, fulfilling the orders received from the General Prefect in Rome, used all their influence at the Court of Lisbon to obtain from D. JOSÉ I., who on the 31st of July, 1750, had succeeded D. JOÃO V, the annulment of the Treaty of Limits.

The Portuguese and English merchants interested in the trade of Colonia do Sacramento also raised a great outcry against the surrender of that port and city to the Spaniards, and General VASCONCELLOS, who had victoriously defended the same stronghold during the siege from 1735 to 1737, attempted to prove in a Report, that the Treaty was very prejudicial to the interests of Portugal and endangered the security of its Dominions in America.

The Treaty of 1750 attacked in Portugal.

It was under these evil auspices, public opinion in the two Countries being irritated against the Treaty, that it was endeavored to begin its execution by carrying out the surrender of the ceded territories and the survey and demarcation of the frontiers. *The demarcation begins.*

The Commissioners proceeded slowly with their work from Castillos Grandes as far as Santa Thecla on the head waters of the Rio Negro and of the Ibicuhy. Having reached this point, they were obliged to go back because a body of Guaranys of the Missions came out (1754), summoning them to retreat and declaring that "there was no right to take from the Guaranys those lands which God and Saint Michael had given them." Shortly afterwards other Guaranys attacked the Portuguese Fort of Rio Pardo. *Insurrection of the Guaranys of the Jesuit Missions.*

From the XVIIth century the Jesuits had armed their Indians and brought them under military discipline in order to resist the attacks of the Paulistas. At that moment, and at the summit of their power, they conceived that they could oppose with advantage the decisions of the two Crowns of Portugal and Spain. As early as 1748 the Superior of the Missions, in an arrogant letter, said: "Exterorum acies non timemus. Nihil foris contubare nos potest."

All means of persuasion having been exhausted, a small army, formed with some troops of Brazil and Buenos-Aires under the command of Generals Gomes Freire de Andrada and Joseph Andonaegui, marched against the Uruguay Missions. On the 10th of February, 1756, the Guaranys were completely beaten in the Battle of Caá-ibaté, near the sources *War of Misiones.* *Battle of Caá-ibaté.*

of the Cacequy, and the allied troops were able, almost without resistance, to occupy the Oriental Missions.

These events delayed the Demarcators, and the Second Party was unable to begin its labors till 1759.

The Joint Commission which made the Demarcation in 1759-1760.
It was composed, on the part of Portugal, of the Colonel of Engineers (afterwards General) JOSEPH FERNANDES PINTO ALPOYM, First Commissioner; Captain ANTONIO DA VEIGA D' ANDRADA, Second Commissioner and Astronomer; Ensign MANOEL PACHECO DE CHRISTO, Geographer; and one hundred and nine men more. On the part of Spain, of D. FRANCISCO DE ARGUEDAS, of the King's Council; 1st Lieutenant of the Royal Navy (afterwards Rear Admiral), D. FRANCISCO MILLAU Y MARAVAL, 2d Commissioner and Geographer; 1st Lieutenant, also of the Navy, D. JUAN NORBERTO MARRON, Astronomer; and one hundred and eleven men.

The Brazilian Special Mission can produce the original *Diary*[1] written and signed by the three Portu-

---

[1] "DIARIO / DA / SEGUNDA PARTIDA DA / DEUIZÃO DA AMERICA / *feita pelo Coronel da Artelharia* / JOZÉ FERNANDES PINTO / ALPUYM." ("*Diary of the second Party of the division of America made by Colonel of Artillery, Jozé Fernandes Pinto Alpuym.*") This Commissioner always signed—JOSEPH FERNANDES PINTO ALPOYM, and not *Alpuym*.

The original Manuscript belongs to the Brazilian Foreign Office and was never published. The publication in Vol. VII. of the *Collecção de Noticias para a Historia e Geographia das Nações Ultramarinas*, Lisbon, 1841 (*Collection of Materials for the History and Geography of Nations beyond the Seas*), is a translation of the Spanish Diary, with not very felicitous inversions because the translator aimed at re-constructing the original Portuguese text, which was impossible, and he was careless in his attempt to apply the diplomatic rule of the alternat.

guese Commissioners and an authenticated copy of the Spanish *Diary*.[1]

Diary.

The defenders of the Argentine pretension have constantly said that in the Instructions given to the Commissioners the River Pepiry was distinguished by these features:

An Invention of 1789.

"A full-flowing river, with a bushy island opposite its mouth, a large reef within its bar, *and that the latter is upstream from the Uruguay-Pitá.*"

The Memorandum of the 30th of January, 1883, of DR. VICTORINO DE LA PLAZA, Minister for Foreign Affairs for the Argentine Republic, repeating an invention of the 13th of November, 1789, had said:

"The Manuscript Map expressly made by order of the Courts to serve as a basis for the Treaty, located the River Pepiri or Pequiri higher up the Uruguay-Pitá or to the East of its mouth, and it is known that the said Pepiri or Pequiri was a full-flowing river with a wooded island in front of its mouth and a large reef opposite its bar."

In the Report presented in 1892 to the Argentine Congress, Minister DR. ZEBALLOS, relying on inaccurate information, wrote as follows:

---

[1] " DIARIO / *hecho* / DE ORDEN DE SUS M. M. / C. Y F. / *que comprehende la Demarcacion de / la Linea de division / desde / la boca del Rio Ibicuy siguiendo, por* / LOS RIOS URUGUAY, PEQUIRY, SAN ANTONIO, IGUAZÚ Y / PARANÁ *hasta el Salto Grande de este. Ejecutada / por / las segundas Partidas.* / AÑO DE 1759." ("*Diary made by order of Their Catholic and Most Faithful Majesties which includes the Demarcation of the Line of Division from the mouth of the River Ibicuy following along the rivers Uruguay, Pequiry, San Antonio, Iguazú, and Paraná as far as the Great Fall of the last. Executed by the Second Parties, Year 1759.*")

The original is preserved in the Department of State, at Madrid, and the copy in the possession of the Brazilian Special Mission is authenticated by the Director of the Archive and Library of that Department (2d June, 1893), and by the American Vice-Consul at Madrid (3d June, 1893).

"The Instructions given to the demarcators charged to trace the lines agreed upon, described the river Pequiri in these terms:

"A full-flowing river with a wooded island opposite its mouth, a large reef fronting its mouth, which mouth is upstream of the Uruguay-Pita, a Southern affluent of the Uruguay."[1]

On the 13th of November, 1789 (thirty years after the first survey of the Pepiry), the Spanish Commissioner ALVEAR said in an official letter addressed to his Portuguese associate, Roscio, that the Map of 1749 located the Pepiry above the Uruguay-Pitá and that in 1788 this Pepiry had been found "with the features that characterize it, of being *full-flowing, and of having a wooded island opposite its mouth, and a large reef within its mouth.*"[2]

Transformations through which the invention of 1789 passed.

ALVEAR did not speak of Instructions; he limited himself to applying to the old Pepiry of the treaty of 1750 the features characteristic of the river discovered in 1788, artfully insinuating that in 1759 the Pepiry was known by those features.

This invention was sufficient, however, to lead two other Spanish Commissioners, JURADO and REQUENA, to

---

[1] *Memoria del Ministerio de Relaciones Exteriores presentada al Congresso Nacional por el* DR. ESTANISLAO S. ZEBALLOS, Buenos-Aires, 1892, pag. 6; e ZEBALLOS, *Cuestiones de Limites*, Buenos-Aires, 1893, pag. 7. (Report of the Department of Foreign Affairs presented to the National Congress by DR. ZEBALLOS, 1892, p. 6; and ZEBALLOS, Questions of Limits, 1893, p. 7.)

[2] "Dentro de su barra" (within its mouth), according to the authenticated copy in the possession of the Brazilian Special Mission, of the official letter of 13th November, 1789, of DIEGO DE ALVEAR, and not—"Frente de su barra," (in front of its mouth) as CABRER wrote, when copying this letter into his Diary.

say what follows in their Historical Report of the Demarcation of Limits, dated 1800:

"The features by which in the said Instruction and the Map following it, drawn by mutual agreement, the Pepiri-Guazu was described, were: a full flowing river with a wooded island in front of its mouth; a large reef in front of its mouth; and that this mouth is upstream of the Uruguay-pitá."

Another Spanish Report, written in 1805, inspiring itself from the invention of 1789, and on the addition of 1800, said:

"A full flowing river with a wooded island opposite its mouth, a reef within its mouth, and situated upstream of the Uruguay-puitá."

Subsequently OYÁRVIDE in a Report written at the beginning of this century, and CABRER in another finished at Buenos-Aires in the year 1835, reproduced the invention of ALVEAR but they did not venture to repeat the supposed passage of the Instructions of 1751 and 1758 composed in 1800 and 1805.

The Report of 1892 of the Department of Foreign Affairs of the Argentine Republic, adopting a supposed quotation by one of the numerous writers who have discussed this question in the Press, gives a different wording from the two of 1800 and 1805: and it is thus that the invention of 1789, passing through successive additions and transformations, reaches the presence of the Arbitrator in the final form in which it is about to be destroyed. *Its final form.*

It has already been shown that in the General Instructions (Treaty of the 17th January, 1751) there is no

The invention of 1789 destroyed by two authentic documents. reference whatever to the Pepiry or the Uruguay-Pitã. It is now necessary to show that in the Special Instructions of 27th July, 1758, given to this Second Party, the passage which has been quoted does not occur.

The Argentine Government has doubtless acted in good faith in repeating what is stated in the reports of certain Spanish functionaries written at the end of the last century and the beginning of this, with the object of complicating this question of Limits, in itself so simple.

When the invention of the passage attributed to the Instructions is established, and when it is proved, as it will be proved, that the Pepiry or Pequiry of the Map of 1749 and of the Treaty of 1750 is the same river that was demarcated in 1759, the entire basis will be removed from the argument of the Spanish Commissioners who, after 1789, pretended to correct supposed errors of their predecessors, and to modify the divisional Line defined by the Treaty of 1777, which accepted and confirmed the first demarcation.

The Special Instruction of 27th July, 1758, was only known by some quotations met with in the Diary of the Demarcation of 1759 and 1760. Now, in this last and supreme trial of the suit initiated more than a century ago, and lately revived, it appears for the first time to make the cause of truth and justice triumphant, and to vindicate the memory of the Portuguese and Spanish demarcators of 1759.

The Spanish text of the Special Instruction has recently been found in the General Archives of Simancas, appended to the autograph letter of MARQUIS DE VAL DE LIRIOS, written from S. Nicolas de Misiones, on the

20th of February, 1760, to the Secretary of State, D. RICARDO WALL, and is transcribed and translated among the documents appended to this Statement.[1]

The Portuguese text, according to a copy preserved at the National Library, Lisbon,[2] is as follows[3]:

"Instruction which We, the Principal Commissioners of His Most Faithful Majesty and of His Catholic Majesty Gomes Freire de Andrada, and the Marquis de Valdelirios, have agreed upon and signed for the guidance of the Commissioners of the second Demarcating Party, Joseph Fernandes Pinto e Alpoim, Colonel of the Regiment of Artillery, and D. Francisco de Arguedas, a Member of His Catholic Majesty's Council in the Supreme Court of the Treasury, so that they may execute it in the manner prescribed herein.

Special Instruction of 27th July, 1758.

"*Art. 1.*—Considering that the natives of this country cannot, on account of their customs and natural disposition, be governed by suitable rules, desired

---

[1] Spanish text, Vol. IV., pp. 61–66; English translation, III., 67–75. The original is at Simancas ("Secr² de Estado, Leg? 7,404.")

The copy which the Brazilian Special Mission produces is authenticated by the General Director of the Archives at Simancas (5th October, 1893); by the General Director of Public Instruction (Madrid, 9th October); by the Minister of the Interior, D. SIGISMUNDO MORET Y PRENDERGAST (9th October), and by MR. STEPHEN BONSAL, Secretary to the American Legation (Madrid, 12th October).

[2] National Library of Lisbon, "Archivo do Conselho Ultramarino, Brazil, Avulsos, maço 233." The copy in the possession of the Brazilian Special Mission was authenticated on the 3d January, 1894, by the Director of the same Library, SR. MONTE PERFIRA, and by the Sub-Director of the Section of Political Affairs in the Portuguese Foreign Office, SR. MACHADO DA FRANCA; and on the 5th January, by Mr. CARUTH, American Minister at Lisbon.

[3] As this Vol. I. contains the translation of the Statement of Brazil, written and printed in Portuguese in Vol. II., the Portuguese text of the Instruction will be found in the latter Vol. (II., pp. 64–69).

Offences and punishments.

by both Sovereigns in order to secure the tranquillity of the Expeditions, the Commissioners of the Second Demarcating Party shall endeavor to conform as much as possible to Articles 21, 22, 23, and 24 of the Special Instructions, which treat of offences and punishments. But in cases in which they may find any difficulty, we grant them power to do that which may seem to them most prudent with the greatest concord and conformity, which is that which the Contracting Sovereigns command.

"*Art. 2.*—The Commissioners shall take the greatest care to conform to Articles 25, 27, 28, 29, 30, and 31

Cosmographers.

of the same Instructions, which treat of the duty incumbent on the Cosmographers, because both Their Majesties command that the work they are to do shall not only be accurate, but that it shall also be profitable to the advancement of science.

"*Art. 3.*—Considering that in the wildernesses and rugged places through which this party is to travel, the help of horses cannot be obtained to allow

The Demarcation from S. Xavier, on the Uruguay, to the Pepiry.

them to make the demarcation in the manner prescribed by the Sovereigns, we have resolved that the Commissioner of His Catholic Majesty shall go to the village of S. Nicolas, and see that the Canoes, Guides, and Rowers are ready, so that when the Commissioner of His Most Faithful Majesty arrives, they may at once proceed together to that of *S. Xavier, where they shall embark upon the rafts they will have constructed there with the canoes, and they shall ascend the Uruguay until they meet, on its Western bank the mouth of the river Pequiri,* or

Pepirí which they shall enter, continuing River Pepiry or Pequiry.
up its stream as far as its principal source,
or as far as the canoes can reach. From this point
they shall send a Party on foot to survey on the highest
ground the principal head of the nearest river that
flows into the Yguassù,[1] upon discovering which, if they
find that the canoes can be carried on men's shoulders,
the Commissioner of His Catholic Majesty Nearest river flowing into the Iguaçû.
shall send a canoe which shall return by
the same river with the information, and
with the order that the boats which shall be ready on
the Paraná go up that river at once to await them
at the mouth of the Yguassù, and in the meantime the
provisions and canoes shall be conveyed by land to the
nearest river that empties itself into the Yguassù.

"*Art. 4.*—For the determination of the principal
heads of the Pepirí and of the river nearest to it that
empties itself into the Yguassù, the Commissioners
shall seek those whose waters are most
abundant; but if the want of horses and Headwaters of the Pepiry and of the affluents of the Iguaçû.
baggage (in the event of the provisions
and canoes having to be carried on the
shoulders of Indians) does not allow that determination of the watercourses to be made, they shall
choose that which may seem best to them and
in accordance with Article 31 of the Instructions,[2]
and they can also take advantage of the epicheia[3]

---

[1] In this document the name of this river was written both Yguassù and Iguaçû.

[2] Art. 31 of the General Instructions, Vol. III., page 43 (English translation) and Vol. IV., page 39 (Portuguese text).

[3] "*Epiky*,(obs.) also *epicay*, *epicheia* . . . Reasonableness, equity as opposed to rigid law." (HENRY BRADLEY, *A New English Dictionary on Historical*

offered by Article 12, which in this case may be applied.¹

"*Art. 5.*—They shall go down the River nearest to the Pepiri as far as its mouth in the Iguaçú, and they shall continue down the stream of this as far as its Salto (Falls), where they shall leave the canoes if they cannot easily convey them, and they shall go overland as far as its mouth in the Paraná, where they shall wait for the boats; and, having embarked in them, they shall go up its waters as far as where the whirlpools formed by its Salto Grande (Great Falls) allow the boats to proceed; and, going to its Western bank, they shall send a party, who shall go as close as possible along the bank of the river, and who shall survey it, as well as the ground, to see whether it can find the landmark left there by the Third Party; and when the thickness of the bush and the roughness of the way do not allow this to be done on foot, they shall take in that region the necessary observations to determine as to the course of the river at that spot.

<small>From the affluent of the Iguaçú to the Paraná</small>

"*Art. 6.*—*If the head of the River that empties into the Iguaçú, and which is believed to be near*

Principles, founded mainly on the materials collected by the Philological Society, Oxford, 1891.)

In Portuguese,—*epicheia,*—*epiqueia ;*—in Spanish, *epiqueya* (from the Greek ἐπιείχεια and ἐπιείκεια).

"*Epiqueya.*—In Spanish law.—The benignant and prudent interpretation of the law, according to the circumstances of the time, place, and person. This word is derived from the Greek, and is synonymous with the word equity. See MURILLO, nn. 67, 68." (JOHN BOUVIER, *A Law Dictionary adapted to the Constitution of the United States of America and of the several States of the American Union, with references to the Civil and other systems of Foreign Law.*" Philadelphia, 1883).

¹ In Vol. III., page 34 (English translation), and Vol. IV., page 32 (Portuguese text).

that of the Pepiri, is not found, or if the *[If the headwaters of the Pepiry cannot be reached.]* distance between them is so great, or the ground so rough that they think the canoes cannot be conveyed overland, they shall take their observations at the spot they are able to reach, and they shall return down the course of the Uruguay as far as the village of Conceição (Concepcion), or as that of S. Xavier, whence they shall proceed overland to that of Candelaria, and embarking there, they shall go up the course of the Paraná as far as the mouth *[Return and ascent by the Paraná and Iguaçú.]* of the Iguaçú, which they shall ascend as far as its Salto (Falls), and carrying overland the canoes they may have taken with them, or building others there, if they cannot carry them, they shall go up the latter as far as the mouth of some *[Mouth of an unknown affluent.]* River that may be with a slight difference in the same longitude in which they consider the heads of the Pepiri to be; and, navigating along it[1] as far as they can they shall take the necessary obser- *[If unable to reach the headwaters.]* vations, in order that they may trace upon the Map they are to construct a line connecting the two points observed.

"*Art. 7.—From the place which they reach*[2] they shall go down its waters and those of the Iguaçú as far as the mouth of the latter in the Pa- *[From the affluent of the Iguaçú to the Paraná.]* raná, where they shall take to their boats and shall proceed in the same manner prescribed in Article the 4th.[3] And this operation being completed, they shall withdraw by the same

---

[1] To this river, discovered and surveyed in 1759, the name of *S. Antonio* was given by the Commissioners.

[2] In the river afterwards named S. Antonio.

[3] In the Lisbon copy the number of the Article is wanting. It is supplied here from the Spanish copy at Simancas (Vol. III. of this Statement, p. 71).

river Paraná to the Village of Candelaria, and thence by land to that of Conceição (Concepcion). Hence they shall send in canoes two Cosmographers, one of each nationality, who shall travel down stream, drawing the Plan of the Uruguay as far as where, on its Eastern bank, the Ibicuhy empties itself into it, and hence they shall withdraw whither they may be commanded.

<small>The Survey of the Uruguay, from S. Xavier to the Ibicuhy.</small>

"*Article 8.*—The Commissioner of His Catholic Majesty shall supply the Commissioner of His Most Faithful Majesty with canoes and boats as well as with jerked beef for all the Party under his command, as we, the Principal Commissioners, have agreed. And in all else that either may need they shall assist one another as provided in the Instructions.

<small>Boats and provisions.</small>

"*Article 9.*—The order to be observed in the advance by the rafts and boats of the two Nations shall be the following. The first day the two Commissioners shall draw lots in order to determine who is to lead the advance upon that day, and, this having been ascertained, they shall afterwards proceed alternately. But if this cannot be strictly carried out, either because it seems to them more proper and necessary that the guides of the river should go first, or on account of some other impediment, they shall not attach too much importance to its execution, but shall do what may be possible and may be most conducive to their common convenience and to facilitate the voyage.

<small>Order of the advance.</small>

"*Article 10.*—The scale to which they shall draw the Map shall be the same that was used by the Third

Party, which is ten inches to the degree, of which the Commissioners shall inform the Cosmographers, warning them above all that it must be executed with the greatest clearness, which is what is required, and is in conformity with the intentions of the two Sovereigns. Map.

"*Article 11.—Inasmuch as in the carrying out of the provisions of Articles 3, 4, 5, 6, and 7 of these Instructions there may be some difficulties that will not permit its strict observance, satisfied of the prudence, zeal, and intelligence of the two First Commissioners, we give them power to act as they may think best, according to the nature of the ground through which they travel, in order to conclude this part of the Demarcation, leaving it clear and well marked, conformably to the will of our Sovereigns.* Unlimited powers.

"In witness whereof we, the abovesaid Principal Commissioners, have signed it and sealed it with the Great Seal of our Arms. At the Ford of the River Jacuhy (Passo do Jacuhy), the twenty-seventh of July one thousand seven hundred and fifty-eight."

This Special Instruction does not say, as the Argentine Government supposed, that the mouth of the Pepiry in the Uruguay is above that of the Uruguay-Pitã, neither does it mention the island so much talked of, nor the reef near the mouth of the same Pepiry. The 3d Article.

What may be read in Article 3d is simply this:

PORTUGUESE TEXT.

" Em attenção a que em os dezertos e asperezas por donde deve hir esta Partida não poderá achar soccorros de cavallarias, que lhe permittão fazer a Demarcação em os termos, que prescrevem os Soberanos, temos disposto, que o Commissario de S. M. C. vá ao Povo de S. Nicoláo, e disponha, que as canoas, Praticos e remeiros estejam promptos, para que quando chegue o Commissario de S. M. F. passem logo juntos ao de *S. Xavier, donde se embarcarám em as Balças, que aly formarem das canóas, e subirám pelo Uruguay até encontrar pela sua margem Occidental a bocca do Rio Pequiri, ou Pepiri, pela qual entrarám, e* continuarám aguas arriba delle até a sua origem principal, ou até donde possam chegar as canóas. . . "

SPANISH TEXT.

" En atencion a que en los desiertos, y asperezas por donde debe ir esta Partida no se podrá hallar socorros de Caballerias, que le permitan hazer la damarcacion en los terminos que prescriben los Soberanos, hemos dispuesto que el Comisario de S. M. C. se vaya al Pueblo de San Nicolas, y disponga que las Canoas, Practicos y Remeros esten prontos para que quando llegue el Comisario de S. M. F. passen luego juntos al de *San Xavier, donde se embarcarán en las Balsas, que formaren alli de las Canoas, y subirán por el Uruguay hasta encontrar* por su ribera occidental la boca de el rio Pequiri ó Pepiri, por la que entrarán, y continuarán aguas arriba de el hasta su origen principal, ó hasta donde puedan llegar las canoas. . . . . "

The following is a translation of the two texts:
"Considering that in the deserts and rugged places

to which this Party is to go it will not be able to find the help of horses that will allow them to make the Survey in the conditions the Sovereigns prescribe, we have ordered that the Commissioners of His Catholic Majesty shall proceed to the Village of S. Nicoláo (or San Nicolas) and shall arrange that the canoes, Guides, and rowers shall be ready, in order that when the Commissioner of His Most Faithful Majesty arrives they shall at once pass on together to that of S. Xavier, where they shall embark upon the Rafts they shall there construct with the canoes, and they shall go up the Uruguay until they meet on its Western bank the mouth of the River Pequiri, or Pepiri, which they shall enter, and they shall continue ascending its waters as far as its principal source, or as far as the canoes can reach. . . "

Nothing is said about the Pepiry up stream of the Uruguay-Pitá; nothing concerning any wooded island; nothing about any reef within or without the mouth of the Pepiry. *One of the two documents quoted in support of the Argentine pretension never existed.*

Thus disappears, because it never existed, one of the two documents which the Argentine Government alleged, giving credit to the inventions of the Spanish Commissioners charged with the second delimitation of frontiers, under the Treaty of 1777. The other document is the Map of 1749, which will be considered later on.

An examination of the demarcation of 1759 to 1760 will show that the Commissioners of the two nations appointed under the Treaty of 1750 carried out exactly the instructions they received.[1]

---

[1] The Maps upon which this survey of 1759 can be studied are those num-

On the 1st of February, 1759, they started from S. Xavier,[1] the most northerly of the Missions the Spanish Jesuits had on the Uruguay, and, therefore, the nearest to the Brazilian frontier. From this village to the mouth of the Pepiry, afterwards Pepiry-Guaçú, it is, in a straight line, some 150 kilometres, or 80 English miles.

The Commissioners ascend the Uruguay, starting from S. Xavier.

The expedition continued, embarked on rafts and canoes, making the survey of the Uruguay.

On the 5th, it passed before the mouth of the Mbororé, an affluent of the right bank, and the limit of the Spanish occupation on that side of the Uruguay.

River Mbororé, the limit of the Spanish occupation.

The diary of the Spanish Commissioners, speaking of the river Mbororé, says:

" . . . *it is also the extreme point reached by land by the Indians of Misiones, who do not venture to go beyond it for fear of the Caribs.*"

On the 10th the expedition surveyed the mouth of the Acaraguá or Acaraguay, the former Acarana. There

---

bered 7 A (Map of 1749, of the Plenipotentiaries), 12 A (Map of 1760, appended to the Portuguese Diary of that Demarcation) and 29 A (prepared by the Brazilian Special Mission for the study of this question).

Besides these, the Brazilian Special Mission can produce to the Arbitrator the same Map, No. 12 A, but on a larger scale, from a copy of the very original constructed by the Portuguese and Spanish Commissioners in 1760. The copy in the National Library of Lisbon (Archivo do Conselho Ultramarino. Brazil, maço 93) was photographed, and the copy in the possession of the Brazilian Special Mission is legalized by the Director of the same Library; by the Portuguese Foreign Office; and by the American Minister at Lisbon (5th January, 1894). The title is:—"PLANO DA RAIA MARCA-/ *da nos Estados do Brazil pellos Offici-/ aes da Segunda Divizão pertencente ao / Parlido do Rio Grande de S. Pedro na / Expedição do anno de 1750. Copiado / do proprio original q. se elevou na campanha.*" (" Plan of the border-line demarcated in the States of Brazil by the Officers of the Second Division belonging to the Party of Rio Grande de S. Pedro in the Expedition of the year 1750. Copied from the very original which was constructed on the spot.")

[1] In division II 6 of Map 29 A.

the Jesuits had had, from 1630 to 1637, the mission Assumpcion, which, at the latter date, they removed to the Mbororé, and suppressed in 1641, taking the Indians who composed it to Yapejú, in consequence of the new invasions of the Brazilians of S. Paulo.[1] *River Acaraguá.*

On the 20th February the Commissioners passed the mouth of the Guanumbaca, which already appeared under that name in the old Maps of the Jesuits, and before that of the Mandiy-Guaçû, now Soberbio, both on the right bank ; on the 21st by that of the Paricay, now Turvo, on the left bank ; on the following day by that of the Itacaray,[2] on the right, the last point which, in 1759, the Guaranys of Misiones reached by water, as may be seen in the following passage from the Spanish Diary : *R. Guanumbaca. R. Mandiy-Guaçû. R. Paricay. Itacaray farthest point of the fluvial journeys of the Guaranys of Misiones.*

" The Itacaray is the farthest point reached by the Indians of some villages of Uruguay, when coming to gather the herb which they use in *maté*, although there are very few villages in whose immediate neighborhood it is not cultivated."

In the proper place in this Statement, it will be shown that, as early as 1788, according to the Spaniard OYÁRVIDE, the Indians of Misiones did not come so near the Pepiry in their river voyages.

---

[1] The Diary of the Demarcators says that Assumpcion del Acaraguá was founded about the year 1623. The true date is 1630, as may be seen in TECHO, *Historia Provinciæ Paraquariæ Societatis Jesv*, Lille, 1673, Lib. IX, Cap. XXVI. In 1657 these Indians separated themselves from those of the mission of Yapejú, to form that of La Cruz to the South of the Aguapey (division L 2 in Map N° 29 A).

[2] Division F 10 in Map N° 29 A.

The Spanish Diary continues:

"Twenty-third day" (February 23, 1759).—"The Spanish Party led the advance. As far as the Itacaray, we have several Indian guides, but thence forward the only one we had was FRANCISCO XAVIER ARIRAPY, who had gone up many years before in the last journey the Indians of San Xavier made to the place which they called Espia" (lookout), "because men of the said village used to scout there in order not to be surprised by the inroads of the Paulistas, to which they were at first much exposed."

The guide Arirapy.

Ancient lookout to watch the movements of the Brazilians of S. Paulo.

Further on (5th day of March) the Spanish Diary says that ARIRAPY was in the Pepiry "some years before" and not "many years before":—" . . . and that by this name he had known it in a voyage he had made *some years before* with others from his village to the place called Espia."

That voyage could only have been made after 1749, that is to say, within the ten years which preceded this survey and demarcation, because,—as will be shown,—even in 1749 the Jesuits of Misiones, knowing nothing about the Upper Uruguay, gave the name of Pepiry to a river below the Great Falls (Salto Grande), and not to the Pequiry or Pepiry of the Paulistas, the first river above the same Salto Grande of the Uruguay.

The journey of Arirapy to the Pepiry.

ARIRAPY, therefore, did not make the voyage when a child ("cuando niño") as the supporters of the Argentine pretension have said. In this survey of 1759 there was at least one guide; in the surveys made after the second Treaty, the Spanish Commissioners did not find a single one. There was not in 1788 and

1789 in Misiones one single Indian who had gone up the Uruguay beyond the mouth of the Paricay, then called Cebollaty, and now Turvo.[1]

On the 23d February, the Commissioners passed before the mouth of the Jaboty-Guaçû, a river which to this day keeps the name of Jaboty, but is better known by that of Pepiry-Mini, that is to say, small Pepiry.[2]   *Jaboty-Guaçû or Pepiry-Mini.*

On the following day they advanced but little. From the place at which they halted to rest they already heard the sound of the Great Falls (Salto Grande), also called now Salto de Moconã.   *Great Falls of the Uruguay.*

The days from the 25th to the 27th were spent in surveying the banks of the river and the cataract; the following days to the 4th of March in overcoming this obstacle which completely obstructed the navigation.

The fall of the river presented at that time a height of about 11 metres on the Western steep rock (36 English feet) and 6 metres of the East (over 19 feet).

On the 4th of March, leaving the Great Falls, the expedition advanced only one league and encamped

---

[1] OYARVIDE, in CALVO, *Recueil de Traités*, Vol. IX., p. 188.

[2] Besides Maps N° 29 A (prepared by the Brazilian Special Mission) and N° 12 A (Commissioners of 1759) the two maps constructed by the Brazilian-Argentine Joint Commission, which, under the Treaty of 28th September, 1885, made the survey of the rivers which limit the Brazilian territory claimed by the Argentine Republic since 1881, should now be consulted. The facsimiles of those are numbered 25 A (the one drawn by the Brazilian Commission) and 26 A (the one drawn by the Argentine Commission). The survey of the river Uruguay began in 1887 at the mouth of the Pepiry-Mini or Jaboty (Division F 2 in Map. N° 25 A).

The *Diary* written by the Argentine Commission says:

"On the 13th day (July, 1887), the survey of the Uruguay was begun, the first station being situated on the right bank of the mouth of *the river known to the inhabitants of the place as the Pepiry-Mini and to which others give the name of Jaboti which it has in the region of the village of San Pedro.*"

Itayoá Stream.

near the mouth of the Itayoá streamlet, a small affluent on the right bank.[1] On the following day, navigating two thirds of a league more, it reached the mouth of the Pepiry, which, therefore, was found five miles above the Great Falls (Salto Grande).

River Pepiry or Pequiry.

The Diary of the Spanish Demarcators says:

"Fifth Day "(5th March,1759).—"The Spanish Party led the advance and we followed the same Western bank[2] upon which we were, and, turning to S.S.E., in which direction the river flows, and there are two small reefs close together, we left two torrents which fell from between the rocks, which we believed were produced by the heavy rain of the previous night. And the numerous boulders and the shallowness of the river, which turns to the E.S.E., caused no slight fatigue. *In this direction there is a reef terminating in a small*

Small island near the mouth of the Pepiry.

island of rock and sarandí[3] trees, and lying close to the northern bank, which island is covered over at flood time, and behind it, at a distance of ⅔ of a league of the Itayoá, is the mouth of a river which can only be seen after having doubled the point of the island, which river, the guide said, was the Pepiri, of which we were in search.[4] The Commissioners summoned him to their presence, and, all the other officers of the two Nations having assembled, asked

---

[1] In the Map of the Brazilian Commission (N.º 25 A) it is named Itapua.

[2] Right bank of the Uruguay.

[3] *Sarandí*, a shrub, whose scientific name is *Phyllanthus Sellowianus*. The species was described by M. MUELLER (d'Argovie), in the *Monographie des Suphorbiacées* (Prodr. de CANDOLLE, Vol. XV., 2d Part, p. 397).

[4] Under N.º 27 A (Vol. VI.) is a fac-simile of the *Plan of the mouth of the Pepiry-Guaçú* (in 1759 Pepiry or Pequiry) drawn after survey, in 1887, by the Brazilian-Argentine Joint Commission.

him what river that was; and he replied again that it was the Pepirí, and that by this name he had known it in a voyage he had made some years before with others from his village to the place they called Espia. At this time there was so little water in the river that it was evident that it was navigable for only a short distance. *And knowing from other information that the Pepirí had a reef near its mouth*, the Commissioners and the Astronomer of Portugal went to explore it; and it was found at half a league from there. *Notwithstanding this, seeing that we had not arrived at the latitude at which the Pepirí is represented in the Map issued by the Courts, and, furthermore, that the situation of the river on which we were, below the Uruguay-pitá, which empties itself on the opposite bank, was not in accordance with the said Map, where it is represented as being above the Uruguay-pitá; in order to correct this Map, and to remove any sort of doubt* which might be raised against the testimony of the guide who *was the only one, not merely among those present, but among the inhabitants of all the villages of Misiones, who could give any evidence*, there not then *remaining any other Indian who had navigated the river above the Falls*, and as, many years having passed since he had navigated it a single time, he might have forgotten it, the two Commissioners resolved to go up the Uruguay on the following day, and also that a plan of this section of it should be jointly drawn after survey, so that the comparison of the evidence he had previously given of the rivers Apiterebí, and Uruguay-pitá, to the point he said he had reached, with their true situation, might assure us as to his knowledge and experience."

A reef near the mouth.

Voyage on the Uruguay above the mouth of the Pepiry.

On the following day the Commissioners, Astronomers, and Geographers went up the Uruguay in canoes. At a quarter of a league from the Pepiry they saw on the left bank of the Uruguay the mouth of an unnamed rivulet, now the Pari. Continuing in the N.E. direction, they passed by the reefs which form the Rapids, at present called Corredeira do Pari, and farther on, when the river made a bend which comes from East and South-east, they crossed other rapids, now known as the Corredeira dos Macacos Brancos. Here, near a rocky island, they saw on the right bank the mouth of the river "which the guide called *Api-terebí*," a league and a quarter distant from the Pepiry. Continuing in the direction of S.S.E. and afterwards E., they reached a curve of the river, which came from N.E., and then they met other rapids, now named Corredeira do Guarita.

<small>River Apitereby.</small>

The Diary then says:

"The river continues its bend to the N.E. and N.E. ¼ N., and at the beginning of this direction, at a distance of about 2½ leagues of the Pepiri, it receives by the Eastern bank a large river which the guide said was the *Uruguay-pitã*, the furthest point to which his knowledge extended."

<small>R. Uruguay-Pitã, or Uruguay-Puitã.</small>

This distance of 2½ leagues between the mouth of the Pepiry to the West, and that of the Uruguay-Pitã to the East, is an important point, as it will appear in the Spanish Instructions given subsequently to the Commissioners charged to make the demarcation of boundaries under the Treaty of 1777.

<small>Distance between the Pepiry and the 2nd Uruguay-Pitã.</small>

The expedition entered the Uruguay-Pitã:

"We went up this (river) some distance to see

whether the colors of its waters corresponded with its name which means the *Red Uruguay*, and it was found that they partook somewhat of its color. Its width, which was measured at a very short distance from its mouth, is 49 Toises and 4 feet; and its depth is 6, 11, 12, 14, and 16 King's feet; and in a navigation of nearly half a league, we found that it keeps its depth of 12 feet, the Great Uruguay having no part in this, as being so low, its waters could not contain those of the Pitá, which is the largest river we met from S. Xavier."

This river *Uruguay-Pitã*, or *Uruguay-Puitã*, of the demarcators of 1759, has been known since the middle of the present century by the name of Rio da Guarita, which in the Map of the Brazilian-Argentine Joint Commission appears between brackets after the name Mberuy.[1] *Two Historical errors to be corrected.*

The Brazilian Government and the Brazilian Special Mission do not accept this erroneous application of the name Mberuy, invented by the Spanish Commissioners after 1789; nor do they accept that of Uruguay-Pitã, wrongly applied in the same Map to the old river Trigoty, now Rio da Varzea.[2] These are denominations adopted by the Spaniards of the second demarcation, but repudiated then by the Portuguese, and afterwards by all Brazilians who have studied the two demarcations. Among the latter may be mentioned General CHAGAS SANTOS and VISCOUNT DE S. LEOPOLDO, whose Maps are appended to this Statement.[3]

[1] In division F 2 of Map No. 25 A (Joint Commission), and Division F 10 of No. 29 A (Brazilian Special Mission).
[2] Division F 4 in Map 25 A; Division F 12 in No. 29 A.
[3] Map of CHAGAS SANTOS, of the beginning of this century, No. 21 A, and of S. LEOPOLDO, of 1839, No. 22 A. In both the river surveyed by the Portuguese and Spanish demarcators in 1759 appears under the name of *Uruguay-Pitã*.

This point must be made absolutely clear in order to avoid confusion. The name Mberuy, applied to the Uruguay-Pitã of the demarcators of 1759, and that of Uruguay-Pitã, transferred to a river more to the East, formerly named Trigoty, and called by the Portuguese Rio da Picada (now Rio da Varzea), are creations of the Spanish Commissioners much subsequent to the second Treaty, dated 1777.

The Brazilian and Argentine Governments, in the Instructions of 1885, charged the Joint Commission to make a Plan after survey of the disputed territory, but did not direct them to attribute to the rivers ancient or historical names.

Returning to the Uruguay on the same 6th day of March, the Commissioners continued their expedition up stream in the direction of the E.N.E., passing two reefs and rapids now called Corredeira da Pedra Branca and Corredeira da Jacutinga. They passed the night above this.

The Commissioners continue to ascend the Uruguay in 1759.

The Spanish Diary then says:

"Not far from this second reef, on the bank, an old mortar was found which, from its make, the Paulistas recognized as having belonged to their people, who had probably left it behind in one of their former malocas (inroads which they used to make against the Indians of these settlements to take them as slaves), and there was also seen a small and very old clearing of trees which was attributed to the same.

Signs of the old Brazilian rule.

"The banks on the bottom of the river are for the most part of rock with high steep bank and a mountain on either side, although not so high as in the neighborhood of the Falls, and always covered with trees."

On the 7th of March the Commissioners continued the ascent of the Uruguay, passing by a rocky island (Ilha da Fortaleza) and they reached the small cataract of two metres in height (6 English feet) known as Salto da Fortaleza.[1] Thence they returned to the Pepiry, as may be seen in the following passage of the Spanish Diary: *Rocky Island and Small cataract.*

"Seventh Day" (7th March, 1759).—"We continued our advance in the direction of the E.N.E., from which by the slope of the hill a stream enters the river on the Northern bank; which turning to the S.E. ¼ E., receives another on the opposite side. It turns to the S. ¼ S.E., and in this direction, at a little more than half a league, there is a rocky island, small but high,[2] having passed which we saw a large Waterfall, which we judged to be a toise in *Now called Small Falls of Fortaleza.*
height, forming steps over which the water leaped impetuously, obstructing the advance.[3] We stopped in front of the island, and sent a small boat forward to examine the Fall, and with orders that, if on either side a passage could be found, the advance should be continued around a point which could be seen in the distance, and that it should be ascertained whether on the Western side any river entered which would agree better with the Map issued by the Courts. The small boat was accompanied to the foot of the Fall by some of the officers who reported that in order to continue the navigation it would be necessary to execute a

---

[1] Division F 3 in Map No. 25 A (of the Joint Commission); Division F 11 of Map No. 29 A (of the Brazilian Special Mission).

[2] The island of Fortaleza.

[3] Falls of Fortaleza.

manœuvre of hauling the boats (a carry) such as we had made at the Great Falls, and the crew of the small boat, who went some distance by land, did not find any river whatever.

"In view of this difficulty, and of the fact that the various small streams which so repeatedly discharge into that side (of the Uruguay) gave us no hope of there being a larger river near by, the Commissioners called together the Astronomers and Geographers of the two Nations; and, when they had all assembled,[1] the Commissioner of His Catholic Majesty explained his motives for the precaution which he had taken, and for the fear he had that the Pepiri might not be the river which the guide had pointed out, both because its latitude and position did not agree with those laid down in the aforesaid Map, and because after so many years he might have forgotten the features of the land and the rivers. He also explained the reasons which removed his doubt after this examination had been made, which reasons were based on the assertion of the said guide, who, in the month of November in the year 1757, had assured him, at the village of S. Xavier, that not only had he been to the Pepiri, which should be reached on the same day after leaving the Salto Grande (Great Falls) of the Uruguay, which furthermore he had repeated on different occasions in the course of the journey, but that he had gone beyond it, now stating that he had only reached the Uruguay-pitá; he (the

Conference of 7th March, 1759.

Statement made by the first Spanish Commissioner Arguedas.

Doubts he had.

---

[1] This conference of the 7th March, 1759, took place near the Salto Pequeno or Saltinho da Fortaleza (Small Falls of Fortaleza).

Spanish Commissioner) was convinced that the river he (the guide) had known by the name of Pepirí was behind, and that it could be no other than that he (the guide) had pointed out and said, because this was the only river which could be reached on the same day after leaving the Salto (Falls). And inasmuch as, on the other hand, the information he had given concerning the two other rivers Apiterebí and Uruguay-Pitá, which he knew, was found to agree with their true location, it was evident that he had not forgotten their features. Besides this, his testimony was proved by other printed Maps, and by some manuscripts made by the Indians during the time when they used to navigate in these parts,[1] which place the Uruguay-pitá above the Pepirí, near the mouth of which latter they had found the reef, which according to information, was known to be there; and the said Commissioner concluded by saying that, if, notwithstanding these reasons, any one entertained still any suspicion or doubt, or if there occurred to any one any further investigation that could be undertaken in order to attain, if possible, a greater certainty in the identification of the river, the suggestion should be made, inasmuch as we were still in time to carry it into execution.

The information of the guide confirmed.

Pepiry near the Great Falls (Salto Grande).

Other Maps confirm the information of the guide.

---

[1] The *Report* of 1892 of the Argentine Foreign Office attributes to Councillor PARANHOS (VISCOUNT DE RIO-BRANCO) this quotation of printed and Manuscript Maps locating the Uruguay-Pitá above the Pepiry. It is true that this is the reading in the Memorandum of 1857 (Portuguese text Vol. IV.; English translation, Vol. III.), but the first who made this assertion was the Spanish Commissioner ARGUEDAS, at the Conference of 7th March, 1759. And in this Statement it will be proved that ARGUEDAS spoke the truth, because *all the Maps printed before that of the Plenipotentiaries, of 1749, give the mouth of the former Pepiry, in the Uruguay, below that of the former Uruguay-Pitá.*

<small>All agree that the river pointed out by the guide is the Pepiry of the Treaty.</small> "All agreed that there was no doubt that the river was the Pepirí, which was always a very large river, although at this time we found little water in it, as was also the case with the Uruguay itself; and upon this agreement it was resolved to turn back to the camp where we arrived after four and a half hours' navigation down stream, having passed the reefs at great risk but without accident, by their channels in which the head winds raised furious waves which, repeatedly breaking into the boats, wetted us all. And, just after we had arrived, a heavy rain fall which continued during part of the night."

Next, under date of 8th March, 1759, comes the Act of recognition and identification of the River Pepiry or Pequiry.

<small>Act of identification of the Pepiry.</small> The Spanish Diary for the 8th day begins thus:

"All being certain that the river at the mouth of which we were was the Pepirí, the following Act of identification was made and signed by all."

This is the document reproduced according to the two Portuguese and Spanish originals:

PORTUGUESE TEXT.	SPANISH TEXT.
"Os Commissarios da Segunda Partida de Demarcação JOSEPH FERNANDES PINTO ALPOYM por S. M. F., e D. FRANCISCO ARGUEDAS por S. M. C., ouvido o parecer unanime dos Astronomos, Geographos, e officiaes das	"Los Commissarios de la Segunda Partida de Demarcacion D. FRANCISCO ARGUEDAS por S. M. C. y JOSEPH FERNANDES PINTO ALPOYM por S. M. F. oido el parecer unanime de los Astronomos, Geographos y Oficiales de las dos Na-

duas Nações, os quaes em
virtude das razoens expostas
na junta antecedente,
e da affirmação do Indio
vaqueano FRANCISCO XAVIER ARIRAPÍ, Sargento do
seo Povo de S. Xavier, cujo
conhecimento, e noticia
destes rios se comprovou
com a conformidade que
se achou entre as que delles
dava e sua verdadeira
situação, disserão lhes não
ficava a menor duvida, de
que era o Pepirí o rio que
o ditto vaqueano assignava
e em cuja bocca estavão
campadas as Partidas; e
assim declaramos, que reconhecemos
este pelo Rio
Pepirí determinado no Art.
5º do Tratado de limites,
por fronteira dos Dominios
de Suas Magestades Fidellissima, e Catholica; em
consequencia do que a
Demarcação começada no
Povo de S. Xavier, e seguida
agoas acima do Uruguay
até a bocca deste,
deve continuar por elle seguindo
o seo curso até as
suas cabeceiras, sem embargo
de se não achar a

ciones, quienes (en fuerza
de las razones expuestas
en la junta antecedente, y
de la asercion del Indio
vaqueano FRANCISCO XAVIER ARIRAPÍ, Sargento
de su Pueblo de San Xavier,
cuyo conocimiento, y
noticia de estos rios se
comprobó con la conformidad
que se halló entre
las que de ellos daba, y su
verdadera situacion) dijeron
no les quedaba la
menor duda de que era el
Pepiri el rio, que dicho
vaqueano designaba, y en
cuya boca estaban acampadas
las Partidas, declaramos
este por el Rio
Pepirí determinado en el
Articulo quinto del Tratado
de Límites por frontera
de los Dominios de
Sus Magestades Catholica
y Fidelisima y en su consequencia,
que la demarcacion
empezada en el Pueblo
de San Xavier, y seguida
aguas arriba del Uruguay
hasta la boca de este debe
continuar siguiendo su curso
hazia sus cabezeras, sin
embargo de no hallarse su

sua effectiva posição conforme a que se dá no Mappa de Demarcação dado pelas duas Cortes, não devendo conforme a declaração assignáda nas costas delle pelos Excellentissimos Senhores Plenipotenciarios Thomaz da Sylva Telles, Visconde de Ponte de Lima, e D. Joseph de Carvalhal e Lancastre, attender-se ao dito Mappa senão em quanto este se acha conforme ao Tratado; e para que em todo o tempo conste este Acto de reconhecimento, e termo da Divizão de Limites fizemos a presente declaração, firmada por todos os abaixo assignados.

" Bocca do Rio Pepirí, oito de Março de mil settecentos cincoenta e nove.

" Joseph Frz. P^{to} Alpoym.

" Antonio da Veiga d'Andrada.

" Manoel Pacheco de Christo.

efectiva posicion conforme á la que le dá el Mapa de la Demarcacion dada por las dos Cortes, no debiendo, segun la declaracion signada en el reverso de el por los Ex^{mos} Sres. Plenipotenciarios Don Joseph de Carvajal y Lancaster, y Vizconde Don Thomas da Sylva Telles, attenderse á dicho Mapa sino en quanto este se halle conforme al Tratado, y para que en todo tiempo conste este acto de reconocimiento, y lindero de la division de terminos, hicimos la presente declaracion firmada por todoslos infrascritos.

" Boca del Rio Pepirí, y Marzo 8 de 1759.

" Fran^{co} Arguedas.

" Francisco Millau.

" Juan Marron." [1]

---

[1] Each one of the two documents registered in the Portuguese and in the Spanish Diary, has these six signatures.

This is the translation of the above document:[1]

"*The Commissioners of the Second Party of Demarcation, JOSEPH FERNANDES PINTO ALPOYM, for His Most Faithful Majesty, and D. FRANCISCO ARGUEDAS, for His Catholic Majesty, having heard the unanimous opinions of the Astronomers, Geographers, and Officers of the two Nations, who, in view of the reasons stated at their previous meeting, and of the affirmation of the Indian Guide, FRANCISCO XAVIER ARIKAPÍ, sergeant in his village of S. Xavier, whose acquaintance with and information as to these rivers were confirmed by the agreement which is found between the information he gave concerning them and their true situation, have declared that not the least doubt remains in their minds that the river which the said guide pointed out and at whose mouth the Party were encamped, was the Pepiri; and we accordingly declare that we recognize this as the River Pepiri referred to in Article 5 of the Treaty of Limits as the Boundary between the Dominions of Their Most Faithful and Catholic Majesties; and consequently that the Demarcation begun at the village of S. Xavier and continued up the course of the Uruguay to the mouth of this river, must follow its course up to its headwaters, although it was found that its real situation does not agree with that which the Map for the Demarcation, issued by the two Courts, attributes to it, as according to the declaration at the back thereof signed by Their Excellencies the Plenipotentiaries THOMAZ DA SILVA TELLES, VISCOUNT DE PONTE LIMA and D. JOSEPH DE CARVALHAL E LANCASTRE, no attention must be paid to the said Map except so far it may be in conformity with the*

---

[1] The translation of the Portuguese text only is given because that of the Spanish text would present the same result with the mere differences resulting from the application of the diplomatic rule of the alternat.

Treaty; and, in order that through all time this Act of recognition and Instrument of Division of Limits may bear witness thereto, we have made the present declaration signed by all as hereunder.

"*Mouth of the river Pepirí, eighth of March, one thousand seven hundred and fifty-nine.*"

The Spanish Diary thus continues:

"The *River Pepirí*, is also called *Pequirí*, and it seems that this name, which means river of the mojarras,[1] suits it better on account of those fish being found there; nevertheless we will retain for it the first name *Pepirí* because the pronunciation is softer and in order to distinguish it from another Pequirí which flows into the Paraná by its Eastern bank above the Great Falls (Salto Grande)[2] of the latter, and it is the first important river that may be called a full-flowing one (caudaloso) which also enters the Northern bank of the Uruguay above the Great Falls, the Demarcation that is made by it agreeing with that made along the river Gatimí by the Third Party, as in both cases the terminal boundary, in the rivers Paraná and Uruguay is the first full-flowing affluent above

<small>Pepiry or Pequiry. The Commissioners prefer the former name.</small>

<small>Because there is another Pequirí, an affluent of the Paraná.</small>

<small>Pepiry, first important river above the Great Falls.</small>

[1] *Mojarra:* Spanish] name of a small fresh-water fish known in Brazil as *Piaba*.

[2] In the Portuguese Diary this passage begins thus:

"Although the River Pepirí should more properly be called the Piquirí, which name means river of Piabas (small fish), on account of those that are found in it, yet we will retain for it the former name of Pepirí, because the pronunciation is softer, and in order to distinguish it from another Pequirí which flows into the Paraná by its eastern bank above the Great Falls (Salto Grande)."

The position of the other Pequirí, an affluent of the Paraná, is shown in the *Map of Southern Brazil*, and in that of the *Itineracy of Cabeza de Vaca* (No. 31 in the small Atlas which forms Vol. V. of this Statement).

their Falls; and although the Falls of the Uruguay, from which the Pepiri is only little more than a league distant, are a natural landmark of the most visible and durable sort for the recognition of this river at all times, as is also the *Great Falls a natural mark.* island lying immediately at its mouth, when the Uruguay is low, nevertheless, as being one of the most important points of our Division, we stopped there to take some observations of longitude and latitude, in order to be able to fix its position with more precision and security; and, on a point which the Eastern bank of the Pepirí forms with the Northern bank of the Uruguay, a clearing was made, leaving in the middle only a single tree of thirteen feet in height, on which a Cross was placed and on the arms of the Cross these letters were carved : R. F. AÑO DE 1759."

In the Portuguese Diary the last lines of the above passage are as follows :

". . . and on a point which the Eastern bank of the Pepirí forms with the Northern bank, a clearing of trees was made, leaving in the middle only one of thirteen feet in height, upon which a Cross was placed, and upon its arms these letters were carved : R. F. (Most Faithful King) ANNO DE 1759."

In the Instructions given, after the Treaty of 1777, to the Spanish Commissioners, charged with the second delimitation of frontiers, mention of this mark of 1759 will be found, and of the latitude then observed, which constitute two other undeniable proofs that the River Pequiry or Pepiry-Guaçù of the second and last Treaty of Limits concluded between Portugal and Spain was the same Pepiry or Pequiry demarcated in 1759, that is to say, the same river that has formed since the XVIIth century the boundary of Brazil in the territory which the Argentine Republic has claimed since 1881.

The average of seventeen observations gave as the Latitude of the mouth of the Pepiry 27° 09′ 23″. In 1789, the new demarcators found 27° 10′ 30″, and in 1887, after more than one hundred observations, the Brazilian-Argentine Joint Commission adopted the average of 27° 10′ 03″.

Latitude of the mouth of the Pepiry.

The Longitude could not be determined with precision in 1759. The astronomers remained at that point nearly two months, but almost incessant rains and fogs only allowed them to observe the immersion of one satellite of Jupiter. The correspondence with the times of Paris and Greenwich could not be established because the calculations made according to the Tables of CASSINI and BRADLEY gave unacceptable results, the former presenting for the phenomenon, at the more easterly of those Observatories, less time than the other gave for the more westerly Observatory. This placed the Pepiry nearer the Meridian of Paris than to that of Greenwich, or, better, located Greenwich to the East of Paris. Moreover, the pendulum used by the observers could not inspire confidence, after so many shakings in the passage of rapids and waterfalls, and because the observation was taken in unfavorable weather. "It was thought that it was not to be trusted," says the Diary, "while there were no corresponding observations of known places with which to compare it."

Longitude.

In the second demarcation it was reckoned that the mouth of the Pepiry (then already Pepiry-Guaçú) was 53° 54′ 08″ West of Greenwich. In 1887 the Brazilian-Argentine Joint Commission began to determine provisionally, by the chronometric method, the Longitude of 53° 46′ 06″.8 West of Greenwich (Field Book and Plan of the mouth of the Pepiry-Guaçú), but subsequently the Brazilian Commission adopted that of 53° 48′ 19″, which, when the triangulation was finished, resulted from the position of that point referred to the Meridian of Palmas which it was possible to establish with all precision, this town being in telegraphic communication with the Observatory of Rio de Janeiro. The Argentine Commission in its Map locates the mouth of the Pepiry-Guaçú at 53° 50′ 11″.

<small>Survey of the Pepiry, 1759.</small>

Obeying the Instructions they had received, the First Commissioners determined to order the survey of the Pepiry as far as its principal headwater, *if it were possible*.

The Spanish Diary says (13th March, 1759):

"With this information the Commissioners determined to send by land the Party which, according to Article 3 of the Special Instructions was to be sent from the place whence forward the Pepiry could not be navigated, with orders to survey its course *if possible* to its source, which did not appear to be very distant; and that from this, following the highest ground, it should seek the source of the nearest river flowing to the Iguaçú."

On the 14th of March this expedition set out, led by the Portuguese and Spanish Geographers, PACHECO DE CHRISTO and FRANCISCO MILLAU, taking provisions for twenty days.

On the 28th it passed by the mouth of an Eastern affluent which the geographers called *Trahiras* (in Spanish *Tarayras*, the name of a fish), and immediately after by "a large and very high sheer rock with some excavations at

<small>Trahiras stream.</small>

its base produced by the continued beating of the waters . . ." They gave this place the name of *Cocas*.

On the 29th the Spanish Diary says:

"We set out at 6 in the morning, and after having navigated to N.W. about 385 toises, we came to a fork where the river divides into two nearly equal branches, both of which were examined to ascertain which of the two was the larger by which we were to continue our course. The one on the right, coming from the N.E., had a sufficient volume of water with little current, and was narrower than that on the left, whose waters, besides exceeding in volume those of the other, had more current. *To the former the name of Pepiri-Mini was given, and we went up the second which at a short distance upstream widens again*." [1]

<small>River Pepiry-Mini.</small>

Therefore this name of *Pepiry-Mini*, which means —small Pepiry—was given, on the 29th of March, 1759, to an Eastern affluent of the old Pepiry, and by Commissioners who were authorized to do so under Article XI of the Treaty of 1750.[2]

Thence upwards the difficulties of the navigation increased until, two days later, the expedition was detained by another Fall (Salto). In view of this obstacle, and being without provisions to carry the survey to the sources of the Pepiry, the Geographers determined to go back, leaving at that place a wooden mark, as shown by the following passage of the Spanish Diary:

<small>Falls.</small>

<small>They determine to go back.</small>

"Thirty-first day" (31st March, 1759).—"We went out at six o'clock in the morning, and at eight, having

---

[1] Division E 3 in Map No. 25 A and division E 11 in No. 29 A.
[2] English translation, Vol. III., 14; Portuguese text, IV., 13.

passed a brook on the Eastern bank, and travelled more than a league in the direction of W.S.W., S.W., S.S.E., S.W. ¼ W., and W.S.W., we came to a very large Fall which crossed the river from side to side, whose height was two toises, and only on the Eastern side there was a little channel two spans wide which rushed very swiftly between two high rocks near which there was a great depth of water, which prevented the pushing of the canoes. Considering the difficulty of passing this Fall, and the risk of wrecking the said canoes if we attempted to do so, we resolved to turn back from this place and, before doing so, set up a Landmark which should serve as a signal that we could recognize when coming from the source downwards. On the Western bank, from which a very high mountain range rises, we cut down all the trees and bushes on the bank, leaving standing only a very large one of the kind called Tapiá, 15 Toises distant from the water; and at the height of about 8 spans, its trunk divided into three very large high and much bent limbs; and on one which pointed towards the direction of the sources a Cross was carved, the perpendicular of which was two spans and the arms one. From the foot of this tree a track was opened towards the North, ending half way up the mountain range, and we, the two Geographers, made a plan of the ground and a drawing of the tree. At midday, we began our downward navigation, and, when it was nearly dark, we reached the place where the canoes had been left. . . ."

Then, going down the river, the two Geographers reached the camp at the mouth on the 4th of April, and delivered to the First Commissioners the Journal of the expedition and the Plans drawn after survey.

Arrival at the mouth of the Pepiry.

Section of the Pepiry explored. According to their calculations, the distance travelled from the mouth of the Pepiry to the Falls (Salto) where the mark was left was 24½ leagues, and they supposed the sources to be distant from that point only 12 or 15 leagues.

Unexplored section. In fact, on account of the numerous windings of the river, the journey was more than 127 kilometres, or approximately 69 miles. From the Falls of the Marca (Mark) to the principal source of the Pepiry the distance, in a straight line, is 58 kilometres or 31 miles, but, counting the bends in the river, the length of the upper course that was not explored is 116 kilometres or 62 miles.

The Spanish Diary says, under date of 5th April, 1759:

Impossibility of continuing by the Pepiry. "The foregoing Diary having been examined by the Commissioners" (that of the Geographers PACHECO DE CHRISTO and F. MILLAU), and the Plans presented by the Geographers having been compared and both found to be in agreement, the former considered the manner in which they could examine the river farther up than had already been done; but from the said reports and from the Geographers, they thought that to do this would require a greater delay than was justified by the scarcity of the provisions which the Indians were beginning to feel, because, on account of the limited space on their rafts, they had not been able to bring sufficient quantities. Besides this, the exploration of the source could only be carried out in very small and light canoes, of which there were only two which carried so few men that they would not suffice to haul them over the Falls and to open the tracks when, the river not being navigable, it should be indispensable to do this work, and much less if any Wild Indians should attack them on their march.

"In view of these embarrassments and difficulties, they resolved, in conformity with Art. 6 of the Special Instructions, to go down the Uruguay and, ascending the Iguaçù, to seek the river which should unite with the Pepiri, in order to search by it for the source of the latter which could not be found from this side; and they approved this part of the Demarcation made by the Geographers of the two Nations, and by virtue thereof, they recognized as appertaining to the Dominions of His Catholic Majesty all the land lying to the West of the River Pepiri, and to those of His Most Faithful Majesty, that which stretches to the East of the same River, according to Art. 5 of the Treaty of Limits." {The Commissioners determine to come down the Uruguay. And to go up the Iguaçù. They approve the Demarcation by the Pepiry.}

The quoted Article 6 of the Special Instructions of the 27th of July, 1758, fully justifies the action of the Commissioners, since it provides as follows: {The action of the Commissioners justified.}

"If the head of the River that empties itself into the Iguaçù, and which is believed to be near that of the Pepiri, is not found, or if the distance between them is so great, or the ground so rough that they think the canoes cannot be conveyed overland, *they shall take their observations at the spot they are able to reach, and they shall return down the course of the Uruguay* as far as the village of Concepcion, or as that of San Xavier, whence they shall proceed overland to that of Candelaria and, embarking there, *they shall go up the course of the Paraná as far as its Salto (Falls,) and, carrying overland the canoes they may have taken with them, or building others there, if they cannot carry them, they shall go up the latter as far as the mouth of some River, that may be with a slight difference in the same longitude in which they consider the heads of the Pepiri to be ; and, navigating along it as far as they can, they shall take the necessary observations in order that they may trace upon the Map they are to construct a line connecting the two points observed."*

The Commissioners were not obliged, therefore, to survey the two rivers as far as their sources, but they used all possible efforts to arrive at this result.

On the 7th day of April, the Commissioners, with the bulk of the Second Party, began to go down the Uruguay, the two Astronomers and a small escort remaining at the mouth of the Pepiry. These latter only joined the Party again on the 26th of May.

<small>Journey to the Paraná.</small>

On the 15th of April the Commission arrived at S. Xavier; on the 23d at Concepcion, and thence it went on by land as far as Candelaria on the left bank of the Paraná. During that time the two Geographers surveyed the Uruguay from S. Xavier to Concepcion.

Then from Candelaria the Commission transferred itself to Corpus, the last and Northernmost settlement of the Spanish Jesuit Missions on the Upper Paraná.

<small>Corpus.</small>

The distance from that point to the mouth of the Pepiry, in a straight line, is approximately 169 kilometres, or 91.2 miles, but the intermediate territory was never occupied by the Jesuits or the Spaniards, nor did the Guaranys of Misiones ever venture to enter it.

The necessary preparations having been made at Corpus, the expedition embarked on rafts and canoes and began to ascend the Paraná. *Departure from Corpus.*

After a journey of twenty-one days it reached the Iguaçù on the 10th of July, 1759, and entered that river. The observations taken determined the latitude of the mouth at 25° 35′ 51″. *Arrival at the Iguaçù.*

On the 12th day the Commissioners decided to encamp below the Great Falls (Salto Grande), near a creek of which the Spanish Diary speaks in the following terms:

"On the 12th at a distance of 3¼ leagues from the mouth of the Iguazù (Iguaçù), and a little more than one from its Falls (Salto), we found a little sandy creek near a stream presenting a very high fall, which stream empties itself on the Southern side, and this place being less inconvenient for mooring the boats, the navigation of which was already very difficult and perilous, it was determined to build a camp here and there to take the necessary measures for the continuation of the voyage. . . ."

Having explored the Great Falls and seen how steep were the two banks of the Iguaçù, they set about overcoming the obstacle and reaching the upper level of the river. With great difficulty some canoes were lifted to a height of 60 metres, or 203 English feet (31 Toises and 2 ft.), and afterwards hauled through the wood for a space of 6,596 metres, or 21,960 feet, as far as the regular current of the Iguaçù above its Great Falls, called Salto de Santa Maria by the Brazilians and Salto de la Victoria by the Argentines. *Great Falls of the Iguaçù.*

As all these details are to appear in the Spanish Instructions of 1778, it is expedient to go on recording them here for the better understanding of the Treaty of 1777 and of the orders then issued by the Government of Madrid.

The Spanish Diary says:

"Besides this it was necessary, in order that they might be hauled, to open in the wood a sufficiently wide track, cutting down trees, and in places levelling the ground, particularly in five streams they had to cross; all this was done successfully, and having been carried *a distance of 3,400 Toises*, they were all placed on the waters above the Falls on the 29th. This work having been completed, the building of the new canoes was commenced."

Above the Great Falls the Commissioners pitched a second camp and the store of provisions.

On the 28th of August the Portuguese and Spanish geographers, PACHECO DE CHRISTO and FRANCISCO MILLAU went out in two light canoes to make the first exploration of the Iguaçú.

Discovery of the rivers of S. Francisco and S. Antonio.

Thirteen days afterwards they returned, having discovered two affluents to which they gave the names of *São Francisco* and *Santo Antonio*, as may be seen from the following passage of the Spanish Diary:

"The officers who had gone up the Iguazú (Iguaçú) returned on the 10th September, after a navigation of more than 20 leagues as far as the mouth of the larger river of those they had found emptying on the Southern side, and *to which they gave the name of San Antonio;* a little below they had left another, smaller, which they named *San Francisco;* and it appearing to them that the San Antonio being the larger, its course would extend farther and its headwaters would lie more to the

South, they entered it and explored a part of the two branches which formed a fork two leagues from its mouth, and they judged from the direction in which it runs that its sources could not be far distant from that of the Pepirí. . . .

"With this information they thought to start quickly and to go in by the River S. Antonio as far as its waters would allow it to be navigated, in order to send thence, in accordance with Article 3 of the Special Instructions, a Party with the Geographers which should endeavor to connect the line of demarcation, exploring the sources of this river and of the Pepirí. But the Spanish Geographer, who already knew the difficulties of the River Iguazú" (Iguaçù), "seeing that if the larger canoes went (as was necessary) laden with provisions for many men . . . . they would not be able to hasten the journey, proposed to go forward in light canoes, which would make the speed greater, so that when the Commissioners with the rest of the parties should arrive, they might have advanced in the knowledge of the interior of the country.

It is determined to explore the S. Antonio.

"This mode of proceeding seemed expedient, as it might advance the desired discovery, and instead of awaiting their arrival at that river to decide on the despatch of the Party, then it was determined that the Geographers of the two Nations should go out from there, and that going up the said river S. Antonio (whose plan after survey as well as that of the Iguazú they were to make jointly) as far as its waters would allow, they should leave the canoes at the place where they could no longer navigate it, and should order the necessary track to be made, giving the pioneers the course which in conformity with their maps ought most directly to lead to the Pepirí, which they should endeavor to identify by finding the mark they left there when they had entered it by its mouth; or, if on account of the difficulties of the way they could not find the mark, then to identify the river by such other signs, as the distance that they had gone, the course in which it flows, its configuration, its waters, the character of its banks, and the other things which they had noticed in the journey from its mouth to the mark; which matters, the men who were with the Party and were experts in mountains and rivers, knew well how to distinguish."

On the 20th of September the two Geographers of Portugal and Spain set out in canoes to carry out these instructions, but nine days afterwards the order was sent to the former to return immediately, because the first Commissioners had determined to advance the work of the demarcation, by making at once the survey of the Upper Paraná as far as the Great Falls (Salto Grande) or Salto das Séte Quédas. It was expedient not to delay the operation, because in December the annual flooding of the river began.

Survey of the S. Antonio.

In this manner, the exploration of the River Santo Antonio and of its headwaters and of the upper course of the Pepiry was entrusted solely to the Spanish Geographer, FRANCISCO MILLAU.

This officer entering the S. Antonio, gave the name of *S. Antonio-Mini* to the Western affluent, which he had already visited in part, and navigated by the principal river as far as the Falls then called Salto de S. Antonio, now Salto Patri-

S. Antonio-Mini.

cio. Thence he set out on the 15th of October travelling, in the direction of the S.E., across dense forests, in search of the headwaters of the Pepiry. He reached the mountainous region in which, very near one another, numerous branches of the affluents of the Iguaçú, the Paraná and the Uruguay take their origin, and on the 23d of November he began to go down one which, by the direction of its course for about four leagues and by other signs seemed to be the Pepiry. After nearly two months of labor and privations, and threatened by the wild Indians, he wrote to the First Commissioners asking for succours and a reinforcement of soldiers in order to prosecute the examination in which he was engaged.

<small>Supposed source of the Pepiry.</small>

Already then ALPOYM and ARGUEDAS, having returned from the Paraná, were encamped near the S. Antonio Falls.

The Diary of the Demarcation gives a detailed account of the conference of the 13th of December, 1759, in which, having heard the unanimous opinion of the other officers of the Party, they determined to suspend the efforts that MILLAU was making in order to reach the mark left on the Pepiry. After referring to the sad circumstances in which they were, to the necessity of promptly going out from those deserts and to the impossibility of sending help to the Spanish Geographer, the Diary says:

"By the force of these reasons they were led to decide that, instead of the twelve soldiers who could not be sent to him, two should be added to the number the Geographer had with him, so that he might go up and explore the principal source of that river, which was unanimously believed to be the Pepiri, and thence seek the nearest source, which was supposed to be very near at hand, and which, according to the nature of the range and the sources he had passed, should go to the very river concerning which they did not know yet whether it was the same S. Antonio or another: *and he was to make use of the permission granted by Article 6 of the Special Instructions; for if the latter provides that corresponding observations shall be taken at the point that can be reached of a river the mouth of which may lie, within a little, in the same longitude in which the main headwaters of the Pepiri may be supposed to be, in order to draw upon the Map a line connecting the two points observed, if the distance were too great, or the ground too rough to carry the canoes over it*, with much greater reason must it be done in this case, in which there only remains 5 or 6 leagues to be surveyed, and in which the difficulties already referred to still occur."[1]

Having received these orders MILLAU began the return journey, going up the river on which he was and which he supposed to be the Pepiry. From the principal source of that river he went to that of the S. Antonio, distant from the other "half a quarter of a league," or 694.5 metres (about the third of a mile); he came down by the S. Antonio and reached the camp of the Commissioners on the 30th of December.

Source of the S. Antonio.

The complete survey of the S. Antonio was made, in two separate sections, by the same MILLAU and by the Portuguese Geographer, PACHECO DE CHRISTO.

Convinced that the river whose source lay nearest

[1] Spanish Diary, 13th day of December, 1759.

to that of the S. Antonio and on the opposite slope of the same range was the Pepiry they had surveyed from the Uruguay to the Salto da Marca, the Commissioners wrote the following in their Diary: *(Declaration signed by the Commissioners.)*

"In the manner stated it was possible to accomplish this part of the Demarcation with such effort and labor as may be supposed to overcome the ruggedness of some towering, impenetrable, and completely unknown mountains, without any track but that which the arms of the soldiers opened up, with no other guide than the compass. . . . The river upon which we were, instead of fish presented reefs which, delaying the advance and the provisions, added to the wretchedness to which, without exception, we were reduced at the end of a journey of six months and a half without any food except beans and maize and without being able to count on any help except the very remote and rare assistance the village of Corpus could afford.

"Notwithstanding all these obstacles, means were found, after the principal source of the Pepirí had been discovered, of surveying also the principal head and following all the course of the nearest river flowing to the Iguaçú; to which, as has been stated, the name of Rio de Santo Antonio was given (and it might with propriety have been named the 'desired river'), and the demarcation having been made along it, the Divisional Line was connected, and, by virtue of Article 5 of the Treaty, all the territory which lies to the East and North of the rivers Pepirí, Santo Antonio, and Iguaçú was recognized as belonging to the Dominions of His Most Faithful Majesty; and, as appertaining to those of His Catholic Majesty, the territory extending to the West and South of the said rivers; and in witness to all time of its firmness and validity, the present was signed by all, at this encampment of the river Santo Antonio, on the 3d January, 1760."

On the following day the expedition began the return journey, coming down the Santo Antonio, the Iguaçú and the Paraná as far as Candelaria, where it disembarked. Thence it went on by land to Concepcion and, crossing the Uruguay, reached S. Nicolas. The two Geographers then made the survey of the Uruguay from Concepcion to the mouth of the Ibicuhy.

Report by the Principal Spanish Commissioner.
The MARQUIS DE VAL DE LIRIOS, Principal Commissioner and Plenipotentiary of Spain, charged to direct the operations of the three Spanish Parties which made the demarcation from Castillos Grandes to Matto Grosso, said the following to the Secretary of State, D. RICARDO WALL, in a letter written from S. Nicolas, under date of 20th February, 1760:

"Although this demarcation has been attended with all the difficulties presented by the navigation of rivers so important as are the Uruguay, the Paraguay, and the Iguazú whose great reefs, falls, and rapids make their navigation laborious and dangerous, it has been possible, by the zeal and activity of DON FRANCISCO DE ARGUEDAS, to carry it out almost completely, since there has only remained to explore in the whole of it the space of five leagues of the River Pepiri, whose headwaters were connected with those of the River to which the name of San Antonio was given, whose course was surveyed like the Pepiri with the exception of this small distance.

"*The whole of this work met with no opposition whatever on the part of the Commissioner of Portugal, who, submitting to the direction and dispositions of the King's Commissioner, suffered all the most prolix examinations without attempting to avoid the work by virtue of the choice* **Condescension of the Portuguese Commissioner.** *which our Instructions offered him*, and so this work was happily concluded, and they returned to these Settlements on January 31."

The work of the Second Party of demarcation terminated at S. Nicolas with the signature, on the 8th of April, of the Map constructed by the Geographers PACHECO DE CHRISTO and MILLAU. **Map of 1760.**

The Diary concludes thus:

"According to the course pursued by the other Parties, the Longitudes were not marked on the Maps for want of corresponding observations in known places, and the said Maps having been constructed in the manner stated, they, as well as the copies prescribed by Article the Eleventh of this Treaty, and the Diary were signed by the Commissioners, Astronomers, and Geographers of the two Nations, at the Village of Sam Nicoláu, April 8, 1760."

Map No. 12 A is a fac-simile of the one appended to the Portuguese Diary of the demarcation. It has the same date from S. Nicolas, April 8, 1760, and the signature of MANUEL PACHECO DE CHRISTO.

This document shows that in 1760 the demarcators already designated the old Pepiry by the name of *Pepiry-Guaçú*, that is to say, **River Pepiry-Guaçú.** the *Great Pepiry*, to distinguish it from its tributary the *Pepiry-Mini*, or *Small Pepiry*.

In fact, whenever an affluent has the same name as the principal river, accompanied by the adjective *mini* or *mirim*, the adjective *guaçú* or *guazú*[1] is added to the name of the river of which it is a tributary.

<small>The adjectives "guaçú" and "mirim."</small>

That is why the Spanish Commissioners of the Second Demarcation often gave to the Uruguay the name of Uruguay-Guazú. At that time the affluent now called Rio do Passo Fundo was known as the Uruguay-Mirim.

The Ibicuhy, although generally designated by this single name, is also called Ibicuhy-Guaçú, because it has as tributaries an Ibicuhy-Mirim on the North and another on the South.

In the Spanish Instructions of 1778 another example is found in the river Ipané, sometimes designated by this name, sometimes by that of Ipané-Guazú, to distinguish it from the affluent Ipané-Miní.

The official Map of 1760 is a document of the greatest importance in this controversy, because the supporters of the Argentine cause have asserted that in using the adjective *guaçú*, it was intended in the Treaty of 1777 to designate a different river from the one surveyed in 1759.

As these questions of names have caused much confusion, it is necessary to establish at once the fact that the old *Pepiry* or *Pequiry* came, from 1760, to be called *Pepiry-Guaçú*, but that it also preserved the old name of *Pequiry* in some Spanish maps.

<small>Pepiry-Guaçú or Pequiry.</small>

With the name of *Pepiry-Guaçú* it appears in the Map of 1760, of the Commissioners of the first demarcation (No. 12 A); in that of SYLVEIRA PEIXOTO, of

---

[1] Note, page 3 in this Vol.

1768 (No. 15 A); in that of Captain MONTANHA, of 1773 (No. 16 A); and in that of OLMEDILLA, of 1775 (No. 17 A), this being the Map used by the Spanish negotiator of the Treaty of 1777 in the discussion with the Portuguese Plenipotentiary.

Under the old name of *Pequiry* it figures in two Maps constructed in 1768 and 1770 by the same MILLAU who explored it in 1759 (Nos. 13 A and 14 A).

VI.

Now is the time to examine this first demarcation of 1759 and the errors that have been attributed to it.

The first fault, according to the Argentine Government, consists in the Portuguese and Spanish Commissioners having demarcated a false Pepiry, in disregard of the instructions and of the Map of the Plenipotentiaries, dated 1749, which had been given them for their guidance. The second, in the same Commissioners having left their work incomplete, inasmuch as they did not go up as far as the sources of the river indicated by the Indian ARMAPY. The third, in their having made a mistake in giving as the head-waters of the Pepiry those of another river which flows to the Paraná. *Examination of the Argentine allegations against the first demarcation.*

The first supposed defect will be examined further on, because consideration of this point requires a greater development. The two other affirmations of the Argentine Government are rigorously accurate as to the questions of fact, but the consequences which it attempts to deduce from those two facts have no foundation whatever in view of the instructions given to the demarcating Commissioners.

The Argentine Government was not acquainted with the Instructions of 1758 which only now appear in this controversy. It referred to them, giving credit to the quotations made by the Spanish Commissioners who worked in the demarcation subsequent to the Treaty of 1777. With the appearance of the Instructions of 1758 it cannot fail to acknowledge that the Commissioners of the second demarcation were unjust towards their predecessors, going so far as to invent Instructions and orders that never existed.

The surveys made in 1887 by the Brazilian-Argentine Joint Commission, appointed under the Treaty of 28th September, 1885, made evident an error in the demarcation of 1759, but an error which could in no wise invalidate that operation or prejudice the interests of the two countries.

An error in the demarcation, but of no importance.

As may be seen in the Map of the Joint Commission of 1887 (No. 25 A), the distance between the principal headwaters of the S. Antonio and of the Pepiry or Pepiry-Guaçú is 17,400 metres (9.4 miles) and not 694 metres (about a third of a mile). Therefore, it is beyond doubt that the Spanish Geographer MILLAU was not in 1759 at the headwaters of the Pepiry, nor did he explore, as he supposed, 12 miles of its upper course. The river on which he was, and whose sources are near those of the S. Antonio, is one of the branches of the Urugualiy, an affluent of the Paraná.[1]

In consequence of that mistake, the Commissioners of 1759 believed that they had surveyed nearly all the course of the Pepiry, excepting merely a section of 18 miles (5 to 6 leagues, they

Extent surveyed in 1759.

---

[1] Map No. 29 A, division C 10.

said) between the Falls called Salto da Marca[1] and the point which MILLAU reached, starting from the supposed headwater of the river. In fact they only surveyed, as is known to-day, the course of the S. Antonio —that is, 131.5 kilometres, or 70.98 miles,—and that of the Pepiry, from its mouth in the Uruguay, as far as the Salto da Marca, over an extent of 127 kilometres, or about 69 miles.

The total extension of the boundary line surveyed was, therefore, 258.5 kilometres, or 140 miles.

All the upper course of the Pepiry, from the Salto da Marca to the principal headwater, remained unexplored, and it has already been said that this section, counting the windings of the river, is 116 kilometres, or 62 miles.

But the Instructions did not make the complete survey of the two rivers and their sources indispensable and obligatory. Foreseeing the great difficulties there would be in that exploration, the two Principal Commissioners and Plenipotentiaries of Portugal and Spain, with the previous and entire approval of their respective Governments, decided that *the essential thing was to survey the mouths of the two rivers and to go up them as far as possible.* {The survey of the source of the Pepiry in 1759 was not indispensable. The essential thing was to survey the mouth of the Pepiry and that of the affluent of the Iguaçú.}

The Principal Commissioner of Spain, the MARQUIS DE VAL DE LIRIOS, in a letter dated February 20th, 1760, addressed to the Secretary of State, D. RICARDO WALL, referred as follows to the proposal he had made in 1757 and which had been approved:

"I have already informed Your Excellency in a letter

---
[1] *Ibidem*, division C 10.

of December 12, 1757, that the Principal Commissioner of Portugal, in consideration of these difficulties, has proposed to me *that only the mouths of the rivers which flow into the Uruguay and the Iguazú, or Rio Grande de Curitiba*, should be sought and their situation determined, because he believed it impossible to travel through the inland country in which they run, and that their headwaters should be connected. I agreed to this proposal as it afforded the opportunity for all to arrive at the conclusion of this matter."

The decision arrived at by the two Governments to have a survey made only of the mouth and of the principal part of the two fluvial courses, which, in a desert region difficult of access, formed a secondary and a relatively unimportant section of the extensive divisional line, was no doubt very prudent and well advised. It was so well advised that without having any knowledge of it, and writing many years afterwards, the Spanish Commissioner OYÁRVIDE, taught by the experience of hard work and privations in those same regions, was of opinion that much less should be done than was accomplished in 1759.

In his *Memoria* on the second demarcation he says[1]:

"For these powerful reasons, and for the better execution of this matter, we may conclude by saying that *whatever may be the divisional line that may divide in this region the territory of Spain from that of Portugal, it is quite sufficient to survey and mark the confluence of the rivers along which it is to pass, and to suppose the line as effective and recognized in the spaces or intervening places where there may be mountains and hilly and uncultivated parts of the country, as happens*

---

[1] OYÁRVIDE, in CALVO, *Recueil de Traités*, Vol. IX., p. 172.

in the whole distance or space over which the line is to run from the Uruguay to the Iguazú. If from this previous suggestion it should result that such enterprises may never be repeated, because future Treaties of limits shall have removed the necessity for them, we would from this moment congratulate ourselves, not only because it must shorten the surveys without detriment to their accuracy, but because it will be a manifest benefit to humanity."

The object in view in 1759 was that the mouth of the *affluent of the Iguaçú should be within a little in the same longitude as the Pepiry.* If the Commissioners met with difficulties in reaching the headwaters of the two rivers, they were according to Article 6 of the Instructions of 27th July, 1758, to trace upon the Map an imaginary line, connecting the two points observed.

<small>The affluent of the Iguaçú was to be approximately on the meridian of the Pepiry. The S. Antonio satisfies this condition.</small>

To leave unexplored the upper course of both rivers and their headwaters was, therefore, a case foreseen and authorized by the Instructions and it cannot be pleaded as a reason of nullity. If the Commissioners, avoiding trouble and work, had limited themselves to tracing upon the Map they constructed an imaginary line from the Salto (Falls) de S. Antonio, now Salto Patricio, to the Salto da Marca, on the Pepiry, that is to say, if the unexplored tract were almost double what it was, they would have accomplished the provisions of Article 6 without laying themselves open to the reproach of any error whatever. The demarcation which would have been perfectly valid in the case of an extent of 241 kilometres (131 miles) of the frontier having remained unexplored, cannot be considered invalidated by the fact that this distance was reduced to one half. Suppressing the 12 miles of the river which were taken for the Upper Pepiry, there remain as the extreme points of the survey of 1759 the Salto da Marca, in the Pepiry, and the principal headwater of the S. Antonio in the same mountainous region in which the Pepiry takes its origin.

The line traced between these two points scarcely departs at all from the course of the Pepiry or Pepiry-Guaçù and even cuts it in several places.

The principal source of the Pepiry-Guaçù is in 53° 37′ 34″ of Longitude West of Greenwich, and the mouth of the S. Antonio in 53° 57′ 50″.

The difference is 20′ 16″.

The mouth of the Pepiry-Guaçù was located by the Brazilian Commission in longitude 53° 48′ 19″. This, compared with that of the confluence of the S. Antonio, gives a difference of only 9′ 31″.

These comparisons and an examination of the Map of the territory now disputed [1] show clearly that the Commissioners of the Second Party of Demarcation in 1759 exactly carried out the orders they had received, since the S. Antonio is indisputably the river which forms with the Pepiry the most natural line directed to the North that the two Governments desired to establish between the Uruguay and the Iguaçù.

And it has already been demonstrated, by a document of February 8, 1749, that this purpose, so expressly manifested in the Instructions of 1758, was that which inspired the two Governments in drawing up Article 5 of the Treaty of 1750.

It is true that Article 5 speaks of the connection of

---

[1] Maps Nos. 25 A and 29 A.

the principal headwaters of the Pepiry with that of the nearest river running to the Iguaçû; but the provision must be understood in accordance with the thought manifested in 1749 and 1758, keeping also in view Article 31 of the Treaty of January 17, 1751, in which this declaration occurs:

"That the Commissioners shall avoid contentions regarding the demarcation, especially on matters of little importance, and that they should rather settle at once among themselves any differences that may arise, because it is not the intention of Their Majesties that any part of the work shall be left incomplete without very weighty reasons, *nor shall the Commissioners take into consideration any small portion of territory, provided the Line is located by the most visible and lasting natural Boundaries.*"

Those who argue from the literal sense of Article 5 of the Treaty of 1750 must take into consideration that this provision of the Treaty of 1751 and the Instructions of 1758 have reduced to nothing the significance of the direction regarding the proximity of the headwaters.

Some claim that if the Commissioners of 1759 had ascended the Pepiry as far as the sources of its principal arm, they would not have demarcated the S. Antonio, but the river which in former maps bore the name of Rio da America, and which in that of the Brazilian Commission of 1887 appears under the name of Capanema.[1]

It has already been proved that the two essential points in the demarcation of that part of the boundary were the mouths of the two affluents and not their

---

[1] VIRASORO, *Misiones y Arbitraje* (Buenos-Aires, 1892), p. 132 (§ VII.).

headwaters. But, admitting that they were these, no one in view of the Map of the Brazilian-Argentine Commission can safely affirm that the principal headwater of the America is nearer that of the Pepiry-Guaçú than the headwater of the S. Antonio.

The course of the America across dense forests was never regularly explored and does not appear on the Map of the Joint Commission. If only the lower courses of the Chopim and Chapecó were known, no one could foresee that their headwaters were under meridians so distant to the East from those of the mouth. It is possible that the America may run in the same direction as the Chopim, and in that case the source of its principal arm would be very distant from that of the Pepiry-Guaçú. Notwithstanding, accepting as a positive fact the supposition or suspicion that the principal headwaters of the Pepiry-Guaçú and the America are very near one another, the loss to Spain —resulting from the orders and instructions which it gave to its Commissioners, and not from any error committed by them—was truly insignificant, seeing that the approximate area of the triangle, whose angles are the principal headwater of the Pepiry-Guaçú and the mouths of the S. Antonio and America, is only 47 square leagues—a very trifling wedge of land, indeed, for Sovereigns who possessed such vast dominions and could calmly dictate to their Commissioners the order contained in the quoted Article of the Treaty of 1751.

But, as has been said, the chief error of the Com-

Another Argentine allegation:— characteristic features of the Pepiry.

missioners of 1759, according to the Argentine Government, was in the demarcation of a false Pepiry, which did not present the characteristic features described in the Instructions, nor correspond with the position indicated in the Map of the Plenipotentiaries, commonly called "Map of the Courts" ("Mappa das Côrtes, or " Mapa de las Cortes ").

The Argentine Government asserts that the true *Pepiry* or *Pequiry* of the Treaty of 1750 is the river more to the East, discovered in 1788, that is to say, the Chapecó or Pequirí-Guazú.

The characteristic features of the Pepiry or Pequiry of 1750, according to a passage, already quoted, attributed to the Instructions given to the Commissioners of 1759, were:

"*A full-flowing river* (caudaloso) with *a wooded island opposite its mouth: a reef within its mouth*, and that it is *upstream of the Uruguay-puita.*"

That is the passage, as it was quoted in 1805 by the renowned D. FELIX DE AZARA,[1] who had the credulity to accept as true the invention of 1789, whose history has already been given.

After the composition of 1805, by which AZARA was deceived, there is the last, that of 1892, which is as follows:

"*A full-flowing river* with *a wooded island in front of its mouth, a large reef in front of its mouth* which is *upstream of the Uruguay-pita, a southern affluent of the Uruguay.*"

Even though such a passage had been in the Instructions of 1751 and 1758, it would prove nothing against the demarcation of 1759 and the right of Brazil.

To be full flowing (caudaloso) is not a distinctive feature of any particular river, as AZARA himself very truly said in 1785, in the following terms:

A full flowing river.

[1] *Memoria sobre el Tratado de Limites de la America Meridional*, dated Madrid, May 14th, 1805, among the *Memorias . . . de* D. FELIX DE AZARA, Madrid, 1847.

"I do not consider this reason as powerful as it appears, because the word *caudaloso* is very general and in its strict sense expresses nothing, since every river is *caudaloso*."[1]

The Pepiry or Pepiry-Guaçú also has an island opposite its mouth.[2] It is much smaller than that of the Chapecó or Pequiry-Guazú, but it is an island, according to the scientific definition, notwithstanding the endeavor of the Argentine Commissioners who, in 1887, wished to reduce it to a bank, preoccupied with the idea of the Instructions composed in 1789. The circumstance that it is submerged during the freshets of the Uruguay is not sufficient to take from it its normal quality of an island, since the accidents presented by the bed of a river and its banks are always referred to the average level of the waters and not to the occasions when, overflowing those banks, they cover the least elevated islands and invade the adjacent lands. No hydrographer would graphically represent the course of a river according to the appearance it presented during an inundation.[3]

An island in front of the mouth of the Pepiry.

---

[1] Letter of the Spanish Commissioner D. FELIX DE AZARA written at Asuncion of Paraguay, on February 7, 1785, and transcribed in CALVO, *Recueil de Traités*, Vol. VI., p. 387. AZARA spoke of the rivers Iguatemy and Igurey.

[2] Plan No. 27 A in Vol. VI., and No. 28 in Vol. V.

[3] In the pamphlet *Misiones*, by DR. ZEBALLOS (Buenos-Aires, 1893), the following may be read at page 51 in a letter of Colonel RHODE:

"It is true, that when the Plan of the mouth was constructed, the Brazilian Commission wished to give the name of *island* to the bank, but it is also a fact that the Argentine Commission protested and that the Plan signed by us all, Brazilians and Argentines, and lodged in our Foreign Office, calls *bank that which is a bank*."

The question of *bank* or *island* has no importance whatever, because the presentation of the Instructions of 1751 and 1758 to the Arbitrator will show that these documents speak neither of *island* nor *bank*, as the Argentine Commissioners believed in the discussion of 1887.

In the meantime, it is necessary to say, that the Brazilian Commission gave

The feature of an island, attributed to the Instructions of 1751 and 1758, was invented in 1789 because near the mouth of the Chapecó there is one and in the " Map issued by the Courts " of 1749, it seems indisputable, to any one who has no knowledge of geographical and cartographical history, that there is also an island near the mouth of the Pepiry or Pequiry, afterwards Pepiry-Guaçú. But the island of the Chapecó, in the Uruguay, is in fact above *the mouth of the Chapecó*, only a small part of the island being in front of the mouth ;[1] and the supposed island in the Map of the Plenipotentiaries is *below the mouth of the Pepiry or Pequiry of the Treaty of 1750*, and at a distance of 10 kilometres or 5⅓ miles.[2] The comparison of that Map of 1749 with the previous ones and an examination of the print in which are reproduced parts of various maps of the XVIIIth century representing the Falls of the Paraná, Uruguay,

Motive for the invention of the island in 1789.

The supposed island in the Map of 1749 is the Great Falls of the Uruguay.

the name of *island* to that which the Spanish Commissioners of 1759 and the Spanish Instructions of 1778 called an island, and that in the two Plans of the mouth of the Pepiry-Guaçú, which are in the keeping of the Brazilian Special Mission, the following is to be read :

" An island of stones and boulders covered with sarandy-trees, submerged in freshets."

One of the Plans dated from the Pepiry-Guaçú July 4th, 1887, has the signatures of the Brazilian Commissioners and Assistant Commissioners, and those of the following Argentines : Commissioners SEELSTRANG and VIRASORO ; Assistants RHODE and PICASSO. Another is signed by the First Brazilian Commissioner and by the First Argentine Commissioner, General GARMENDIA.

But this does not mean that the Argentines had renounced the opinion that the island is a bank, but simply that they authenticated the Plans of the Brazilians, as the latter authenticated those of the Argentines. The two opinions were recorded in the Diary.

[1] Plan of the mouth of the Chapecó, No. 28 A in Vol. VI.
[2] No. 7 A (Vol. VI.), fac-simile of the size of the original ; No. 10 (Vol. V.), fac-simile enlarged by photography.

Ivahy, and Iguaçû,[1] show that the supposed island below the mouth of the Pepiry is the indication of the Great Falls (Salto Grande) of the Uruguay. The cartographers of that time represented cataracts by a widening of the river, nearly always placing an island in the centre.

The other features indicative of the Pequiry of 1750, in the imaginary passage of the Instructions, have reference to a reef and to the relative positions of the Pepiry and the Uruguay-Pitã. This last point will be examined at the same time as the Map of 1749. As to the reef near the mouth of the Pepiry, what ALVEAR said in 1789 was that it lay "*within its mouth*," and not "opposite its mouth," as CABRER wrote inadvertently, when copying the letter of November 13, 1789, of that Commissioner, and as was repeated by mistake in 1892.[2] It did not suit ALVEAR to say that the Pepiry of the Treaty of 1750 should have a reef in front of its mouth, since the river surveyed in 1759 presents this feature, which the Chapecó has not, as the Brazilian-Argentine Joint Commission ascertained. The reef of the Chapecó is within the river and does not answer the description of 1892.[3] The Pepiry, surveyed in 1759, however, can satisfy the two different wordings of the passage attributed to the Instructions, because it has a reef *both within and without its mouth*. The outer reef is evident in the Plan drawn after the survey by the

A reef within or without the mouth of the Pepiry.

---

[1] Print No. 27 in Vol. V.

[2] The Brazilian Special Mission has a copy of the quoted letter of ALVEAR, authenticated by the Portuguese Commissioner ROSCIO, to whom it was addressed.

[3] Speaking of the Chapecó the Diary of the Argentine Commission says (August 19, 1887): " . . . no reef whatever being seen between the mouth and the opposite bank of the Uruguay and only at 800 metres above its mouth."

Brazilian-Argentine Joint Commission; the one within, at 3 kilometres of the mouth according to the Field Books of the Commissioners, is mentioned in the Diary of the Spanish demarcators of 1759 where the following may be read under date of March 5, 1759: " . . . and knowing from other information that the Pepirí had a reef near its mouth, the Commissioners and the Astronomer of Portugal went to explore it, *and it was found at half a league from there.*" And at the date of March 14th, when the Party commissioned to survey the Pepiry commenced to ascend the river: "At one o'clock in the day the party left the mouth of the Pepirí, navigating in canoes as far as the place from which, as they could not advance, the overland track was to begin, and with the Party the Commissioners and Astronomers went as far as the same place. The navigation was begun towards the N.N.W., whence the river continues its course towards the W. N.W., and turning by the intermediate directions to the N.N.E., it narrows a little; *and at half a league from its mouth the first reef is reached,* when the canoes were able to pass with less difficulty, although they had to be hauled on account of the waters it had received from the repeated rains of the previous days."

The only news the Commissioners of 1759 had upon the Pepiry, as is seen in their Diary, were those regarding *the reef* and to the effect that *on the same day on which they should start from the Great Falls of the Uruguay they were to reach the mouth of the Pepiry.*

<small>The only true information the Commissioners of 1759 had concerning the Pepiry.</small>

Now, on the same day on which one leaves the Great Falls, ascending the Uruguay, it is easy to reach

<small>Distance from the Pepiry to the Great Falls.</small> the mouth of the Pepiry or Pepiry-Guaçú which is only distant from it 8,390 metres or 4¼ miles, but there is no craft that can in less than a week overcome the current of the Uruguay and the difficulties which are met in <small>Distance from the Chapecó to the Falls.</small> the 149.5 kilometres or 80.7 miles, that separate the Great Falls of the Uruguay from the mouth of the Chapecó, the Pequirí-Guazú of the Argentine pretension.

VII.

It has been sufficiently shown that the features imagined in 1789 could equally be found in the Pepiry <small>Examination of maps anterior to 1749.</small> surveyed in 1759 and in the Chapecó, except the point relating to the Uruguay-Pitá which can only be discussed while studying the Map of 1749.

The Argentine Government drew its arguments from the Instructions given to the Commissioners and from the Map of 1749.

The Instructions do not contain the passage which has been quoted, nor would this passage prove anything against the demarcation of 1759.

One of the two points in support of the Argentine line of argument therefore disappears.

<small>A declaration of the Argentine Government.</small> The other document upon which the Argentine Government endeavors to rest is the official Map of 1749, used by the Plenipotentiaries in the drawing up of the first Treaty of Limits.

The Argentine Memorandum of 1883 said:

"If it is possible to determine which were the boundaries traced upon that Map, *the question will be implicitly and authoritatively solved.*"

It is possible and even easy to prove that the Commissioners of 1759 surveyed the same Pequiry along which, in the Map of the Plenipotentiaries, the divisional line runs, and that the river of the Argentine pretension is much to the East of the Pequiry or Pepiry of the same Map.

But, in order to understand the *reason of the difference between the positions of the mouth of the Uruguay-Pitá, which was located in 1759 above the Great Falls of the Uruguay and shown below the same Falls in the Map of 1749*, it is necessary to ascertain in the cartographical documents and in the records of the XVIth and XVIIth centuries the acquaintance then possessed with regard to the Upper Uruguay and its affluents.

The first document in which mention is made of a tributary of the Uruguay under the name of Pepiry is *La Argentina*, a chronicle of the Provinces of the River Plate, written by the Paraguayan RUI DIAZ DE GUZMAN, and concluded at Charcas in the year 1612.

The Pepiry, 1612.

Above the mouth of the Rio Negro, GUZMAN only mentions the said tributary, so that it is impossible to know in what section of the Uruguay the confluence was. He says that it was then reported that there was gold in the Pepiry, an inexact statement made by some Indian because, as Father PEDRO LOZANO wrote in 1745, *the Spaniards never saw the Pepiry.*

The first map in which an affluent of the right bank of the Uruguay appears under that name, is that which

The Caraffa Map. The first one presenting a Pepiry.
the Jesuits of Paraguay presented to Father CARAFFA, Prefect General of the Society of Jesus from 1645 to 1649.[1] It was engraved at Amsterdam by GERARD COECK for Vol. XI. of the *Atlas Major* of JOHAN BLAEUW, published at Amsterdam in the year 1662.

It is very valuable and the best of the maps of the Jesuits for the study of the history of the Missions in the XVIIth century and for the understanding of the texts of DURAN, MONTOYA, TECHO, and other Jesuits, and very interesting from the abundance of geographical information which it presents for the first time, showing all the great features of a good part of the interior of South America. HUMBOLDT said very truly, speaking especially of America in the XVIIth and XVIIIth centuries: ". . . The Missionaries were then the only geographers of the most inland parts of continents."[2]

The map must have been drawn between the years 1637 and 1641 because it was during that time that the mission of Assumpcion, removed from Acaraguá (Acarana), was near the Mbororé.

In a work recently published DR. ZEBALLOS[3] has

---

[1] The part of this Map in which the territory now contested is to be found is reproduced under No. 1 in Vol. V. ; and in VI., under No. 1 A, is a fac-simile of the whole map whose title is:

"PARAQUARIA / *vulgo* / PARAGUAY / *Cum adjacentibus*. / *Adm. R^{do} Nr̃ō.* / *P. VICENTIO CARRAFA / Praposito Grali. Soc^{tis} Jesu.* / Gerard Coeck *sculpsit. Ioannes Blaeu Exc. Amsteladami.*"

[2] Vol. III., p. 430 of *Personal Narrative of Travels to the Equinoctial Regions of America during the Years 1799–1807* . . . *Written by* ALEXANDER VON HUMBOLDT, *translated by* T. ROSS, London, 1853, 3 vols.

[3] *Misiones, Exposicion hecha por el ex-Ministro de Relaciones Exteriores de la República Argentina*, DR. ESTANISLAO S. ZEBALLOS, *para refutar errores de origen brasilero é ilustrar la opinion publica en Sur y en Norte America*, Buenos-

seemed to give the impression that this document, deservedly praised by D'ANVILLE, is favorable to the Argentine cause. The document, however, reveals the strongest evidence that the Jesuits of Paraguay had until then only very vague information regarding the Upper Uruguay, since the Great Falls do not yet appear, a feature which no explorer would omit, and which must necessarily have struck the most uncivilized and ignorant Indian of the Missions who might pass that way.

The first meridian is not shown in the Map, but on comparison of this with that of Brazil in the same Atlas, it is seen that the Dutch cartographer referred the longitudes to the meridian of Recife de Pernambuco, which was still occupied by the Dutch between the years 1645 to 1649, and where there was at Mauritzstadt, an Observatory founded by PRINCE MAURICE OF NASSAU. The publication of Vol. XI. in 1662 does not prove that all the maps were engraved in that year.

The first meridian being thus known, and referring to that of Greenwich the Longitudes marked on the Map, it is seen that the Pepiry is much to the West of the Pepiry-Guaçù, the boundary of Brazil, and, therefore, in the actual Argentine territory of Misiones.

But in a discussion of this kind—and in any discussion—affirmations which have not a sound basis should be avoided, and, therefore, on the part of Brazil it will only be said that the Map under consideration cannot benefit either one cause or the other.

Aires, 1893. (Translation :—"*Misiones, Statement made by Ex-Minister for Foreign Affairs of the Argentine Republic, Dr. Estanislao S. Zeballos, in refutation of errors of Brazilian origin and to enlighten public opinion in South and North America.*")

The course of the Upper Uruguay is represented too much to the North, and known points of reference are not found in it to make an approximate location of the Pepiry possible. The location of the Iguaçú and of all the other rivers shows that there had been no exploration worthy of the name, and that all the topographical accidents were traced almost wholly on supposition and based on information obtained from Indians who were necessarily inaccurate as to distances and directions. As to Longitudes, the very position of the continent being still uncertain in the XVIIth century, it is clear that no argument can be deduced from meridians traced by a mere estimate.

After this comes the *second Map of the Jesuits*,— that of 1722.

The Map of G. SANSON (1668), which has been cited,[1] can be considered a Map of the Jesuits only in the particular that it is a reproduction of their first Map with omissions, with names incorrectly written, and with some not very felicitous changes, such as the exaggerated widening of the continent; but if there were any reason for attributing to that Religious Order the Map of a geographer who was inspired by theirs, it would then be necessary to quote many other maps which are in the same case, as, for example, that of CORONELLI in which the Pepiri of the Jesuits is seen transformed into Papiri, as SANSON also wrote by mistake.

G. Sanson, 1668.

It must also be said—with due respect to the contrary opinion—that the Map of Paraguay by GUILLAUME DE L'ISLE, composed in 1703,[2] and considered by DR. ZEBALLOS "the first

De l'Isle, 1703.

---

[1] LE / PARAGUAY / *Tiré des Relations les plus Recentes* / *Par* G. SANSON, *Geographe ordinaire du Roy*. / Paris, 1668."

[2] "CARTE / DU PARAGUAY / DU CHILI / *du Detroit de Magellan, &c.*, /

Map in importance and authority,"[1] is not a Map of the Jesuits, but of that geographer.

DE L'ISLE asserts that he did his work according to the descriptions of Fathers NICOLAS DEL TECHO (NICOLAS DU TOICT) and ALONSO DE OVALLE, but it cannot be inferred from this that these two Jesuits personally gave him information for the drawing of the Map,[2] for OVALLE died in 1651, and DE L'ISLE was five years old when TECHO died in 1680. In the Map of the former of these Jesuits the French geographer could find very little, and that only upon Chile; in the *Historia Provinciæ Paraquariæ*, of the latter, there is no Map whatever. DE L'ISLE did not read with attention the work of TECHO, since he represents, as still existing, missions whose destruction or desertion, between the

---

Dressée sur les Descriptions / des P. P. Alfonse d'Ovalle et Nicolas Techo, / et sur les Relations et Memoires de Brower, Narbouroug, Mr. de Beauchesne, &c.,/ par GUILLAUME DE L'ISLE *Geographe / de l'Academie Royale des Sciences / A Paris. . . . 1703."

D. ANDRÉS LAMAS said in the introduction to the *Hist. de la Conquista del Paraguay* by LOZANO that the copy in his collection has between the water-marks the shield of the Society of Jesus. There may have been a mistake in the interpretation, because other copies examined, and one in the possession of the Brazilian Special Mission, also has water-marks, but not the sign of the Society of Jesus. In any case, the mark, if it exists, can only mean that some special impression was made for the Jesuits, since the Map is indisputably the work of the geographer DE L'ISLE ; it resulted from the ill-digested reading of the documents he quotes ; it does not contain the declaration that it was constructed by order of the Jesuits ; and it became an article of trade, seeing that it was on sale at the house of the author, on the Quai de l'Horloge, in Paris.

[1] " . . . the *third* known Map of the Jesuits . . .; but *the first in importance and* authority . . ." (*Misiones*, § XXI., p. 66.)

[2] " Two of the most notable figures of the Jesuitic legion in South America, Fathers D. ALONSO DE OVALLE, a scholar and writer . . . . and D. NICOLAS TECHO . . . . gave the data for the drawing of this Map." (DR. ZEBALLOS, *Misiones*, § XXI., p. 64.)

years 1630 and 1638, the latter historian describes with the greatest clearness, and which had already appeared in the first Map of the Jesuits with a sign indicating that they had been destroyed or evacuated.[1] The mission of Assumpcion, removed in 1637 from the Acaraguá or Acarana to the Mbororé, was re-installed by DE L'ISLE on the first of those rivers in spite of TECHO'S *Historia* and of the first Map of the Jesuits. Two villages of the itinerary of CABEZA DE VACA, located with more accuracy near the Tibagy in previous maps,[2] are much more to the South in this Map.

The passage quoted in the pamphlet *Misiones*[3] for the purpose of showing that D'ANVILLE recognized the merit of the Map of 1703, has no reference whatever to this Map or to DE L'ISLE.

D'Anville did not praise the Map of De l'Isle.

This is what D'ANVILLE wrote[4]:

"In composing the Map of Paraguay I have made use of several maps given by the Rev. Jesuit Fathers,

---

[1] No. 2, in Vol. V., is an enlarged fac-simile of a section of the Paraguay of DE L'ISLE. On comparing it with No. 1, it is seen that the Missions destroyed or deserted, according to TECHO, and represented in N° 1 by a cross, are re-established, as existing settlements, by DE L'ISLE. In the first Map of the Jesuits (No. 1 A, Vol. VI.) it may be read before this sign, in the *Notularum explicatio :* " *Reduct. indor. Christianoru PP. S*^{tis} *Iesu destructe.*"

[2] For example, in that of G. BLAEUW, No. 32, in Vol. V.

[3] In the pamphlet *Misiones*, p. 71 :

" D'ANVILLE says, in the place quoted, in commenting on the Map of RETZ and his own, *referring* to the *Map of 1703 and to its previous sources*, what follows . . . " Next comes the end of the passage transcribed above, of D'ANVILLE, from the words : " *This first Map* . . ."

Having made the transcription, DR. ZEBALLOS says : " *Having thus recognized the singular merit of the Map of 1703 and of those which served as a basis for it, superior to the subsequent ones of 1726 and 1732* . . ." (*Misiones,* § XXI., p. 71.)

[4] *Observations Géographiques sur la Carte du Paraguay par l'Auteur de cette Carte,* in Vol. XXI., p. 429, of the *Lettres Édifiantes et Curieuses écrites des Missions Étrangères, par quelques Missionnaires de la Compagnie de Jesus,* 1734.

Missionaries in that country. In 1727, the Fathers presented a large Map of Paraguay to the R. F. General MICHELANGELO TAMBURINI. This same Map, renovated, as it seemed to me, however, by changes in several places, has been presented to the R. P. General FRANCESCO RETZ, in 1732. An old Map of Paraguay was already known, dedicated to the R. P. VINCENZO CARAFFA, who was the seventh General of the Society from the year 1645 to the year 1649. This first Map, which must yield to the more recent maps for the location of inhabited places, which are subject to change, has seemed, in compensation, to preserve an advantage over those maps, with regard to a greater abundance and accuracy in the details, excepting only the neighborhood of the town of Assumption."

It is thus seen that the only maps D'ANVILLE quotes are those which the Jesuits presented to CARAFFA (1645-1649), TAMBURINI (1722), and RETZ (1732), and, therefore, the "*more recent maps*" of which he speaks in contradistinction to the "first map" are those of 1722 and 1732, of the Jesuits, and not that of 1703, of DE L'ISLE.

Far from praising the last named map, D'ANVILLE corrects it, and, in a note written on the *Carte du Paraguay*, of 1733, he points out an error of DE L'ISLE, regarding the exaggerated width of the continent, although he does not state the name of this geographer.

DR. ZEBALLOS says, speaking of the Map of 1703:

The Map of De l'Isle in no way favors the Argentine cause.

"The disputed territory is only sketched in this Map; but it *already gives two rivers*, the Pequiry or Pepiry Guazú, that of *the Argentines and that of the Brazilians . . . Those rivers have been indicated without names."*

The comparison of the first Map of the Jesuits (No. 1, Vol. V.), with that of DE L'ISLE (No. 2) shows that the two rivers without names to the East of the Acaraguá or Acarana are the Guanumbaca and the Pepirí of the former.

Now, the Guanumbaca never was the Pepiry of the Brazilians, for it is a river in the present Argentine territory of Misiones[1], and the Pepiry of the Maps of the Jesuits was neither the Pequiry Guazú of the Argentines (Chapecó), nor the Pepiry-Guaçú of the Brazilians, but, as will be proved, *a river below the Great Falls of the Uruguay.*

The Map of DE L'ISLE was sent from Buenos-Aires to the Argentine Special Mission at Washington, according to published information.[2] That Map, however, does not serve to prove anything, because it is not possible to point out in it the rivers of the controversy, and because the line indicating the Western boundary of Brazil in that region is drawn arbitrarily. It is not a line defined by any Treaty, nor is it that of the *uti possidetis* of that time. Spain did not admit such a line, nor did Portugal. And, lastly, in arguing from the limit of Brazil improvised by DE L'ISLE, that line must also be accepted which he traces on the side of the Andes and of the Terra Magellanica, giving to Chile the present Argentine Province of Mendoza, the Government of Nauquen and the whole of Patagonia.

After the Map of DE L'ISLE, without doubt very

---

[1] Division F 9, in Map 29 A.
[2] DR. ZEBALLOS, *Misiones*, p. 64.

inferior to the first of the Jesuits, the only one that deserves mention, on account of the official title of the author, is that of *Chili and Paraguay*, by NICOLAS DE FER, "Geographer to His Catholic Majesty." This Map, which was published in 1720,[1] thoroughly reveals the want of information of the Geographer to the King of Spain regarding the course and affluents of the Upper Uruguay. The last affluent it gives is the Acaraguá. N. de Fer, 1720.

The learned WALCKENAER mentions[2] a Map of Paraguay by D'ANVILLE, drawn in 1721 for the *Lettres Édifiantes*, but he was probably mistaken in writing that date instead of 1733, for no copy of 1721 is to be found among the known editions of the collection in question, either at the French Foreign Office, or in the National Library of Paris, where all the printed documents and manuscripts left by the great Geographer are to be found.

So, then, observing chronological order, the next Map to be mentioned is *the second of the Jesuits*, dated 1722, engraved at Rome by PETROSCHI in the year 1726, and dedicated to the General Prefect TAMBURINI.[3] The Second Map of the Jesuits of Paraguay, 1722.

---

[1] "PARTIE / LA PLUS MÉRIDIONALE DE L'AMÉRIQUE OU SE TROUVE / LE CHILI / LE PARAGUAY / . . . *par* N. DE FER, *Geographe de sa Majesté Catholique*."

[2] *Notice sur Don Felix de Azara* par WALCKENAER, in Vol. 1., p. xxii., of AZARA, *Voyages dans l'Amérique Méridionale* (Paris, 1889).

[3] A reduced fac-simile of the whole map is in Vol. VI., under No. 2 A. Another, of the essential section of the Map, and on the same scale as the original, is No. 3 in Vol. V.

The reproduction was made from the copy that belonged to D'ANVILLE, preserved in the Geographical Depot of the French Foreign Office. The Brazilian Special Mission can also produce a copy belonging to the cartographical collection of the Brazilian Foreign Office.

Title and dedication: "PARAQVARIÆ PROVINCIÆ SOC. JESU CUM ADJACENTIB⁵ NOVISSIMA DESCRIPTIO / *Post iteratas peregrinationes, & plures*

In this Map appear for the first time in the Upper Uruguay the Great Falls and the rivers *Uruguay-Pitá* and *Uruguay-Mini*, affluents of the left bank, besides other unnamed tributaries.

It is, therefore, the first Map in which the positions of the Pepiry and of the Uruguay-Pitá can be examined, because in it is seen the Salto Grande (Great Falls), a safe and indisputable point of reference. It is easy to get confused as to rivers and to transfer the name of one to others; but *there is only one Salto Grande* (Great Falls) *in all the Upper Uruguay*.

None of the maps printed after this and before the Treaty of 1750 contains any new information on the course of the Uruguay and the names or the positions of its affluents.

In 1730, a second edition of the Map of 1722[1] was published at Augsburg by SEUTTER.

Seutter, 1730.

In 1732, PETROSCHI engraved at Rome *the third Map sent from Paraguay by the Jesuits of that Province*, and presented by them to Father F. RETZ, General Prefect of the Society.[2] Although it was written in 1892 that this Map was made at Rome by Father RETZ, the dedication which

The third Map of the Jesuits of Paraguay.

---

observationes Patrum Missionariorum eiusdem Soc. tum huius Provinciæ, cum & Peruanæ accuratissime delineata Anno 1722. / ADMODUM R. IN CHTO. PATRI SUO / P. MICHAELI ANGELO TAMBURINO / SOC. JESU PRÆP. GENERALI XIV. *Hanc Terrarum Filiorum Suorum / sudore, et sanguine excultarum et rigatarum tabulam* / D. D. D. / *Provincia Paraquariæ Soc. Jesu / Anno 1726.* / Joannes Petroschi Sculp. Romæ Sup. perm. Ann. 1726."

[1] "PARAQUARIÆ PROVINCIÆ / SOC. IESU / CUM ADJACENTIBUS Novissima Descriptio . . . *delin / à /* MATTHÆO SEUTTERO, S. C. M. G. August."

[2] "PARAQVARIÆ PROVINCIÆ SOC. JESV CVM ADIACENTIB: NOVISSIMA DESCRIPTIO *Post iteratas peregrinationes, & plures observationes Patrum Missionariorum eiusdem Soc, tum huius Provinciæ, cum & Peruanæ accuratissime delineata, & emendata. Ann. 1732.* . . . Ioannes Petroschi Sculp. Romæ Sup. perm. Anno 1732."

is inscribed on the document itself removes the confusion.

In 1733, D'ANVILLE, in view of the two Maps engraved by J. PETROSCHI (1722 and 1732) and of that previously engraved by G. COECK (XVIIth century), that is, in view of the three Maps sent and dedicated to three different General Prefects of the Society of Jesus at Rome *by the Jesuits of the Province of Paraguay*, composed his *Carte du Paraguay*, appended to Vol. XXI. of the *Lettres Édifiantes et Curieuses écrites des Missions Étrangeres, par quelques Missionnaires de la Compagnie de Jesus*,[1] Father DU HALDE, the editor of the Letters, says in the Preface: "In order to satisfy you completely regarding these Missions, I have thought it my duty, Reverend Fathers, to give you an accurate Map of that vast tract of land, over which they are scattered: M. DANVILLE, Geographer in ordinary to the King, has drawn it expressly with very great care, from various Maps, and, among others, from a quite recent one, *given by the Missionaries of Paraguay themselves*. You will find at the end of the Report which has come from Spain, an address in which the Author of this Map makes a sort of analysis of it, in order that you may judge for yourselves how accurately it has been worked out."

D'Anville, 1733.

Indeed, in the same volume of the *Lettres Édifiantes*, from page 429 to 465, "*Geographical Remarks upon the Map of Paraguay by the Author of that Map*" are found.

[1] "LE PARAGUAY / où les R.R. PP. de la Compagnie de JESUS / ont répandu leurs MISSIONS / par le S! D'ANVILLE / Géographe du Roi / Octobre 1733."

There is a Spanish edition of this Map in the translation of the *Edifying Letters*, Madrid, 1757, *Cartas Edificantes*, Vol. XVI.

D'Anville, 1748. In 1748 the Map of South America by D'Anville was published.[1]

These are the only maps published between the years 1722 and 1750 in which are seen, in the Uruguay, the *Great Falls*, the *Pepiry*, the *Uruguay-Pitā* or *Puitā*, and the *Uruguay-Miní*.

This Statement is accompanied by fac-similes of all the maps quoted.

In Vol. VI. are the following full reproductions:

No. 2 A: Map of 1722 of the Jesuits of Paraguay, engraved in 1726 at Rome.

No. 3 A: The same Map, engraved in 1730 at Augsburg.

No. 4 A: New Map of the Jesuits of Paraguay, engraved at Rome in the year 1732.

No. 5 A: Map of Paraguay by D'ANVILLE, of 1733, appended to Vol. XXI. of the *Lettres Édifiantes* of the Jesuits.

No. 6 A: One of the sheets of South America by D'ANVILLE, of 1748.

In Vol. V. of this Statement are fac-similes of the sections of those maps in which the territory of the present controversy is represented. Besides the two of D'ANVILLE quoted, another manuscript Map of the same author, which is preserved in the Geographical Depot of the French Foreign Office, is reproduced.

It is in the reproductions of Vol. V. that this question

---

[1] "AMÉRIQUE / MÉRIDIONALE / PUBLIÉE SOUS LES AUSPICES / DE MONSEIGNEUR LE DUC D'ORLÉANS / PREMIER PRINCE DU SANG / PAR LE S! D'ANVILLE / MDCCXLVIII. / *Avec Privilège.* / *A Paris* / *Chez l'Auteur, aux Galeries du Louvre.*"

There is a London edition, 1775, of this Map, and another of Venice, 1779.

The part of Paraguay and adjacent territories was reproduced in 1760 under this title:—" LE PARAGUAY / *tiré de la Carte de l'Amérique Méridionale de M. d'Anville.*"

BOUNDARY QUESTION. 137

of limits can best be studied, because nearly all the maps have been drawn to the same scale, by the process of photogravure, in order to facilitate comparisons. Those now cited are all on the same scale.

In Vol. V. the maps to be studied at this point are those published from 1722 to 1750, that is, since the *Great Falls of Uruguay* and the affluents of the *Uruguay-Pitá* and *Uruguay-Miní* were for the first time represented in the Upper Uruguay (where previously the Pepiry and some affluents without names only appeared) to the conclusion of the Treaty of Limits of 1750.

These are the maps:

No. 3: Second Map of the Jesuits of Paraguay, composed in 1722, engraved at Rome in the year 1726 and dedicated to the General Prefect TAMBURINI.

No. 4: Edition of Augsburg of the preceding Map, also dedicated to TAMBURINI.

No. 5: Third Map of the Jesuits of Paraguay, engraved at Rome in 1732 and dedicated to the General Prefect RETZ.

No. 6: *Paraguay* of D'ANVILLE, 1733.

No. 7: The *Upper Uruguay* according to the original drawing of D'ANVILLE, in the French Foreign Office.

No. 8: Fragment of *South America* by D'ANVILLE, year 1748.

In his pamphlet *Misiones*, Dr. ZEBALLOS acknowledges that the *Pepiry* in the maps of the Jesuits of 1722 and 1732, and the *Pepiry* or *Pequiry* (the two names in the Treaty of 1750) in the Map by D'ANVILLE, dated 1733, are not the river of the present Argentine pretension. He endeavors by this to prove that those maps

Not one of the Maps quoted favors the Argentine cause.

were constructed according to information of the Portuguese Jesuits, and accuses the Prefect Retz and D'Anville of having suppressed the river which in the Map of 1703 of De l'Isle (No. 2), has the name of *Acaraguá*, giving to the two rivers, which in that Map have no names, those of *Guarumbaca* and *Pepiry*.

Neither of these allegations can be sustained.

A comparison of Maps 1 and 2 shows that the *Acaraguá* was also named *Acarana*. On the *Acaraguá or Acarana* was situated until 1637 the mission of Assumpcion, then transferred to Mbororé, below the Uruguay, as is seen in Map No. 1. De l'Isle, without paying attention to what Techo says, placed on the *Acaraguá or Acarana*, as has heretofore been said, the mission which, in a Map constructed half a century earlier, was represented no longer there.

In the disapproved maps of 1722, 1732, and 1733 (Nos. 3, 4, and 6), the Acaraguá was not suppressed, as it appears in them all under the name of *Acarana*.

The two rivers above the mouth of the *Acaraguá* or *Acarana* already have the names of *Guanumbaca* and *Pepiry* in the first Map of the Jesuits (No. 1). Therefore, the Jesuits in 1722 and 1732, and D'Anville in 1733 (Nos. 3, 4, and 6), did not make the innovation attributed to them by the pamphlet *Misiones*.

It is also impossible to make the Portuguese Jesuits responsible for the position, which is truly very inconvenient for the Argentine cause, in which, in those maps, the rivers *Pepiry* and *Uruguay-Pitá* are located. Any one who knows the discipline that always prevailed in the Society of Jesus, will understand that the Jesuits of Portugal and Brazil would never give information contrary to that afforded by their brethren of the Province of Paraguay.

The Jesuits of that Province were not Portuguese, and in the maps of 1722 and 1732 it is stated that the "*Province of the Society of Jesus in Paraguay*" presents and dedicates to the General Prefect those maps "wherein are represented lands that have been cultivated and watered with the sweat and blood of his children."

The dedication of the first of those maps says:
"Admodum R. in Christo Patri suo P. MICHAELI ANGELO TAMBURINO, Soc. Iesu Praep. Generali XIV. Hanc terrarum filiorum suorum sudore, et sanguine excultarum et rigatarum tabulam, D. D. D. *Provincia Paraquariae Soc. Jes.*"

In the second Map the dedication is written in identical words, by the Province of Paraguay, the only difference being in the name of the General Prefect, who was then RETZ.

In the Map of 1733, as has been proved by a transcription of D'ANVILLE, this geographer was guided by the two most recent maps of the Jesuits, which were those of 1722 and 1732.

In all the maps which are now under examination,—Nos. 3, 4, 5, 6, 7, and 8, —the *Uruguay-Pitã is seen below the Great Falls of the Uruguay*, as an affluent of the left bank, and, *lower still*, on the opposite bank, the *Pepiry* of the Jesuits. In all the maps of Spanish origin anterior to 1749 the Pepiry and the Uruguay-Pitã are below the Great Falls.

Therefore, *the Pepiry of the Jesuits is a river situated in the present Argentine territory of Misiones*: it is not the *Pepiry* or *Pequiry* of the Map of 1749, since this *is the first river above the Great Falls*, and still less can it be the Chapecó (Pequiry Guazú of the Argentines) because The Pequiry or Pepiry of the Paulistas.

this is much more distant from the Great Falls (Salto Grande) and from the Pepiry of the maps of the Jesuits and d'ANVILLE.

Father PEDRO LOZANO, the "Chronicler of the Society of Jesus in the Province of Paraguay," ter-minated in 1745 his *Historia de la Conquista del Paraguay, Rio de la Plata, y Tucuman*,[1] and from it the knowledge possessed by the Jesuits of that time concerning the upper course of the Uruguay can be seen.

<small>Lozano's description of the Uruguay, 1745.</small>

LOZANO was not a Portuguese. He was born at Madrid September 16, 1697.

His description of the Uruguay entirely agrees with the maps of 1722 and 1732 (Nos. 3 and 5) and with those of D'ANVILLE of 1733, the undated manuscript, and that of 1748 (Nos. 6, 7, and 8).

The description of LOZANO can be followed in any of the five maps cited, and it is sufficient to take it from the river Yyuí (afterward Ijuhy), on the left bank of the Uruguay. LOZANO goes up the Uruguay, naming the affluents of the left bank, and afterward comes down the river, mentioning those of the right.

In the ascent of the river:

"From the *Yyuí*, up the Uruguay, following one another along this bank,[2] the rivers *Yaguarapé, Nucora, San Juan, Yriboba*, and *Uruguay-Pitá*, which are tributaries of the Uruguay: *not far from the Uruguay-Pitá, this great river takes a prodigious leap (Salto), hurling the whole of its waters from a very high elevation with an astounding roar*."[3]

---

[1] Published for the first time at Buenos-Aires by D ANDRÉS LAMAS, in 1874.
[2] Left bank.
[3] LOZANO, *Hist. de la Conquista*, I., 34.

Therefore according to LOZANO, the Uruguay-Pitã *was a river whose mouth lay below the Great Falls*, as it is represented in the maps of the Jesuits and in those of D'AN-VILLE.

<small>Uruguay-Pitã below the Great Falls.</small>

LOZANO continues :

"A short distance before this Uruguay-Pitã is an impenetrable circle of pine trees enclosing a large space of ground, some ninety leagues wide, which extends from the sources where the Uruguay rises as far as the said place, and where pine trees are wanting to complete the circle, this gap is defended by a very high mountain range which runs behind the island of Santa Catalina, opposite the lake of Patos, until it meets the said pine forests, and which is so steep that, while pack animals cannot climb it at all, men can only do so with the greatest difficulty and toil. From it the sea can be discovered, and some Portuguese villages can be seen. *From a short distance after the Salto (falls) mentioned, the stream of the Uruguay changes its direction, because, flowing as far as this from North to South, from its source to the Salto (falls) it runs from East to West.*"

<small>The two general directions of the Uruguay.</small>

In this passage the two general directions of the course of the river are well marked: the Upper Uruguay, running from East to West as far as the Great Falls ; and the Lower, in the general direction of North to South from the Falls to the River Plate.

The position of the Great Falls, nearly at the point of deflection of the Uruguay, is also well determined, as can be ascertained by examining Map No. 29 A. The informants of the Jesuits were Indians, but the two general directions of the

<small>Position of the Great Falls.</small>

river, which were so different, and the extent and grandeur of the Falls, were circumstances which the most ignorant Indian would necessarily keep in mind and would be capable of indicating with clearness.

The Great Falls of the Uruguay have an extent of about two kilometres or one mile. The waters are precipitated over a steep and sheer diorite rock. The height of the fall is 10 metres or 32½ feet. Above that fall, and before reaching the Chapecó, there are other small falls. The most important is the Saltinho da Fortaleza, which is as far as the demarcating Commissioners reached in 1759. This is about 2 metres or 6½ feet in height, but it is composed of three ledges.[1]

* Saltinho da Fortaleza.

Above the Great Falls (Salto Grande), LOZANO only mentioned one affluent, which is the *Uruguay-Mini*.

Speaking of the sources of the Uruguay, he says (p. 35):

"Its source, then, is in the mountain range lately mentioned, farther on than the island of Santa Catalina in 26½°, almost in the same latitude as the river San Francisco; at its source it has but a small volume of water, and divides into two branches, of which that to the South is called the *Uruguay-Mini*, and the one to the North, *Uruguay-Guazú*, into which, before they unite, so many rivulets flow that from there it runs in a great volume; *and from here, as we have ascended giving the description of its left or Eastern bank, we will go down along the opposite side* until we stop again at the point where it loses its name and gives the volume of its waters to the River Plate."

---

[1] SR. VIRASORO, now the Minister for Foreign Affairs of the Argentine Republic, shows in § VI. of his pamphlet, *Misiones y Arbitraje*, the insignificance of this small Fall.

LOZANO, it is seen, is about to begin the descent of the Uruguay from the point where the Uruguay-Mini unites with this river, and he will now proceed to point out the affluents of the right bank.

The first he mentions *is a Pepiry below the Great Falls* (Salto Grande), as in the maps of the Jesuits.

This is what the chronicler of the Society of Jesus says (p. 36) :

"From these sources of the Uruguay towards the North and West, there are some fifty leagues of *very dense forests as far as the Plains of Guayrá*, which belong to the government of Paraguay, and in them wander many unconverted Indians, *Guayanás, Ibirayarís, Gualachos*, most fierce people, and the *Yraitis*, so called because they are accustomed to wear caps of wax upon their heads. In the direction of the East, the said sources may be some ninety leagues from the true boundaries of Brazil,[1] and *running by the bank, after the Falls, the first river to enter the Uruguay is the Pepiri, a very full stream, of which only from the accounts of the Indians, for the Spaniards did not see it*, it was very constantly reported among the first conquerors and their descendants that its fine sands were very auriferous. . . ."

The Pepiry of the Jesuits below the Great Falls.

After the Great Falls and the Pepiri (that of the Jesuits), says LOZANO, continuing down the Uruguay and naming the tributaries of the right bank :

"*Travelling towards the South*, came successively

---

[1] At this point, like a good Spaniard, LOZANO contested the right of Portugal to the lands to which it was in possession North of the Uruguay.

It has already been said (page 60 in this Vol.) that this Father LOZANO was the writer of the representations addressed by the Jesuits of Paraguay to the Court of Madrid, petitioning for the annulment of the Treaty of 1750.

after this river, the *Guanumbaca*, *Acaraguay*, and *Mbororé*. . . ."

This is a second proof that the *Acaraguá*, or *Acaraguay* was not suppressed in the Maps of 1722 and 1732 and in those of D'ANVILLE, as DR. ZEBALLOS has supposed in his pamphlet *Misiones*, since, under the name of *Acarana*, which it also had, it appears in those maps between the *Guanumbaca* and the *Mbororé*, that is to say, in the position indicated by LOZANO.

It is unnecessary to proceed further with the transcription of the text of LOZANO, since immediately below the Mbororé is the Mission of S. Xavier, the starting point of the Commissioners of 1759 when they went up the Uruguay to survey the Pepiry or Pequiry of the Treaty of 1750.

In the pamphlet quoted, written "to refute errors of Brazilian origin and to enlighten public opinion in North and South America" there are two propositions which need a rapid examination.

The Pepiry in d'Anville is not the river of the Argentine pretension.

MR. MINISTER ZEBALLOS asserts in this pamphlet that the errors attributed by him to the Map of Paraguay (1733) by D'ANVILLE were corrected in the Map of South America (1748) by the same geographer, and affirms that the Pepiry in the second of those maps is the river of the Argentine pretension.[1]

---

[1] "D'ANVILLE corrects in the American Map the *Portuguese datum* of his map of Paraguay of 1733. . . . I can, therefore, affirm that the river to the *East* in this Map (1748), called Pequiry, is the one which corresponds to the boundary. D'ANVILLE did not rectify the situation *of the Uruguay-Pitá which in all the maps of that period is vaguely indicated*" (this proposition is very exact and important). "The new position of the rivers given by D'ANVILLE, is no longer that of the Portuguese in the map of 1733, nor that of the Spaniards. It is that of Nature, because it is the one which Argentines and

A mere comparison of the two maps (Nos. 6 and 8) shows that in both the Pepiry has its mouth *to the West and below the Great Falls*, and, therefore, it is a river which, drawn upon the Map of the Brazilian-Argentine Joint Commission (No. 25 A), or in that of the Brazilian Special Mission at Washington (No. 29 A), would be within the present Argentine territory of Misiones. The Chapecó, or Pequiri-Guazú of the Argentine pretension, is far to the East of the Great Falls (Salto Grande), and within the Brazilian territory.

Disregarding the Great Falls, and considering only the co-ordinates of the mouth of the Pepiry in both the maps and in that of the Joint Commission, the result is no less contrary to the second affirmation made in the pamphlet.

It is not possible to deduce any argument whatever from the Latitudes, because in all maps previous to the survey made in 1759 by the Portuguese and Spanish Commissioners the upper course of the Uruguay is drawn on a parallel too much to the North. Only the Longitudes can be compared.

In both the maps under consideration, D'ANVILLE took as the first meridian that of Ferro Island, but in the *Map of Paraguay* (1733) he located this first meridian at 19° 51′ 33″ West of the Observatory of Paris,[1] and in that of *South America* at 20° West.[2] In

Brazilians trace on their Joint Map, with the natural differences between the empirical data of travellers, as were those of 1745, and those which were obtained in 1887 by approximately accurate scientific operations." (DR. ZEBALLOS, *Misiones*, p. 73.)

[1] " The longitude of these places, compared with the determination of Ferro Island, observed last by Father FEUILLÉE, of the Order of the Minims, at 19° 51′ 33″ of the meridian of Paris, has served as a basis for the longitude laid down in the Map." (D'ANVILLE, in his *Observations sur la Carte du Paraguay*, p. 431 of Vol. XXI., 1st ed., of the *Lettres Édifiantes*.)

[2] " . . . having agreed to fix the Longitude from Paris at 20° in round

accordance with these declarations of the author the degrees of Longitude from the meridian of Greenwich, which is 2° 20′ 14″ West of Paris, were marked on Maps Nos. 6 and 8.

In both the maps the Pepiry lies, with an insignificant difference, on the same meridian as the mouth of the Pepiry-Gauçú, the Brazilian boundary, which is 53° 18′ 19″ West of Greenwich, while the mouth of the Chapecó, the boundary claimed by the Argentine Republic, is in Longitude 52° 59′ 55″ West of Greenwich.

Consequently, by this process, and by the first and more exact, of referring the rivers of the controversy to the position of the Great Falls (Salto Grande), the Pepiry of the Map of *South America* of D'ANVILLE is not the river of the Argentine pretension, as has been affirmed. By the second process, it would undisputably be the river of the present Brazilian boundary.

As to the boundary line of Southern Brazil drawn by D'ANVILLE in his Map of 1748, and quoted by DR. ZEBALLOS, it also proves that that Geographer was guided by information of the Spanish Missionaries of Paraguay, inasmuch as this line is not that of the *uti possidetis* of 1748, as is seen on the "Map issued by the Courts" of 1749, nor was it defined in any Treaty whatever between Portugal and Spain. D'ANVILLE in the same Map of *South America* gives to Chile all the territory of Cuyo and nearly all Patagonia. If it were entitled to any weight in the present controversy, consistency requires that the Argentine

---

numbers from the same meridian . . . I do not think that 7 to 8 minutes are an object that should be very strongly insisted upon." (*Lettre de* M. D'ANVILLE *à* MM. *du Journal des Savans, sur une Carte de l'Amérique Méridionale qu'il vient de publier*, in the *Journal des Savans*, Paris, March, 1750.)

Republic, in the settlement of the question of Limits with Chile, should conform to the same authority.[1]

It has been proved that in the Maps of the Jesuits of Paraguay, in those of D'ANVILLE, and in the description of the Uruguay by LOZANO, the *Pepiry* and the *Uruguay-Pitá,*—or, more exactly, the two rivers to which the Jesuits gave those names, —emptied themselves into the Uruguay *below and to the West of the Salto Grande (Great Falls)*.

Conclusions.

It has also been proved that all of these documents were of Spanish origin.

1st. Because the Maps of the Jesuits were drawn in the Missions and presented to the General Prefect in the name of the whole " Province of Paraguay of the Society of Jesus";

2d. Because LOZANO was a Spanish Jesuit, a known defender in boundary questions of the old but exaggerated pretensions of the Government of his country, and one of the warmest adversaries of the Treaty of 1750;

3d. Because D'ANVILLE declared that he had constructed his Map of Paraguay, utilizing the information contained in the Maps of 1722 and 1732 of the same Jesuits.

---

[1] The pamphlet *Misiones* quotes a passage in which D'ANVILLE speaks of Portuguese information. That passage refers solely to the neighborhood of S. Paulo, and nobody, looking at a Map, will say that the city of S. Paulo lies near the Pepiry. The beginning, already transcribed, of the *Observations* of D'ANVILLE (1733), fully answers the quotation of that isolated passage.

For the Map of South America, he also had much new information of Spanish origin, as appears from the following passage of another work of his:

" What must take a great part of the advantages which distinguish the *Map of South America*, is the having acquired in the countries occupied by the Spaniards a degree of perfection with which one would not have ventured to flatter oneself." (D'ANVILLE, *Considérations Générales sur l'Étude et les Connoissances que demande la Composition des Ouvrages de Géographie*, Paris, 1777.)

Evidence of Portuguese origin as to the true position of the Pequiry of the Brazilians of S. Paulo, or Paulistas,—*the first river above the Great Falls (Salto Grande)*,—will now appear with all clearness in the manuscript Map of 1749, upon which was drawn the divisional line as agreed upon in the Treaty of Limits of January 13, 1750.

<small>The Brazilian Pepiry in the Map of 1749: first river above the Great Falls.</small>

This is, however, the second document upon which it is proposed to base the Argentine claim.

Map No. 7 A, appended to this Statement (Vol. VI.), is a faithful reproduction of the original used by the Plenipotentiaries of Portugal and Spain in the discussion of the Treaty.

No. 8 A is this same Map, examined by M. EMILE LEVASSEUR, of the Institute of France.

No. 10, in Vol. V., is a reproduction of the section of this Map in which the territory now contested is situated. The section was raised to the scale of the maps of the Jesuits and those of D'ANVILLE.

In No. 8 A, the following conditions have been made under the supervision of M. EMILE LEVASSEUR, after he had studied the projection of the Map:

a) the degrees of Longitude have been traced with reference to the meridians of Rio de Janeiro, Paris, and Greenwich;

b) the coast-line has been marked in red, from Cape S. Roque to the River Plate, and also the lower courses of the Uruguay, the Paraná, and the Paraguay, in accordance with the projection of the Map and the French Admiralty Charts by MOUCHEZ; and

c) in the same red color, the rivers of the contested territory have been marked, in accordance with the Map of the Brazilian-Argentine Joint Commission.

It has already been stated and proved by two letters of June 24 and July 12, 1751, of the Portuguese Ambassador at Madrid, that the Map of 1749 was executed at Lisbon.

How the Portuguese Map of 1749 was executed.

The most conclusive proof, however, that it is a Portuguese Map is in the following beginning of the Official Letter of February 8, 1749, addressed by the Minister for Foreign Affairs of Portugal to the Ambassador at Madrid :

"*I hand to Your Excellency the Map I had promised, showing, by a red line, the boundaries indicated in the Draft Treaty. The part of this Map which refers to the Spanish lands in the South is taken from the Map in Vol. 21 of the* Edifying Letters *produced by the Spanish Missionaries. That which refers to our lands in the same Southern part is taken from the Geographical Map of F*ᴿ· D*IOGO* S*OARES*. *The part which follows from the River Paraná to the Cuiabá is taken from the Map sent by* G*OMES* F*REIRE DE* A*NDRADA, and from other reports of travellers.* The River Guaporé and the Missions of Moxos are drawn according to the reports and sketches of some miners at Matto Grosso, who were there twice, and from some information they gathered there. The situation of our Missions of the river Madeira, and of the River Tapajoz, and their neighborhood, is taken from maps and reports which have come from Pará. The river Amazonas was copied from the Map of L*A* C*ON-* DAMINE, the Orinoco from the book of Fᴱ G*UMILLA*, and the country lying between these rivers is drawn according to some imperfect information given by the Carmelite Missionaries of the Rio Negro. That which lies between the river Amazonas and the Province of

Chareas is imaginary, and has no foundation except in the knowledge that the large rivers which empty themselves into the Amazonas come from that part, and that there is a chain of mountains which follows the course of the river Amazonas from East to West although distant from this river.

"Referring now what has been said in the draft to that which is seen in this Map, *there can be no doubt regarding the whole part of the borders which runs from the disputed territory on the bank of the river Plate to the Great Falls of the Paraná*, because it is a known country in which the Spanish maps agree with ours in that which refers to the country bordering on Colonia, Rio Negro, Uruguai, Iguaçú, and Paraná, and their surroundings. With regard to Lake Merim and its neighborhood, concerning which the Spaniards had no information, we can affirm that they are as in the Map, because various geographical maps, by different Authors, which have come to us from those parts, agree on that point. *If there be any scruple as to the name of the river Piquiri, along which the draft leads the boundary to reach the Iguaçú, it may be said, that it (the boundary) is to be along the river which, discharging into the Uruguai, shall form with the course of the same Uruguai the line nearest to the North direction, and that from the headwaters of such river those of the nearest river that empties itself into the Iguaçú shall be sought, and that along it the boundary shall be established. . ."*[1]

---

[1] Official letter of February 8, 1749, of MARCO ANTONIO DE AZEREDO COUTINHO, Secretary of State for Foreign Affairs for Portugal, addressed to VISCOUNT THOMAZ DA SILVA TELLES, Ambassador at Madrid. The copy in the possession of the Brazilian Special Mission was authenticated on October 31, 1893, by the Portuguese Foreign Office, where the original minute is preserved.

This last passage has already been quoted, but it is expedient to reproduce it here.

The "Map issued by the Courts," of 1749, is, therefore, indisputably a Portuguese Map, as was stated in 1776 by the MARQUIS DI GRIMALDI, Secretary of State in Spain.

It was constructed in view of the best Portuguese, Spanish, and French geographical documents then existing, and, as was natural, many errors of previous maps were corrected, according to information from the Portuguese authorities in Brazil, and above all of the Paulistas, who were the explorers of its whole interior. WALCKENAER indirectly acknowledged the superiority of this map over that of Paraguay by D'ANVILLE, since that of BELLIN of 1756, to which he refers, is a mere copy of it.[1]

On examining No. 8 A, which was studied by M. EMILE LEVASSEUR, No. 29 A, and the *Map of Southern Brazil*, it is at once seen that the difference between the Latitude of the mouth of the Pepiry in the "Map issued by the Courts" and that which was observed upon the ground, could not disappear, even though the Portuguese and Spanish Commissioners in 1759 had continued to ascend the river as far as the confluence of the Pelotas and of the Canoas, where the Uruguay begins. The course of this river is represented in the "Map issued by the Latitude of the upper course of the Uruguay.

---
[1] The Map of BELLIN is appended to this Statement under No. 10 A, (Vol. VI.) and will be treated of shortly.

WALCKENAER says, speaking of the Map of Paraguay by D'ANVILLE:

" He brought this work to perfection in his Map of South America ; but, although he corrected that part of his Map in 1765 and 1779, it is still less accurate in the outlining of the coasts after the last correction, than that which was published by BELLIN, in 1756, in the *Histoire du Paraguay* by Father CHARLEVOIX." (WALCKENAER, *Notice sur Don Felix de Azara.*)

Courts," some forty miles to the North of the parallel in which it should be, and the same error is noticed in all previous maps.

This difference in the Latitude was the cause of the chief doubt entertained by the Spanish Commissioner ARGUEDAS, a doubt immediately removed, because it was impossible to go and seek further a river which the "Map issued by the Courts" located so near the Great Falls (Salto Grande).

The Latitude of these Falls was also wrong on the Map, and the Treaty of January 17, 1751, "upon the interpretation of the Geographical Maps," anticipated the inevitable inaccuracies that would be found when the Demarcating Commissioners should proceed upon the ground to a survey never before undertaken.

This difference in the Latitude does not benefit the Argentine cause, because neither is that of the mouth of the Chapecó in accordance with that of the Pequiry or Pepiry of the Map.

The other doubt of Commissioner ARGUEDAS, as was

Relative positions of the Pepiry and Uruguay-Pitá.
seen by his statement at the conference of March 7, 1759, had reference to the relative positions occupied in the Map by the Pepiry or Pequiry and the Uruguay-Pitá.

In the Map, the mouth of the Uruguay-Pitá is below that of the Pepiry. On the ground, and according to the information of the guide ARIRAPY, it was found above the mouth of the Pepiry.

The explanation of this is very simple.

In the maps of the Jesuits, as has been shown,

Pepiry above the Great Falls, Uruguay-Pitá below.
both the Pepiry and the Uruguay-Pitá have their mouths *below the Great Falls*. The Portuguese Government in the Map of 1749 located the Pepiry or Pequiry,

according to the information of the Paulistas, *above the Great Falls*, and it made no change whatever in the position which the maps of the Jesuits and those of D'ANVILLE attributed to the Uruguay-Pitá. [margin: Pequiry or Pepiry of the Paulistas.]

The divisional line did not pass along this river and, thus, its position on the Map was not a point of importance or interest. And the Instructions given to the Commissioners in 1758 do not say, as was asserted in 1789, that the Pepiry was to be sought above the Uruguay-Pitá.

It has already been proved in another place,[1] and when quoting Print No. 27 (Vol. V. of this Statement), that the Great Falls are represented in the "Map issued by the Courts" immediately below the mouth of the Pepiry. The Portuguese cartographer of 1749 omitted to write the word—Salto (Falls),—but made the distinctive sign of cataracts, according to the custom of that time. [margin: The Great Falls.]

In 1759 and, it appears, since 1750, the Jesuits of the Missions gave the name of Pepiry to the first river above the Falls (Salto), no doubt because they preferred as a limit the Brazilian Pequiry or Pepiry, more to the East, to their old Pequiry below the Falls. Until 1749, as may be seen in a Map of that date by Father JOSEPH QUIROGA,[2] they called the first river above [margin: Transfer of names.] [margin: Map of Quiroga.]

---

[1] Pages 121 and 122 in this Vol.
[2] No. 9, Vol. V., Title: "MAPA DE LAS MISSIONES DE LA COMPAÑIA DE JESUS EN / LOS RIOS PARANÁ, Y URUGUAY *conforme à las mas modernas observaciones de Latitud y Longitud; hechas en los pueblos de dichas Missiones, y à las relaciones anti- / guas y modernas de los Padres Missioneros de ambos rios. Por el Padre* JOSEPH QUIROGA *de la misma Campañia de Jesus en la Provincia de el Paraguay* / Ano 1749, / Ferdinandus Franceschelli sculp. Romæ 1753."

This Map is much inferior to the previous ones of the Jesuits. It is only interesting as showing that at that date the Jesuits still knew by the name of the Falls Apitereby, because until then—as in the description of LOZANO (1745)—the river to which they gave the name of *Pepiry* was the one which in the demarcation of 1759 appeared under the name of *Mandiy Guaçú* and is now called *Soberbio*, in the Argentine Territory of Misiones.¹

The Apitereby of the Jesuits.

The Mandiy Guaçú was the Pepiry of the Jesuits.

All the old names of affluents of the left bank of the Uruguay which are met with in the maps of the Jesuits and in the description of LOZANO were changed when the Commissioners in 1759 made the journey from S. Xavier in search of the Pepiry. The names *Yaguarape*, *Nucorá*, *S. Juan*, *Yriboba*, and *Uruguay-Pitá* (the "Red Uruguay") did not then exist below the Great Falls.²

Names changed.

To the last, the name of *Paricay* or *Piracay* was given in the demarcation of 1759. In 1788 the Spanish geographer OYÁRVIDE found the same river with the name of *Piray* or *Cebolloty*.³ It is now known as the *Turvo*⁴ ("muddy river").

The first Uruguay-Pitá, in 1759 Paricay.

Apitereby the Pepiry or Pequiry of the Paulistas. When it was engraved in 1753, they added to it the divisional line, according to the Treaty of 1750, making it pass along the first river above the Falls of the Uruguay.

¹ Map No. 29 A, division F 9.
² The old names and the changes which subsequently occurred are shown in the following table:

1722	1759	1788	XIX Century.
Yaguarape.	Itapuá.		Camanday ou Mbutuhy.
Nucorá.	Imbutiay-Guaçú.		Santa Rosa.
S. Juan.	Pinday.	Pindayí.	Nhucorá.
Yriboba.	Cavacuá-Guaçú.	Cavacuá Guaçú.	Herval Grande.
Uruguay-Pitá.	Paricay ou Piracay.	Piray ou Cebollaty.	Turvo.

³ OYÁRVIDE, in CALVO, N., 74. It was in 1788 that he passed before the mouth of this river. ⁴ Division F 10 in Map No. 29 A.

In a Spanish manuscript Map, which must have been drawn on the River Plate before 1760 and which was retouched in part during that year, the old *Uruguay-Pitá* of the Jesuits is still seen with its first name and with its mouth between those of the rivers Ipané and Guanumbaca on the opposite bank.[1]

<small>Spanish Map of 1760.</small>

Of these frequent changes of name OYÁRVIDE speaks in the following terms:

". . . The word Toropí of the Guaraní language means bull's hide, and thus it is presumable that from some circumstance of the kind they substituted for the name of Ibicuí that of Toropí, as we see how inclined to such changes are, not only these Indians, but also the Spanish inhabitants among whom we have travelled, who easily changed the names of places and rivers, according to the events that make the greatest impression upon them, and for this reason it is that places well known to the guides themselves come to be strange to them if they are not called by the name by which they distinguish them, although in old records they were always called by the names asked."[2]

<small>Spanish testimony to changes of names of rivers.</small>

The Spanish Commissioners of 1759 also had occa-

---

[1] The fac-simile of a section of this Map is under No. 14, in Vol. V., whereunder No. 21, it is compared with that of 1749. In Vol. VI. is a fac-simile of the whole Eastern part of the Map (No. 11 A).

The original belongs to the Brazilian Foreign Office and is in the keeping of the Brazilian Special Mission. Title: " MAPA / DE LOS CONFINES DE LAS DOS / CORONAS DE ESPAÑA Y PORTUGAL / EN LA / AMERICA MERIDIONAL / *que comprehende desde Castillos Grandes / hasta la boca del Rio Jauru con- / forme á la Linea Divisoria determinada en el Tratado concluido entre Sus Mag.^{des} C.^s y F.^s el año 1751. El color encarnado señala los dominios de España, y el Amarillo los de Portugal.*" Upon a mark is seen the name of FERDINAND VI. This King died in 1760, and, therefore, the Map is not subsequent to that date. The course and the name of the S. Antonio are in different ink, which shows that the Map was retouched according to information supplied by the demarcating Commissioners. [2] OYÁRVIDE, in CALVO, VIII., 218.

sion to notice how the names of the less important rivers in those regions varied, since they wrote as follows in their Diary (July 2, 1759):

"This novelty or variation of names, which is common in rivers of lesser note,—the inhabitants of one settlement calling them by one name, while those of others name them differently, and, what is more peculiar, the inhabitants of the same settlement varying them according to their whim,—produces a confusion which is reflected in the maps, in which a like diversity is seen."

The question relating to the Uruguay-Pitã, raised by the Spanish Commissioners of the second demarcation, has not the importance which the Argentine Government gives it.

Position of the first and second Uruguay-Pitã.

The demarcators of 1759 did not change the position of the Pequiry or Pepiry of the "Map of the Courts"; *it was the name of Uruguay-Pitã that changed its place*, seeing that it had been transferred from a river whose mouth, according to the Map, is 41 kilometres, or 22 miles, below the Great Falls, to another which discharges itself 22 kilometres, or 11.8 miles, above the same Falls and above the mouth of the Pepiry. For this second Uruguay-Pitã, now the Guarita, the Spanish Commissioners invented, after 1788, the name of Mberuy, removing then to another river more to the East the name of Uruguay-Pitã, and wishing, after the two successive removals, to find *above the mouth of the third river of that name* the Pequiry or Pepiry whose mouth, according to the "Map of the Courts," is above an Uruguay-Pitã truly, *but above the first river which had that name*, that is to say,

The 2nd Uruguay-Pitã transformed into Mberuy in 1788.

The Uruguay-Pitã of the Official Map is the 1st below the Great Falls.

the Uruguay-Pitā of the maps of the Jesuits and of D'ANVILLE, below the Great Falls, and below the point where the Uruguay, turning to the South, changes its first direction, as is seen in those maps and in the work of LOZANO.

The position of the Pepiry or Pequiry was perfectly determined on the Map of 1749 by that unalterable and immovable landmark of the Great Falls (Salto Grande), its neighbor. The immovable landmark.

The name—Uruguay-Pitā—is not found either in the Treaty of Limits of 1750, or in the General Instructions of 1751, or in the Special Instructions of 1758 given to the Second Party charged with the survey of the Pepiry or Pequiry. If the Commissioners of 1759 had been charged with the survey of the Uruguay-Pitā it would have been their duty to look The Treaty and the Instructions do not speak of the Uruguay-Pitā.
for it where the "Map of the Courts" located it,—below the Great Falls,—because the question of a name, above all when, as has been proved, names were so capriciously variable in that region, could not be preferred to that of a position determined in the Official Map. Question of name and question of position.
The name could and did change its position, but the place remained where it was. In order that the Pepiry demarcated in 1759 should continue to have an Uruguay-Pitā below its mouth, as it had when the Map was drawn, it was sufficient to replace the name in its old position, suppressing the new name of Paricay, which, in fact, did not last long, because all the names of affluents of the Upper Uruguay were given by Indian travellers of the Spanish Missions, who went up in canoes as far as the Itacaray to gather

maté, and not by the uncivilized inhabitants of the forests crossed by those rivers.

Moreover, a river of unknown course, *whose position was indicated at that time in a vague man-*

River of unknown course. *ner*, as Mr. Minister ZEBALLOS very truly said,[1] could not determine the position of any other affluent of the Uruguay, and still less change that of the Pepiry, which was perfectly defined by its proximity to the Great Falls.

The really important point in the examination of the demarcation of 1759 is to ascertain whether the Pequiry

The position of the Pepiry on the official Map. or Pepiry of the Map of 1749 is the Pepiry, soon afterwards (1760) Pepiry-Guaçú, pointed out by the Indian ARIRAPY and surveyed by the Commissioners ALPOYM

and ARGUEDAS, or whether it is the Chapecó to which the Spanish Commissioners gave after 1789 the name of Pequirí-Guazú.

Let us see, then, which of the two causes, whether that of Brazil or that of the Argentine Republic, the celebrated "Map of the Courts" upholds.

A rapid glance at Map No. 8 A, in which are the superpositions made under the direction of M. EMILE LEVASSEUR, immediately shows that the Pepiry-Guaçú, and not the Chapecó, is the river along which in that Map the divisional line runs.[2]

Comparison of Latitudes. The examination of the Latitudes gives the following results:

---

[1] "D'ANVILLE *did not rectify the position of the Uruguay-Pitá which in all the Maps of that period was vaguely indicated.*" (*Misiones*, p. 73.) The date of the Map of D'ANVILLE analyzed by the author is 1748.

[2] Another graphic comparison of the Map of 1749 with that of the Brazilian-Argentine Joint Commission is presented under No. 22 in Vol. V. In this superposition, it has been assumed that the course of the Uruguay is in the same Latitude in both Maps.

1. Latitude of the mouth of the Pepiry or Pequiry, afterwards Pepiry-Guaçú, the Brazilian Boundary:

              Lat. S.

a. In the Map of the Plenipotentiaries of 1749................................. 26° 27' 48"

b. In the Map of the Joint Commission...... 27° 10' 03"

2. Latitude of the mouth of the Chapecó (Pequiri Guazú of the Argentines), the boundary claimed by the Argentine Republic:

a. In the Map of the Joint Commission..... 27° 05' 41"

b. At the point in the course of the Uruguay which it would occupy on the Map of the Plenipotentiaries if it were represented upon this Map according to the Longitude known at the present day............................. 26° 25' 06"

Difference between the Latitude of the mouth of the Pepiry in the Map of the Plenipotentiaries and in that of the Joint Commission............ 0° 42' 15"

Difference between the Latitude of the mouth of the Chapecó and that of the Pepiry in the Map of the Plenipotentiaries...................... 0° 37' 53"

Difference between the Latitude of the mouth of the Chapecó on the Map of the Joint Commission and that of the point in the course of the Uruguay, corresponding in the Map of the Plenipotentiaries to the Longitude of the mouth of the same river............................ 0° 40' 35"

In the Map of 1749 the course of the Upper Uruguay is not in the Latitude in which it should be, but the error, as is evident, does not benefit the Argentine Republic, since its Pequiri Guazú (Chapecó) has not its mouth in the same Latitude as that of the boundary river in the Map.

The question of Latitude in this case is of no importance. The Treaty describing a boundary running from South to North, only the difference in the degrees of Longitude could modify it, giving more or less land to Portugal or Spain. It is evident that any one travelling along the boundary thus marked, constantly changes the Latitude at every step taken towards the North or South.

The important point, then, is to ascertain the Longitude of the mouth of the boundary river on the Map
Comparison of Longitudes. and its distance from the Great Falls, and to compare the results with those obtained by a corresponding examination on the Map of the Brazilian-Argentine Joint Commission with reference to the mouth of the Pepiry-Guaçú, the Brazilian boundary, and that of the Chapecó or Pequirí Guazú, the boundary of the Argentine claim.

1. *Longitude of the mouth of the Pequiry or Pepiry, afterwards Pepiry-Guaçú, the Brazilian boundary :*
 a. On the Map of the Brazilian-Argentine Joint Commission (No. 25 A)................ 53° 48′ 19″ W. of Greenwich.
 b. On that of 1749 of the Plenipotentiaries, according to M. EMILE LEVASSEUR (No 8 A)..... 53° 46′ 22″

Difference between these two Longitudes....... 0° 01′ 57″
2. *Longitude of the mouth of the Chapecó (Pequiry-Guazú, according to the Argentines), boundary claimed by the Argentine Republic* (Map of the Brazilian-Argentine Joint Commission).................. 52° 59′ 55″
Difference between this Longitude and that of the mouth of the Pequiry or Pepiry in the Map of 1749 referred to above, according to M. E. LEVASSEUR.. 0° 46′ 27″

Therefore, the river which the Map of 1749 designates as the boundary is not the Chapecó or Pequirí-Guazú, as the Argentine Republic asserts; it is the Pepiry-Guaçu, the old Pequiry of the Brazilians of S. Paulo, the boundary of Brazil since the XVIIth century.

A comparison of the distances between the mouths of the two rivers of the controversy and the Great Falls of the Uruguay will give safer and not less conclusive results:

Distance from the Great Falls.

1. *Distance (along the windings of the river) from the Great Falls of the Uruguay to the mouth of the Pequiry or Pepiry, afterwards Pepiry-Guaçú, the Brazilian boundary:*

	Leagues	Miles	Kilometres
a. In the Map of 1749 of the Plenipotentiaries	1.8	5.5	10.2
b. According to the Diary of the demarcators of 1759 (1 league and ¼)	1.6	5.0	9.2
c. In the Map of the Brazilian-Argentine Joint Commission	1.5	4.5	8.3
2. *Distance (along the windings of the river), according to the Map of the Joint Commission, from the Great Falls of the Uruguay to the mouth of the Chapecó (the Pequiri Guazú of the Argentines), the boundary claimed by the Argentine Republic*	26.9	80.7	149.5

Therefore, the river along which, in the Map of 1749, the red line passes which marks the boundary defined in the Treaty of 1750 is the Pepiry-Guaçú which Brazil defends, and not the Pequiri-Guazú of the Argentine pretension.

A mere glance at Map No. 8 A shows besides that the distance between the mouth of the river along which the boundary is drawn and the corresponding point on the sea-coast is approximately the same distance that separates the mouth of the Pepiry-Guaçú from the littoral of Santa Catharina, while the distance between the mouth of the river of the Argentine pretension and the sea-coast is much less and, therefore, reduces the extent of the lands which, according to the Map, belong to Portugal. *Distance from the sea-coast.*

The Memorandum of 1883, of the Minister for Foreign Affairs of the Argentine Republic, Dr. VICTORINO DE LA PLAZA, said: *The question is solved.*

". . . If it is possible to determine which were the boundaries traced upon that Map, the question will be implicitly and authoritatively solved, provided the rivers drawn upon it exist and agree with the geographical positions marked thereon and with the descriptions relating thereto."

The demonstration is made, and, therefore, the question is "implicitly and authoritatively solved." The river of the boundary in the "Map of the Courts" is indisputably the Pepiry-Guaçú and not the Chapecó. This last—the Pequirí-Guazú of the Argentines—is there represented without a name, approximately in its place, to the East of the river of the boundary and to the West of the mouth of the Uruguay-Mirim.

The Argentine Minister acknowledges that the Map of 1749 is favorable to Brazil. This is so evident, that Mr. Minister Estanislao S. Zeballos indirectly acknowledged it in his pamphlet *Misiones* when he analyzed the Map of Paraguay by Bellin dated 1756.

This Map, praised by Walckenaer, is, as has been said, a faithful and accurate copy of a part of the Map of 1749 called "Map of the Courts." There is no difference whatever in the drawing of the sea-coast or in the courses of the rivers, as will be seen by placing the fac-simile No. 10 A (Map of Bellin, in Vol. VI. of this Statement) over No. 7 A ("Map of the Courts," in the same volume).

The Map of Bellin is a copy of the Map of 1749.

The fac-simile No. 10 A represents the original enlarged to the scale of the "Map of the Courts," by the process of photogravure whose strict accuracy cannot be disputed.

The only additions or alterations that Bellin made

when copying the "Map of the Courts," consisted: 1st, in adopting an inexact projection for the drawing already made which he did not study with sufficient care; 2d, in slightly modifying the Latitudes and in asserting that he graduated the Longitudes by the meridian of Paris, but making an error of about two degrees, so that the Longitudes almost correspond to those of Greenwich; 3d, in putting in the name of Lake Xareyes (Xarayes is the name), and in drawing the Oiejones Islands which preceding maps located in those periodical swamps produced by the great inundations of the Upper Paraguay.

The rivers *Pequiri* and *Uruguaypita* of the "Map of the Courts" appear in that of BELLIN under the names of *Pequin* and *Uruguayrosta*, mistakes which can only be imputed to the engraver, as it is easy to read *Pequin* instead of *Pequiri*, and *Uruguayrosta* instead of *Uruguaypuita*, as it would be in the manuscript. The word *pitā* (red) is also written *puitā*.

A reproduction of the part of this Map representing the disputed territory is given under No. 12 in Vol. V., and on it are marked with the letters A, B, and C, the three affluents to which Mr. Minister ZEBALLOS refers in the following passage of his pamphlet *Misiones*[1]:

Dr. Zeballos and the Map of Bellin.

"The work of CHARLEVOIX is entitled: *Histoire du Paraguay par le* P. PIERRE FRANÇOIS XAVIER DE CHARLEVOIX *de la Compagnie de Jésus*. A *Paris, 1757*. To the third Volume is appended the *Carte du Paraguay*

---

[1] *Misiones.—Exposicion hecha por el ex-Ministro de Relaciones Exteriores de la Republica Argentina*, DR D. ESTANISLAO S. ZEBALLOS, *para refutar errores de origen brasilero é ilustrar la opinion pública en Sur y en Norte America*, Buenos-Aires, 1892.
The passage quoted is from § XXII., p. 75.

et des pays voisins sur les Memoires des Espagnols et des Portugais et en particulier ceux des R. R. P. P. *de la Compagnie de Jésus,* par M. BELLIN, *Ing. de la Marine,* 1756.

"In these Maps the names of the Rivers *Guarumbaca and Pepiry* of the maps of 1703 and of the general of D'ANVILLE disappear, *and although it represents three rivers,*[1] *one of them approximately where our Pepiry-*

Important declaration. *Guazú is situated, it omits its name*[2] *and gives that of river Pequin to the Guarumbaca or to the one most to the West*[3] *in the first maps. It would not be said that the Pequin is the Pepiry-Mini*[4] *or the river stated by Brazil, if* BELLIN *had not traced, following its banks with a dotted line, the boundary between Spain and Portugal. . . ."*

Of the passage quoted, this important statement must be remembered :

The Pequiri Guazú, the river of the Argentine pretension, is the unnamed affluent which in the Map of BELLIN *is to the East of the Pequiri (Pequin).*

By placing the Map of BELLIN (No. 10 A) over that of "the Courts" (No. 7 A) and making the coast-line, the courses of the Uruguay, the Paraná, and the Iguaçú coincide, *it is seen that the river Pequin of* BELLIN *co-*

[1] A, B, and C, in the small reproduction No. 12.

[2] *The unnamed river* (C) *to the East of the Pequiri* (Pequin) *is the Pequirí Guazú of the Argentines.*

[3] The river of the boundary in the Map of BELLIN (B) *is more Westerly than the Pequiri Guazú of the Argentine pretension* (C), says DR. ZEBALLOS.

[4] The author gives great importance to the question of the adjectives *Mini* (small) and *Guaçú* (great). In 1789 Commissioner ALVEAR proposed to give the *Pepiry Guaçú* the name of *Pepiry Mini*, but this name continued to be that of an affluent of the Pepiry-Guaçú. Besides this Pepiry-Mini there is another, which is a tributary of the Uruguay, in the Argentine territory, to the West of the Pepiry-Guaçú, as shown in Maps No. 25 A and No. 29 A and in the passage already quoted (page 79 in this Vol.) of the Diary of the Argentine Commission, in 1887.

incides exactly with the Pequiri along which the boundary line runs in the "Map of the Courts," and that the Eastern affluent, *which is, as the author of the pamphlet has very truly said, the Pequiri Guazú (Chapecó) of the Argentine pretension, lies much to the East of the boundary indicated by the "Map of the Courts," and within the Brazilian territory.*

The Argentine Republic based its claim on two documents: the Instructions given to the demarcating Commissioners of 1759, and the Map of 1749, authenticated by the Plenipotentiaries.

The Special Instructions given to these Commissioners have now come to light, and it has been ascertained that they do not contain the passage invented in 1789 which, as well as the Map, served as a pretext for the question raised in the second demarcation by the Spanish Commissioners. The Instructions fully justify the action of the Commissioners of 1759 and the decisions taken by them.

The examination of the Map of 1749 has just proved that this document is favorable to the cause of Brazil and opposed to the Argentine claim.

There does not now remain, therefore, a single document upon which the Argentine Republic can base a condemnation of the demarcation of 1759.

The river indicated by the guide ARIRAPY, and surveyed in 1759 by General ALPOYM and by Councillor ARGUEDAS, Commissioners of Portugal and Spain, is the same Pepiry or Pequiry as that of the Treaty and the "Map of the Courts." The Chapecó, claimed by the Argentine Republic is the river which appears without a name on that Map, to the East of the Pequiry or Pepiry along which the divisional line runs.

An examination of the Treaty of 1777 will show that the Spanish Government approved and ratified the demarcation of 1759.

VIII.

It was only in the Southern Division, from Castillos Grandes to the Jaurù, and with the difficulties already related, that the survey of the frontiers defined by the Treaty of 1750 could be carried out. In consequence of the difficulties raised by the Spanish and Portuguese Missionaries of the Orinoco and Pará against the advance of the demarcators, the Northern Division never entered upon its labors. In 1760 the Principal Commissioner of Spain was still at Cabruta, for want of canoes and Indian rowers, and was unable to meet the Commissioners of Portugal on the Rio Negro.[1]

The Treaty of 1750 annulled.

In the South, there were serious controversies between the Commissioners only as to which of the upper arms of the Ibicuhy was the river of the Treaty, whether that to the South, afterwards river Santa Maria, or the Ibicuhy Mirim in the North, which comes from the range then called Monte Grande.

The labors of the Second Party and of the Third ended without disagreement. In those of the Second, such harmony and mutual trust prevailed, that the Principal Commissioner and Plenipotentiary of Spain, the MARQUIS DE VAL DE LIRIOS, felt justified in saying that the Principal Portuguese Commissioner had shown the greatest condescension, submitting to the direction of the Spanish Commissioner and being in

---

[1] VISCOUNT DE PORTO-SEGURO (VARNHAGEN), *Historia Geral do Brazil*, 926.

favor of all the investigations and explorations proposed by the latter. And the First Portuguese Commissioner of the Second Party was not, as might be supposed, a man of no importance: he was General ALPOYM, distinguished as a soldier on the battlefield, and as the master of the military youth of Rio de Janeiro, —the illustrious ALPOYM,—as he is called in his *Uruguay*, by the first Brazilian epic poet.

All decisions were made by the unanimous vote of the Commissioners and in full compliance with their Instructions, so that it is impossible now to maintain that the question of the demarcation of the Pepiry and S. Antonio contributed to the annulment of the Treaty of 1750.

An authority above suspicion, COUNT DE FLORIDA-BLANCA, First Secretary of State in Spain, explains this matter as follows:

" For these reasons, so much importance was given during the preceding reign (that of FERDINAND VI., who was succeeded in 1760 by CARLOS III.) to Colonia del Sacramento that, in order to acquire it, all the territory of the Ibicuí, including more than five hundred leagues in Paraguay, was ceded by the Treaty of 1750 with Portugal. *The opposition and the intrigues of the Jesuits, as well as the reluctance of the Portuguese to the surrender of Colonia, compelled Your Majesty to annul the Treaty.*"[1]

---

[1] *Memorial presentado á el Rey Cárlos III. y repetido á Carlos IV. por el* CONDE DE FLORIDABLANCA, *renunciando el Ministerio.* The memorial presented to Carlos III. is dated San Lorenzo, October 10, 1788. It is published in Vol. 59 of the *Biblioteca de Autores Españoles*, in which occur the *Obras Originales del* CONDE DE FLORIDABLANCA (Madrid, 1867).

The passage quoted is also in CALVO, *Recueil de Traités*, VII., pp. xvii. to xxii.

D. José I. of Portugal and Carlos III. of Spain did not hold the same views as D. João V. and Ferdinand VI., regarding the reciprocal advantages of the exchange of Colonia do Sacramento, and the right bank of the River Plate, for the territory of the Seven Oriental Missions of Uruguay, and they resolved to annul the Treaty of 1750 solely in order to avoid the division of the contested territory therein stipulated.

Each one of the two Sovereigns preferred to preserve in their integrity their rights or pretensions to the whole of the territory called Colonia do Sacramento. For Portugal it was bounded by the North bank of the River Plate, where Spain already held Montevidéo, and by the Eastern bank of the Uruguay, where the Seven Oriental Missions were situated.

The Treaty of annulment, signed at El Pardo on February 12, 1761, provided as follows in Article 1:

"The aforesaid Treaty of Limits in Asia and America, concluded at Madrid on January 13, 1750, with all the other Treaties or Conventions, which afterwards were concluded in consequence of it, fixing the Instructions to the respective Commissioners who until now have been engaged in the demarcations of the said boundaries, and all that was drawn up by virtue thereof, is now agreed to be, and to be held, by virtue of the present Treaty, as cancelled, quashed, and annulled, as if they had never existed nor never been executed; so that all things relating to Boundaries in America and Asia are restored to the provisions of the Treaties, Compacts, and Conventions which had been concluded between the two Contracting Sovereigns before the said year 1750: in such manner that only those Treaties, Compacts, and

Conventions that were concluded before the year 1750 shall hereafter remain in force and vigor."

Article 2 said :

" As soon as this Treaty shall have been ratified, the above named Most Serene Kings will cause authentic copies thereof to be transmitted to Their respective Commissioners and Governors within the boundaries of America; declaring to them as cancelled, quashed, and annulled the said Treaty of Limits, signed on the 13th of January, one thousand seven hundred and fifty, with all the Conventions that were derived therefrom and followed it; and commanding them that, holding as of no effect and causing to cease all operations relating to its execution, they shall overturn the monuments or landmarks that were erected in consequence of it, and immediately evacuate the lands that were occupied under title of the same execution or by reason of the said Treaty, demolishing the dwellings, houses, or fortresses which in consideration of the aforesaid repealed Treaty may have been built or raised by either party ; and declaring to them that from the very day of the ratification of the present Treaty forward, they shall have no other rules to guide them except the other Treaties, Compacts, and Conventions, that had been stipulated between the two Crowns before the said year one thousand seven hundred and fifty ; because each and all of them are hereby reinstated and restored to their original and proper force, as though the aforesaid Treaty of the thirteenth of January one thousand seven hundred and fifty, with the others that followed from it, had never existed ; and these orders shall be delivered in duplicate from one Court to the other for its guidance and for their prompt fulfilment."

The Preamble gave as reasons for the annulment of the Treaty the great difficulties encountered in its execution in countries so distant and so little known, the contradictory information received regarding them, and the fact that while it had been concluded to establish perfect harmony between the two Crowns and an unalterable union between their subjects, it had, on the contrary, given rise since 1752, and would in future give rise, to many controversies and disputes opposed to those aims.

In the very next year war broke out between Spain and Portugal, because the latter Power had preferred an English alliance to that of the Sovereigns of the House of Bourbon, which had concluded the Family Compact. General D. PEDRO DE CEVALLOS, Governor of the Provinces of the River Plate, took Colonia do Sacramento (1762), invaded the territory of Rio Grande do Sul, and occupied both banks of the channel of that name, between the Lake dos Patos and the sea (1763).

War of 1762-1763.

By the Treaty of Peace signed at Paris on February 10, 1763, it was provided as follows (Art. 21):

Peace of Paris, 1763.

"The Spanish and French troops shall evacuate all Territories, Country places, Cities, Forts, and Castles of His Most Faithful Majesty situated in Europe, that may have been conquered by the armies of France and Spain, without any exception whatever; and they shall restore them in the same condition in which they were when the conquest was made, and with the same artillery and munitions of war that were in them; and *with regard to the Portuguese Colonies in America,* Africa, or in the East Indies, if any change shall have happened, all things shall be restored to the same footing in which they were, and as provided by the Treaties previously existing between the Courts of Spain, France, and Portugal before the present war."

The Spanish General did not carry out this provision of the Treaty, inasmuch as he only restored Colonia do Sacramento, keeping the Islands of Martin Garcia and Dos Hermanas and Rio Grande do Sul.   *Violation of the Treaty of Peace.*

To the protests of Portugal, the MARQUIS DI GRIMALDI, First Secretary of State of CARLOS III., replied, on February 6, 1765, that all the territories conquered during the war belonged of right to Spain, and could not be restored.

From that date to 1777 the opposite occurred to what ALEXANDRE DE GUSMÃO had contemplated in Article 21 of the Treaty of 1750, seeing that while the two Sovereigns of Portugal and Spain remained at peace in Europe, they were almost constantly at war on the frontiers of Brazil.   *Renewed hostilities in Brazil.*

In 1767 the Portuguese troops retook the left bank of the Rio Grande do Sul, and, in 1776, the right bank, as well as all the forts and territories held by the Spaniards in violation of the Treaty of Paris.

Incensed at the reverses suffered by his arms, CARLOS III. sent against Brazil a great expedition, under the command of CEVALLOS, who easily conquered the Island of Santa Catharina and, in 1777, compelled the fortress of Colonia to surrender.

In the same year great changes occurred in the Government of the two Kingdoms of the Peninsula. On the death of D. José I. (February 24) D. Maria I. ascended the throne of Portugal, and Martinho de Mello e Castro succeeded the Marquis de Pombal as principal Secretary of State. In Spain Count de Flodidablanca was appointed Prime Minister (February 19) in the place of Grimaldi.

The resignation of this Genoese Statesman, more than the other changes, facilitated the suspension of hostilities in South America and the negotiation of a new Treaty of Limits.

Negotiations for a Treaty of Limits.

This negotiation had already begun during the administration of Grimaldi while D. Francisco Innocencio de Souza Coutinho was Ambassador of Portugal at Madrid.

In 1776, by order of the King of Spain a Consulting Junta had been formed to consider the question of Limits between the Spanish possessions and Brazil, as may be seen from the following passages of the letter dated Aranjuez, June 3, of that year, and addressed by Grimaldi to the Secretary of State of the Indies, D. José de Gálvez:[1]

Spanish Consulting Junta.

"You are acquainted with the probability that the proposed Congress of Paris will take place, at which Count de Aranda will represent the King, our Master, while the King of Portugal will be represented by His respective Plenipotentiaries, together with the Ministers who may be appointed by Their Most Christian and Britannic Majesties as mediating Princes, for the purpose of examining and treating of the points long since contested between Spain and Portugal regarding the

---

[1] In the General Archives of Simancas, "Secretaria de Estado, Leg°, No. 7,412, f. 33."

The copy in the possession of the Brazilian Special Mission was legalized by the Director of the Archives on December 2, 1893.

Limits of the Dominions of both Crowns in South America, and that an endeavor may be made to arrive at a satisfactory understanding by means of which new dissensions may for the future be avoided.

"In order to draw up the Instructions that will have to be given to COUNT DE ARANDA, I proposed at our Ministerial Conference of the 30th of last month not only the draft of the negotiation, considered under all its aspects, but also various doubts and difficulties that required to be previously removed ; and all this having seemed to you, no less than the other Secretaries of State, to be worthy of the greatest attention, and of the notice of the King, I have duly informed His Majesty thereof by reading, at the last audience I had, the same paper in which I conveyed my opinion to you, as well as to COUNT DE RICLA, D. MIGUEL DE MUZQUIZ, and to the MARQUIS GONZALEZ CASTEJON. . . .

"His Majesty has considered those words equally well founded and opportune, and, in accordance with them, thinks it indispensable, as we do, that a Junta should be formed of competent persons who may combine with talent, learning, and zeal, *local knowledge and accurate information as to the countries in dispute ;* and approves and commands that it shall be composed of Lieutenant General D. PEDRO DE CEBALLOS, the MARQUIS DE VALDELIRIOS, the President of the India Council D. ANTONIO PORLIER, of Major General D. VINCENTE DOZ, and of D. FRANCISCO DE ARGUEDAS.

"The King, therefore, commands me to inform you of this, that you may issue the necessary directions to the subjects mentioned, in order that they may proceed to treat of the matter with due attention. . . ."

The letter concludes in the following manner :

" Persuaded that it will be of some assistance to the members of the Junta to have before them the Map of South America, constructed and engraved by order of His Majesty, as well as the Dissertation on the Meridian of Demarcation, written by D. JORGE JUAN and D. ANTONIO DE ULLOA, and published in the year 1749, I will place at your service five copies of each, in order that you may distribute them as you may think proper."

The above document proves that in the negotiations which preceded the Treaty of 1777, the Cabinet of Madrid consulted the same ARGUEDAS who, as First Commissioner, surveyed the Pepiry and S. Antonio in 1759. It proves besides that the Map preferred for the examination of the question of Limits was that of South America, constructed and engraved by the King's order by OLMEDILLA.

These two facts are of the greatest importance, particularly the second, because the Map of OLMEDILLA, to which reference will be made later on, is one of the most conclusive documents in favor of the cause of Brazil.

From the negotiations between the Ambassador of Portugal, SOUZA COUTINHO and the COUNT DE FLORIDABLANCA resulted the Preliminary Treaty of Limits signed at San Ildefonso on October 1, 1777.

Treaty of S. Ildefonso, Oct. 1, 1777.

This Treaty restored, from the mouth of the Pepiry-Guaçú to the Northern part of the basin of the Amazonas, the boundary line described in that of 1750, but it entirely modified the previous marking of the Southern frontier from the sea-coast to the mouth of that affluent of the Uruguay. Portugal lost territories in the Rio Grande do Sul as well as Colonia do Sacramento. Spain restored to her the Island of Santa Catharina.

The new Southern divisional line, after reaching, having started from the sea, the headwaters of the rivers flowing to the Rio Grande and the Jacuhy, continued along them passing over those of the river Araricá, an affluent of the Jacuhy, and those of the Piratiní and Ybiminí (Yiuiminí or Ijuhyminí), affluents of the Uruguay, and proceeded as far as the left bank of this river opposite the mouth of the Pepiry-Guaçú.

Article 4 of the Treaty deals with this first section of the divisional line. The second section, in which the frontier of the territory now contested is situated, is described in Article 8.

This is, therefore, the article that must be examined. *Article 8 examined.*

The two texts, the Portuguese and Spanish, are as follows:

"ART. VIII.—Ficando já signalados os dominios de ambas as Corôas até a entrada do *Rio Pequiri* ou *Pepiri-guaçú no Uruguay,* convieram os dois Altos Contratantes em que *a linha divisoria seguirá aguas acima do dito Pepiri-guaçú até á sua origem principal; e desde esta pelo mais alto do terreno, debaixo das regras dadas no Artigo VI, continuará*

"ART. VIII.—Quedando ya señaladas las pertenencias de ambas Coronas hasta *la entrada del Rio Pequirí ó Pepiriguazú en el Uruguái,* se han convenido los dos Altos Contrayentes en que *la línea divisoria seguirá aguas arriba de dicho Pepiri hasta su origen principal; y desde este por lo mas alto del terreno, bajo las reglas dadas en el*

a encontrar as correntes do
Rio Santo Antonio, que
desemboca no grande de
Curituba, por outro nome
chamado Iguaçú, seguindo
este aguas abaixo até á sua
entrada no Paraná pela
sua margem oriental, e
continuando então aguas
acima do mesmo Paraná
até donde se lhe ajunta o
Rio Igurei pela sua margem occidental."

Articulo VI, continuará
á encontrar las corrientes
del Rio San Antonio, que
desemboca en el grande de
Curituba, que por otro
nombre llaman Iguazú,
siguiendo este aguas abajo
hasta su entrada en el
Paraná por su ribera oriental, y continuando entonces aguas arriba del
mismo Paraná hasta donde se le junta el Rio
Iguréi por su ribera occidental."

In the following English translation of the two texts, the geographical names written according to the orthography of the Spanish copy are given in brackets:

"Art. 8.—The dominions of both Crowns being already defined as far as the entrance of the *River Pequiri* or *Pepiri-Guaçú* (*Pequiri* or *Pepiri-Guazú*) into the *Uruguay* (*Uruguái*), the two High Contracting Parties have agreed that the divisional line shall follow up the course of the said *Pepiri-Guaçú* (*Pepiri*) as far as its principal source; and thence along the highest ground, under the rules given in Article VI., it shall continue until it meets the waters of the *River Santo Antonio* (*San Antonio*), which empties itself into the Grande de Curituba, otherwise named *Iguaçú Iguazú*) running downwards along the latter until it enters the Paraná by its Eastern bank, and continuing thence up the said Paraná to the point where the river Igurei (Iguréi) joins its Western bank."

As will be seen, the starting point of the divisional line between the Uruguay and the Iguaçû is, according to Article 8 of the Treaty of 1777, the mouth of the river *Pepiry-Guaçû* or *Pequiry*, an affluent of the right bank of the Uruguay. Thence the line runs along the bed of the same Pepiry-Guaçû as far as its principal source, and thence again, over the highest ground, "under the rule laid down in Article 6," it goes on till it meets the source of the River S. Antonio, down whose bed it reaches its confluence with the Iguaçû.

Article 6, to which Article 8 refers, provides as follows:

"In like manner as in the foregoing Article, there shall be also reserved throughout the remainder of the divisional line, both as far as the entrance into the Uruguay of the *River Pepiri-Guaçu* and in the continuation of the said line which shall be specifically set out in the following Articles, a sufficient space between the Boundaries of the two Nations, although it may not be equal in breadth to that of the said Lakes, in which villages may not be built by either of the two parties, nor Forts, Guard-houses, or military Posts erected, so that such spaces may be neutral, durable landmarks and signals being erected to make known to the subjects of each Nation the spot beyond which they are not to pass; for which purpose lakes and rivers shall be sought which can serve as permanent and unalterable limits, and, failing them, the crests of the most prominent mountains, these and their feet constituting the neutral and divisional zone which may not be entered, peopled, built upon, nor fortified by either of the Nations."

This Article, as will be seen, treats of the neutral zone which, according to the Treaty, was to be established along the frontier.

The Argentine Government has expressed surprise that the Government of Brazil should accept Article 8 while at the same time declaring the Treaty annulled.

It has already been explained that Brazil accepts that Article only because the frontier line described therein is the same that is designated by the *uti possidetis* of the period of the Independence.

Neither does the Argentine Government consider the whole Treaty valid, seeing that it has never attached any importance to the clause relating to the neutral zone.

Article 6, therefore, rejected both by Brazil and by the Argentine Republic, is of no importance in the settlement of the present controversy.

Treaties of 1750 and 1777 compared. It is expedient to compare the 8th Article which the two contesting parties accept, with the corresponding Article of the preceding Treaty:

TREATY OF 1750.	TREATY OF 1777.
" Art. V. — From the mouth of the Ibicui, the Line shall run up the course of the Uruguay until reaching the *River Pepiri, or Pequiri, which empties itself by the Western bank of the Uruguay; and it shall continue up the bed of the Pepiri as far*	" Art. VIII. — The dominions of both Crowns being already defined as far as *the entrance of the River Pequiri, or Pepiri-Guacú, into the Uruguay,* the two High Contracting Parties have agreed that *the divisional line shall follow up the course of the*

as the principal source thereof; from which it shall follow along the highest ground to the principal head of the nearest river that may flow into the Rio Grande de Curituba, otherwise named Iguaçú. The Boundary shall continue along the bed of the said river nearest to the source of the Pepiri, and afterwards, along that of the Iguaçú, or Rio Grande de Curituba, until the point where the same Iguaçú empties itself by the Eastern bank of the Paraná; and from that mouth it shall go up the course of the Paraná, to the point where the Igurey joins it on its Western bank."

said Pepirí-Guaçú as far as its principal source: and thence along the highest ground, under the rules given in Article VI., it shall continue until it meets the waters of the River Santo Antonio, which empties itself into the Grande de Curituba, otherwise named Iguaçú, running downwards along the latter until it enters the Paraná by its Eastern bank, and continuing thence up the said Paraná to the point where the River Igurey joins it on its Western bank."

In determining the frontier between the Uruguay and the Iguaçú, the Treaty of 1750 designated a known river, the Pepiry or Pequiry, and an un-named affluent of the Iguaçú. From the principal headwater of the Pepiry the divisional line was to pass on to the principal source of the nearest affluent of the Iguaçú. This condition of neighborhood was explained in the Instructions of 1758, according to which the essential point was that the mouth of the affluent of the Iguaçú should be approximately in the same longitude as the place in which the principal headwater of the Pepiry might be supposed to be situated. The affluent sought was, as we have seen, discovered and explored in 1759, when it received the name of *S. Antonio.*

Differences. Article 8 of the Treaty of 1777 differs from Article 5 of the Treaty of 1750:

1) *In not presenting any condition of neighborhood or proximity between the two rivers or their headwaters;*

2) *In determining by name, not one, but both the rivers, indicating them clearly by the new denominations they received in 1759 and 1760.*

The affluent of the Iguaçù is designated in Article 8 by the only name it had after 1759 and under which it appeared in all maps subsequent to that date; and the affluent of the Uruguay thus named in different Articles of the same Treaty of 1777:

Question of names.

Art. III.: *River Pequiri or Pepiri-Guaçú (Pequiri or Pepiri-Guazú)—Pepiri-Guaçú (Pepiri-Guazú).*

Art. IV.: *Pepiri-Guaçú (Pepiri-Guazú).—Pepiri-Guaçú (Pepiri-Guazú).*

Art. VI.: *Pepiri-Guaçú (PepiriGuazú).*

Art. VIII.: *Pequiri or Pepiri-Guaçú (Pequiri or Pepiri-Guazú). Pepiri-Guaçú (Pepiri).*

In the Portuguese copy: *Pepiri-Guaçú,* seven times; *Pequiry,* twice.

In the Spanish copy: *Pepiri-Guazú,* six times; *Pequiri,* twice; and *Pepiri,* once.

Consequently, the two Governments recognized as designating the same river these three names: *Pequiry, Pepiry-Guaçú,* and *Pepiry.*

The *Report* of 1892 of the Minister for Foreign Affairs of the Argentine Republic asserts that the Treaty in using the adjective *guaçú* (large), intended to designate a river different from the Pepiry or Pequiry of 1750. <small>Refutation of the Argentine Report, 1892, as to the question of names.</small>

The *Report* says:

"Let the text of the Treaty of 1750 be compared with that of 1777, and it will be seen at once, that the former gives as a boundary to the East, in Misiones, the River Pequirí or Pepiri; and as this vague denomination has produced confusion in the minds of the Commissioners of 1759, the second Treaty defined the river, qualifying it from its principal feature of being a *large river*, and not a small stream or rivulet.

"Thus the Treaty of 1777 definitely decides the point, transferring the boundary to the system of *large* or Easterly *rivers*, above the Uruguay Pitá."

This *system of Easterly rivers* was not yet invented when the Treaty of 1777 was written. Nor did the *third Uruguay Pitá* to which the *Report* refers then exist. The Treaty of 1777 does not speak of any river of that name. <small>The system of Eastern rivers an anachronism in 1777.</small>

In another place (pg. 109 and 110) this question of the adjectives *guaçú* (large) and *miní* (small), has been explained, showing that by the fact that in 1759 the name of *Pepiry-Miní* had been given to an affluent of the old Pepiry, the principal river became entitled to the addition of *guaçú* to its name.

It has also been proved by the Map appended to the Diary of the First Demarcators, that from 1760 the old Pepiry or Pequiry came to be called *Pepiry-Guaçú* (pg. 109-111). <small>Maps of 1760.</small>

Under this name it already appears on the maps signed at S. Nicolas of Missions on April 8, 1760, by the Commissioners of the first demarcation. The proof that from 1760 the name *Pepiry-Guaçú* belongs to the river surveyed in 1759 is in the Map referred to, which, with the original Diary, is submitted to the examination of the Arbitrator.[1]

Under the same name of *Pepiry-Guaçú*, the old Pepiry or Pequiry surveyed in 1759 appears in the following maps (besides other manuscript maps) anterior to the Treaty of 1777:—

1) *South America*, by SYLVEIRA PEIXOTO, 1768, Manuscript[2];

2) *Part of South America*, by ALEXANDRE J. MONTANHA, 1773, Manuscript[3];

3) *South America*, by OLMEDILLA, 1775, engraved at Madrid.

Piquiry in Millau's Maps. 1768, 1770.
Under the name of *Pequiri*, in the two following Spanish Maps:—

4) *General Captaincy of the River Plate*, by FRANCISCO MILLAU, 1768, Manuscript[4];

---

[1] Colored fac-simile on the scale of the original, No. 12 A, in Vol. VI. Reduced fac-simile No. 13, Vol. V.

[2] Partial reproduction under No. 15 A, Vol. VI. Its title is: "CARTA GEOGRAPHICA / da / AMERICA MERIDIONAL / Por / ANTONIO MARTINS DA SYLVEIRA PEIXOTO. . . ." Dated Villa Rica (now Ouro-Preto), 1768.

[3] Reproduction of a part of this Map, No. 16 A, in Vol. VI. Title: " MAPPA GEOGRAPHICO / de hña parte da America Meridional desde o Tropico de Capricornio té a barra do Rio da Prata / . . " By ALEXANDRE JOSÉ MONTANHA, Captain of Engineers. Year 1773.

[4] The original is kept in the Department of State at Madrid. The Brazilian Special Mission presents an authenticated copy; a reduced fac-simile of the whole Map, under No. 13 A (Vol. VI.); and a fac-simile of a part in which is included the territory now contested. This partial reproduction is numbered 15 in Vol. V., and is represented with the coloring of the original. Title: " PLANO / DE LA CAPITANIA GENERᴸ / de las tres Provincias del / Rio de la Plata, Paraguay, Tucuman / del mando del Exᵐᵒ Señor Dᴺ FRANᶜᵒ BVCARELI Y VRSVA / . . . AÑO 1768. / . . . Echo por el Teniente de Navio de la Real Armada Dᴺ FRANCISCO MILLAU Y MARAVAL."

5) *Territory of Montevideo and of the Rio Grande*, by the same F. MILLAU, 1770, Manuscript.[1]

The author of these two last maps is the same Spanish geographer who took part in the survey of 1759. Both the maps should be considered as official, and that of 1770 even bears a declaration that it was made by order of BUCARELI, Captain General of the Provinces of the River Plate. The boundary line proposed in it passes along the *Pequiri* and *S. Antonio* demarcated in 1759.

The Map of 1768 by MILLAU (No. 15, Vol. V.) is also very interesting, because it shows the boundaries of the Spanish and Portuguese occupation of that time and the territories inhabited by the Wild Indians.

In the two maps, the *Pequiri* (Pepiry-Guaçù) and the *S. Antonio* are the rivers demarcated in 1759. The *Uruguay-Pitá* is *the second river of that name*, that is to say, the present Guarita, which was visited that year by the first demarcators.

These maps of MILLAU, maintaining the name of *Pequiry*, and that of OLMEDILLA giving to the old Pepiry or Pequiry the name of *Pepiry-Guaçù* adopted in the official maps dated 1760, explain the double denomination which is read in the Treaty of 1777.

The two authorities, OLMEDILLA and MILLAU, are Spaniards and cannot be impugned by the Argentine Republic.

Olmedilla and Millau.

The river Pepiry-Guaçù or Pequiry and the S. Antonio in the maps of those official geographers

---

[1] Authenticated copy of the original in the hydrographical Department at Madrid. Title: "MAPA / que comprehende el / Pays, que se extiende por la Cos / ta de el Mar, entre la Ciudad de Montevideo y el Riogrande . . . Hecho de orden de el Ex.mo Senor D.N FRANCISCO BUCARELI Y URSUA, siendo Capitan general de las Provincias de el Rio de la Plata, por el Teniente de Nazio de la Real Armada, D.N FRANCISCO MILLAU Cosmografo de S. M. en el Año de 1770."

are those of 1759, and, therefore, the rivers referred to by COUNT DE FLORIDABLANCA, when he drew up Article 8 of the Treaty of 1777, were the same as those of 1759, that is to say, the two rivers which form the present boundary of Brazil with the Argentine Republic.

It is an anachronism to attribute to the negotiators of the Treaty of 1777 the "system of Easterly rivers" which was only created in 1789 by the Spanish Commissioners. The question of names and adjectives is explained by the official Spanish maps and by the examples already quoted, which could be multiplied, of rivers (and even rivulets) which are qualified as *guaçús* because they have as affluents a *mirim* or *mini*.

Another graphic proof, and a Spanish one, that, when the Treaty was signed, it was understood that the Pepiry-Guaçú and the S. Antonio were the two rivers surveyed in 1759, is found in the *Map of Paraguay* of 1787 by D. FELIX DE AZARA.[1] In this Map the Brazilian Pepiry-Guaçú has the following names:

Map of Azara of 1787.

The principal river, "*R. Pepiry*," and "*R. Pepiry-Guazú*"; the largest Eastern affluent, "*R. Pequiri or Pepiry-Mini*."

AZARA uses, therefore, the three names: *Pepiry*, *Pequiry*, and *Pepiry-Guaçú*.

From these cartographical documents, all of the greatest importance in the examination of the pres-

---

[1] Partial fac-simile No. 17 in Vol. V.; fac-simile of the whole map, No. 18 A Vol. VI. The document belongs to the Department of State in Madrid. Title: "CARTA *Espherica, ó reducida de las Provincias del Paraguay, y / Misiones Guaranis, con el distrito de Corrientes.*" It is dated, "Assumpcion del Paraguay, August 30, 1787." It was presented by D. FELIX DE AZARA to D. JOSEPH NICOLAS DE AZARA.

ent litigation, the most valuable is the Map of *South America* by D. JUAN DE LA CRUZ CANO Y OLMEDILLA,[1] constructed and engraved by order of the King of Spain, and delivered to the Consulting Junta appointed in the following year to investigate the question of boundaries between Brazil and the Spanish possessions, as has already been shown.[2]

The most important Map is that of Olmedilla of 1777.

The Map of Olmedilla in the negotiation of the Treaty of 1775.

This Map was also used by COUNT DE FLORIDABLANCA, Principal Secretary of State and Plenipotentiary of the King of Spain, in the negotiations which resulted in the Treaty of October 1, 1777.

D.R LUIS DOMINGUEZ confirms this in the following passage of his *Historia Argentina*:

"The drawing of this immense boundary line had been made according to the Map published at Madrid in 1775 by D. JUAN DE LA CRUZ CANO Y OLMEDILLA, constructed from the geodesical surveys of the demarcators under the Treaty of 1750."[3]

The part of this Map in which the contested territory is included, is reproduced under No. 16 in Vol. V. In the same Vol., under No. 24, the comparison of this Map with that of the Brazilian-Argentine Joint Commission is made graphically.

This comparison renders any commentary unnecessary.

---

[1] " MAPA GEOGRAFICO / DE / AMERICA MERIDIONAL / DISPUESTO Y GRAVADO / POR D.N JUAN DE LA CRUZ CANO Y OLMEDILLA, GEOG.FO PENS.DO DE S. M./ *individuo de la R.l Academia de S.n Fernando, y de la Sociedad Bascongada de los Amigos del Pais ; | teniendo presentes varios Mapas y noticias originales | con arreglo á Observaciones astronómicas, | Año de 1775.*"

[2] Official letter of June 3, 1776, of the First Secretary of State of Spain, the MARQUIS DI GRIMALDI (a document already transcribed, page 172-174).

[3] P. 306 of the 4th Edition. DR. DOMINGUEZ was the Argentine Minister in Brazil charged with the discussion of this boundary question, and is now the Argentine Minister in London.

The Map of South America and its author have recently been severely criticised in the press of Buenos-Aires by an illustrious politician,[1] who doubtless wrote that part of his work from notes communicated to him, without having had time to verify personally the accuracy of the texts he quoted.

Reply to recent Argentine allegations.

It is a fact that a Spanish philologist, speaking of OLMEDILLA, mentioned him only as an engraver.[2] But this only proves that the philologist did not study the History of his country seriously. The very Map of South America is there to prove that as early as 1775 OLMEDILLA had the official title of Geographer. Years afterwards he was appointed Chief Cosmographer of the Kingdom of Spain, as may be seen from the following passage of an official letter of October 6, 1790, by the Spanish Commissioner ALVEAR:

Olmedilla was appointed Chief Cosmographer of Spain.

". . . you quote the Map of America by D'ANVILLE with reference to the observations of LA CONDAMINE, BOUGER, *and the one printed in Madrid by the Chief Cosmographer of the Kingdom, D. JUAN DE LA CRUZ. . . .*"[3]

The Spanish Commissioners charged with the demarcation took copies of this Map, "*constructed and engraved by order of His Majesty,*" as was stated on June 3, 1776, by Minister the MARQUIS DI GRIMALDI.

The Spanish Commissioners took with them copies of the Map of Olmedilla.

---

[1] DR. ZEBALLOS, *Misiones*, §§ IX., X., and XI.

[2] ROQUE BARCIA, author of the *Primer Diccionario General Etymologico de la Lengua Española*, Madrid, 1881. In this "Etymological Dictionary of the Spanish Language" are to be found the biographical notes recently quoted to show that OLMEDILLA was an engraver, but not a geographer.

[3] This document was published by MILITON GONZALEZ, one of the supporters of the Argentine cause, in his edition of the *Diary* of CAURER (Vol. III., p. 39).

In the official correspondence of these Commissioners, or in works written by them on the second delimitation survey, references are made to the Map of OLMEDILLA, or of JUAN DE LA CRUZ, as this geographer was more commonly called.

In CABRER this passage may be read: "... features by which it is characterized and distinguished in the printed Plans, *especially the large Map of this America by the Geographer Royal, D. JUAN DE LA CRUZ.*"[1]

In OYÁRVIDE: "... and from all this convinced that this river is called Uruguai-Mini, which *our geographer D. JUAN DE LA CRUZ places in his Map printed at Madrid in 1775.*"[2]

In an official letter of February 10, 1789, from the Principal Spanish Commissioner, VARELA, may be read: "*D. JUAN DE LA CRUZ, Geographer to His Majesty ...*"

It has been asserted that, in the controversy relating to the river Igurey, the Map of OLMEDILLA was never quoted, nevertheless, in the *Memoria de la Linea divisoria* by LASTARRIA the following passage in which the author speaks of the question of the Igurey occurs: "... *like the one of South America published by D. JUAN DE LA CRUZ*, two years before the Preliminary Treaty of 1777, and according to the maps constructed by the Spanish and Portuguese Commissioners under the Treaty of 1750. ..."[3] And further on: "... *the large Map of South America by our Cosmographer D. JUAN DE LA CRUZ* which has been quoted."[4]

---

[1] CABRER, *Diario de la Segunda Subdivision*, Manuscript, p. 112 of Vol. II., and p. 349 of Vol. II. in the edition of MILITON GONZALEZ.
[2] OYÁRVIDE, *Memoria*, in CALVO, *Recueil de Traités*, IX., 283.
[3] LASTARRIA, in CALVO, IV., 331.
[4] *Ibidem*, 372.

Another Spanish Commissioner, D. FELIX DE AZARA, wrote the following:

Opinion of Azara on the Map of Olmedilla.
"I have copied all those rivers and the coasts connected with them from the Map of DON JUAN DE LA CRUZ, engraved in 1775. *This Map is rightly held to be the best of South America.*"[1]

Other quotations, D'Avezac, Humboldt.
Many opinions of European Americanists could be adduced. D'AVEZAC said: "... the most valued maps, such as those of D'ANVILLE, and JEAN DE LA CRUZ...."[2] And the great HUMBOLDT: "Almost all the maps of South America which have appeared since the year 1775 are, in what regards the interior of the country comprised between the steppes of Venezuela and the river of the Amazonas, between the Eastern back of the Andes and the coast of Cayenne, *a simple copy of the great Spanish map* of LA CRUZ OLMEDILLA."[3]

The copy of Olmedilla which belonged to Humboldt.
The copy of the Map of OLMEDILLA, which HUMBOLDT had during his travels in America, is exhibited in the principal room of the American Geographical Society, at New York. On the lower part of the frame may be read the following: "The Map used by HUMBOLDT in exploring South America, with his autograph."

On February 23, 1802, D. FRANCISCO REQUENA, who was also one of the Spanish Commissioners in the demarcation of limits, made the following statement:

Opinion of Requena regarding Olmedilla.
"This work, which was printed in 1775, is an honor to the Nation, to the wise Minister who promoted it, and to the author

---

[1] FELIX DE AZARA, *Voyages*, Vol. I., p. 12.
[2] D'AVEZAC, *Observations Géographiques*, Paris, 1857, p. 129.
[3] HUMBOLDT, *Personal Narrative of Travels to the Equinoctial Regions of America*, London, 1853, Vol. III., p. 28.

himself, on account of the minuteness of detail and the completeness with which he executed the Map . . . At the time when the Map was published, none more accurate could be made."[1]

OLMEDILLA worked at this Map for many years, and consulted all the documents in the possession of the Spanish Government. On December 8, 1767, in a communication addressed to the MARQUIS DI GRIMALDI, he said :

Documents consulted by Olmedilla.

"Sir.—DON JUAN DE LA CRUZ CANO Y OLMEDILLA, a Pensioner of His Majesty, and a Member of His Royal Academy of San Fernando, says,—that his honor being engaged by the confidence placed in him by Your Excellency when you were pleased to command him to execute the Map of South America, he cannot do less than state a second time what occurs to him upon the subject in order that he may be successful in his endeavor to serve the King and Your Excellency. Moved, therefore, by that incentive which should inspire a son of our Country, *and unwilling to limit himself to merely correcting the Map of DON FRANCISCO MILLAU Y MARAVAL; he has found himself under the necessity of constructing another and a new one on a different projection* (although of the same dimensions on account of the size of the plates) *with all the valuable Plans which were taken for this purpose* from the Department of the Indies, which being insufficient,

---

[1] Report presented by D. FRANCISCO REQUENA in fulfilment of a Royal Order (Archives of Alcala de Henares).

Another authority above suspicion for the Argentines is D. PEDRO DE ANGELIS, in his introduction to the *Descripcion de Patagonia by* FALKNER. ANGELIS gives as a proof of the importance of that work the fact that it was used by OLMEDILLA in the Map of South America, and said, in 1835, that to that date he had not seen anything that could throw any doubt on the value of the same Map (ANGELIS, *Colleccion de Documentos,* &c., Vol. I., p. vi., of the Introduction referred to, Buenos-Aires, 1835).

although there are sixty-two of them, it would be advisable that Your Excellency should request DON MANUEL JOSEPH AYALA, Record Keeper of the said Department, to allow those he has to be used . . ."

Gratuity paid to Olmedilla by Royal Order. 1776.

The work having been finished, this geographer and engraver was rewarded by the King, as appears from the following document:

"Palace, April 7, 1776.—To DON FRANCISCO MANUEL DE MENA.—The King has determined that out of the returns of the Gazeta and Mercurio, a gratuity of six thousand reales de vellon shall be paid to DON JUAN DE LA CRUZ *in consideration of the care and accuracy with which he has constructed and engraved the Map of South America. . . .*"[1]

OLMEDILLA was at the same time a geographer and an engraver, but MERCATOR, HONDIUS, and many others were also geographers and engravers.

In his Map of 1775 there are certainly many errors, but the same may be said of all maps of South America subsequent to his, even of the most recent. Until proper surveys of all the interior shall have been made,—an undertaking which it will require many generations to accomplish,—it will be impossible to construct strictly accurate maps. As to the one now referred to, Brazil only has to consider these points:

Olmedilla's Map and the Brazilian cause.

1st. That it is an official Spanish Map;

2d. That it was the Map used by the Plenipotentiary of Spain in the negotiation of the Treaty of 1777, and

---

[1] This document and the preceding one are in the Archives of Alcala de Henares. The Brazilian Special Mission has copies of these and of many others relating to the Map of South America, *constructed and engraved by* OLMEDILLA.

that it was given by the Spanish Government to its demarcating Commissioners;

3d. That in it the Pepiry-Guaçú and the S. Antonio are the rivers forming the present boundary between Brazil and the Argentine Republic[1];

4th. That the rivers of the Argentine pretension are much to the East of the Pepiry-Guaçú and S. Antonio of the official Spanish Map.

An examination of the Map of OLMEDILLA will show that this geographer corrected the mistake of MILLAU with regard to the proximity of the sources of the Pepiry-Guaçú and S. Antonio. As has been said, MILLAU, in 1759, mistook as the source of the Pepiry one of the branches of the Uruguahy, and for this reason, he only found between the two a distance of 694 metres, or ⅓ of a mile. In the Map of OLMEDILLA the distance separating the sources of the Pepiry from those of the S. Antonio is about 17,500 metres, or 9¼ miles. Whether by accident, or as the result of reliable information obtained after the first demarcation, it is certain that when the Treaty of 1777 was concluded, the Spanish Government already knew from this Map that the headwaters of the two rivers were separated from one another by that distance.

Olmedilla corrects Millau's mistake concerning the headwaters of the Pepiry.

Distance between the sources of the Pepiry and S. Antonio according to Olmedilla.

[1] In the pamphlet *Misiones*, DR. ZEBALLOS censures OLMEDILLA, saying that in 1775 he was ignorant of the Treaty of 1761, because he drew the boundary along the Pepiry and the S. Antonio. This censure is another proof that when the distinguished Argentine diplomatist wrote this part of his pamphlet he was guided by notes that were given to him, and without having seen some documents he quoted. OLMEDILLA limited himself to locating the Pepiry-Guaçú and the S. Antonio in their proper places, without drawing any boundary along them. The challenged geographer was acquainted with the Treaty of 1761, and, like a good Spaniard, he drew upon his Map the line of Tordesillas, which GRIMALDI wished to make effective.

The fact is worthy of mention here only because the supporters of the Argentine cause attach great importance to this question of the proximity of headwaters. The question, however, is of no importance whatever. The first Treaty did not establish a standard of measurement for the distance between the headwaters of the rivers which serve as boundaries flowing in opposite directions, and the Treaty of 1777 designates by their names the Pepiry-Guaçú and the S. Antonio without laying down any condition whatever as to the proximity of their headwaters. Nor do the Instructions issued to the Commissioners mention the sources of the two rivers: they only give directions as to the positions of their mouths.

The Treaty of 1777 and the Instructions do not mention the headwaters of the two rivers.

Nevertheless, it is proper to repeat here that the Brazilian-Argentine Joint Commission ascertained in 1887 that, in a straight line, it is 17,400 metres, or nearly 9¼ miles, between the headwaters of the Pepiry-Guaçú and S. Antonio, that is to say, the same distance that can be measured on the Map of OLMEDILLA.

Distance according to the Brazilian-Argentine Joint Commission.

The Commissioners appointed by the two Governments for this demarcation were, according to the Treaty, to establish the boundary along the rivers Pepiry-Guaçú and S. Antonio, and not by other rivers. Article 10 of the Treaty allowed the Commissioners to choose on the spot, for the frontier running between the Jaurú and the Guaporé, in Matto Grosso, such divisional line as might seem to them most suitable[1]; but the sanction was limited to that part of the frontier.

The demarcation Commissioners received limited powers.

---

[1] Portuguese text of this 10th Article, Vol. IV., p. 84; English translation, Vol. III., p. 90.

The Instructions issued by the Spanish Government for this demarcation defined with the greatest clearness the positions of the rivers Pepiry-Guaçù and S. Antonio.

Spanish Instructions, 1778, 1779.

The first is the *Royal Instruction* dated Aranjuez, June 6, 1778, and signed by the Secretary of State for the Indies, D. JOSEF de GÁLVEZ.[1]

This document reproduced almost word for word the Memorandum of May 25, 1778, and signed by COUNT DE FLORIDABLANCA to the Portuguese Ambassador at Madrid.

The second Instruction, which was much more detailed, was drawn up by General VERTIZ, Viceroy of the Provinces of the River Plate, and was approved by CARLOS III. on January 12, 1779. Its title is: *Plano para executar la Demarcacion de esta America (Plan for the execution of the demarcation in this America).*[2]

The First Division of the Commissioners was charged with the demarcation of the Southern frontier from the sea-coast to the Great Falls of the Paraná. It was divided into two Subdivisions or Parties.

The 1st Party was to begin its labors at the Chuy stream, near the sea, and to conclude them on the left bank of the Uruguay, opposite the mouth of the Pepiry-Guaçù. To the Second Party was allotted the demarcation of the frontier from the mouth of the Pepiry-Guaçù to the Great Falls of the Paraná.

The Royal Instruction of June 6, 1778, treating of the First Division, directed as follows:

"But considering that the work of this Division as far as the foot of the Great Falls of the river Paraná

Quotation from the Spanish Royal Instruction, 1778.

[1] Transcribed in Vol. IV., pp. 101-107; translated into English in Vol. III., pp. 107-114.
[2] Transcribed in full in Vol. IV., pp. 108-126; and translated into English in Vol. III., pp. 115-134.

may be impracticable in the terms proposed by the
Court of Lisbon, through thick woods without any
track, *and through rivers of short navigation, the
Pepiri-guazú and San Antonio, distant from all settlements that could give them any help;* His Majesty
has resolved that this Party, after having gone a part
of the way together, shall divide itself, forming two
subdivisions, each composed of one Commissioner, one
Guide, and half of their followers, both Spanish and
Portuguese; and that one shall continue by the crest-
line of the watersheds between the river-basins of the
Uruguay, on the West, and of the Yacuy, on the East,
until it arrives at the mouth of the Pepiri-guazú, and
that the other subdivision shall start from the river
Ybicuy, which has its source in and passes by the Monte
Grande, and, proceeding through the Villages (Pueblos)
of Misiónes, as far as that of Candelaria or that of Corpus, the last of those on the Eastern bank of the Paraná,
*it shall ascend it in boats as far as the foot of the Salto
(Falls) of the river Yguazú or Curitiba, which is distant three leagues from its mouth in the Paraná; and
that hauling by its Northern bank the medium-sized
canoes it may carry, or building new ones above the
Salto, it shall navigate in them as far as the
river San Antonio, which is the second that
enters it on the Southern side; and going up
this river as far as its waters will allow,
shall endeavor to survey its source and to connect it with
the Pepiri-guazú, whose mouth the First Division will
already have surveyed; and on its return it shall lay
down the Demarcation from the mouth of the Iguazú to
the foot of the Salto Grande (Great Falls) of the river
Paraná, in conformity with Article the 8th of the*

S. Antonio, the second southern affluent of the Iguaçú above the Falls.

Treaty, if they do not think it more opportune to do this before entering the Iguazú."

The river S. Antonio, according to this Instruction, is *the second above the Great Falls of the Iguaçú.*

Therefore, the river S. Antonio is the present boundary of Brazil, and not the Jangada (San Antonio Guazú) as asserted by the Argentine Republic, seeing that between the Falls and the Jangada there are more than twenty rivers.

The *Plan* of VERTIZ, approved by the King of Spain in 1779, defined the position of the mouth of the S. Antonio and also that of the Pepiry-Guaçú.

<small>Quotations from the Spanish Special Instruction of 1779.</small>

This document said, referring to the terminal point of the labors of the First Party:

"In order that the Delimitation Commissioners of this Party may attain the end indicated to it at the mouth of the Pepiri-Guazú, they must guide themselves by the course of the River Uruguay-Puitá, as far as its confluence in the River Uruguay, *because at the distance of two leagues and one third, following the bank of the River Uruguay in a Westerly direction, the mouth of the River Pepiri will be found on the side opposite.* The River Uruguay-Puitá is well known to the Indians of Misiones, principally to those of the village of S.º Angel, who are nearest to it, and its sources are crossed at the way leading to the Baqueria.¹

<small>Location of the Pepiry-Guaçú.</small>

"*The mouth of the River Pepiri-Guazú is in Latitude 27° 9′ 23″. When the Uruguay is low, a small island is visible at its mouth, and at the point of the same mouth, on the Eastern side, there will be found a place from which the trees*

<small>Mark left by the former Commissioners.</small>

---
¹ Plains of Vaccaria in the N. E. part of Rio Grande do Sul.

have been cut down, and in the middle of this clearing, one standing-tree, thirteen feet in height, upon which a Cross has been carved, with the characters—R. F. AÑO DE 1759."[1]

The Pepiry-Guaçú was, therefore, the river demarcated in 1759, the same that Brazil now defends.

Location of the S. Antonio. The location of the mouth of the S. Antonio was not less clearly defined in the Plan. This document, referring to the Second Subdivision or Party, says:

"His Majesty commands that this Second Subdivision shall separate from the First from the River Ybicuy, which has its source in and passes by the Montegrande, and that proceeding through the Villages (Pueblos) of Misiones as far as that of Candelaria, or that of Corpus, the last village on the Eastern bank of the Paraná, it shall ascend it in boats *as far as the foot of the Falls (Salto) of the River Yguazú or Curituba,* which is distant three leagues from its mouth in the Paraná; and that, hauling along its Northern bank the medium-sized canoes it may carry, or building new ones *above the Salto, it shall navigate in them as far as the River San Antonio, which is the second that enters it on the Southern side,* and going up this river as far as its waters will allow, shall endeavor to survey its source, and to connect it with the Pepirí-Guazú, whose mouth the First Division will already have surveyed; and on its return, it shall lay down the demarcation from the mouth of the Yguazú to the foot of the Great Falls (Salto Grande) of the River Paraná, in conformity with Article 8 of the Treaty, if it shall not

---

[1] The Spanish Viceroy translated the Portuguese inscription. It said:— R. F. AÑO DE 1759. The two initials R. F. mean : *Most Faithful King,* i. e., King of Portugal.

find it more opportune to do this before entering the Yguazú.

. . . .

"This Party, taking to their boats at the port of the said Village of Corpus, will navigate as far as the mouth of the River Yguazú (in doing which it will spend more than twenty days), and, entering the same, will continue up four leagues as far as its Great Falls, and at three leagues and one fifth from its mouth a small sandy creek will be found, near a stream with a high Fall, which empties itself on the Southern side, where the boats can stop, and a camp can be pitched, until they go up and establish another, which will be necessary also above the Falls.

. . . .

"*From these Falls (Salto) of the Yguazú the river will be navigated for a distance of twenty leagues as far as the mouth of the River San Antonio, which will be reached after an eight days' journey, and which lies in latitude 25° 35' 4". Entering this river, it will be found that at a distance of little more than a league and three quarters it divides into two branches, the smaller bearing the name of San Antonio-Mini, and the Eastern branch, which is the larger, must be followed.*

"This River San Antonio is not navigable, and can only be explored by following on foot the banks to its source, which, nevertheless, presents a number of difficulties to overcome, and those who go on this exploration ought to be on their guard against the wild Indians, who dwell in this district, and they must carry their arms ready, inasmuch as many persons cannot enter it because of the difficulty of carrying supplies.

"From the mouth of the River San Antonio the Party shall return surveying the River Yguazú as far as its mouth, which is in Latitude 25° 35′ 51″, which empties itself into the Rio Paraná, and shall continue the demarcation up this river as far as its great Salto (Falls) which is in Latitude 24° 4′ 27″."

These Spanish Instructions were drawn up in view of OLMEDILLA's Map of South America and of the

Comparison of the Spanish Instructions with the Diary of the Demarcation of 1759. Diary of the delimitation Commissioners of 1759, which is a new and undeniable proof that in the mind of the Spanish Government the Pepiry-Guaçú and the S. Antonio of the Treaty of 1777, were the very rivers that were demarcated in 1759—the same that form the present boundary of Brazil.

The comparison of the two texts will make this evident:

1) *Directions as to the Pepiry-Guaçú:*
1)

a) *Spanish Instruction, 1759 (Plan of Vice Roy VERTIZ, approved by King CARLOS III., January 12, 1779):*

"In order that the Delimitation Commissioners of this Party may attain the end indicated to it at the mouth of the River Pepirí-guazú, they must guide themselves by the course of the River Uruguay-Puitá, as far as its confluence in the River Uruguay, because at *the distance of two leagues and one third*, following the bank of the River Uruguay in a Westerly direction the mouth of the River Pepirí will be found on the opposite side." (In the original, fol. 29 v.)

b) *Diary of the Spanish Commissioners, 1759 ;*
Going up the Uruguay, March 6:

"The river continues its bend to the N.E. and N.E. ¼ N., and at the beginning of this direction, at *a distance of about* 2⅓ *leagues of the Pepiri*, it receives by the Eastern bank a large river which the guide said was the *Uruguay-pitā*, the farthest point to which his knowledge extended." (In the authenticated copy, fol. 30 v.)

2)

a) *Spanish Instruction, 1779*:
"The mouth of the River Pepiri-Guazú is in Latitude 27° 09′ 23″. . ." (Fol. 30.)

b) *Spanish Diary, 1759*:
April 6, 1759: "Mean between seventeen observations: 27° 09′ 23″." (Fol. 41.)

3)

a) *Spanish Instruction, 1779*:
"When the Uruguay is low, a small island is visible at its mouth. . . ." (Fol. 30.)

b) *Spanish Diary, 1759*:
March 5: ". . . in this direction there *is a reef, which terminates in a small island of rock, which is covered of Sarandi-trees, lying close to the Northern bank, which is covered over at flood time*, and behind it, at a distance of ¾ of a league of the *Itayoá*, is the mouth of a river, which can only be seen after having doubled the point of the island, which river, the guide said, was the *Pepiri* of which we were in search." (Fol. 29.)

4)

a) *Spanish Instruction, 1779*:
". . . and at a point of the same mouth, on the Eastern side, there will be found a place from which the trees have been cut down, and in the middle of this clearing, one standing-tree, thirteen feet in height,

upon which a Cross has been carved, with the characters—R. F. AÑO DE 1759." (Fol. 30.)

b) *Spanish Diary, 1759:*

March 8: "... and although the latter (the Falls of the Uruguay), from which the Pepirí is only little more than a league distant, are a natural landmark of the most visible and durable sort for the recognition of this river at all times, as is also the island lying immediately at its mouth, when the Uruguay is low, nevertheless, as being one of the most important points of our Division, we stopped there to take some observations of longitude and latitude, in order to be able to fix its position with more precision and security; and, on a point, formed by the Eastern bank of the Pepirí and by the Northern bank of the Uruguay, a clearing was made, leaving in the middle only a single tree of thirteen feet in height on which a Cross was placed, and on the arms of the Cross these letters were carved—R. F. AÑO 1759." (Fol. 33.)

II) *Directions as to the River S. Antonio.*

1)

a) *Spanish Instruction, 1779:*

"... it shall ascend it in boats as far as the foot of the Salto (Falls) of the River Yguazú or Curituba, *which is distant three leagues from its mouth in the Paraná;* and that, hauling along its Northern bank the medium-sized canoes it may carry, or building new ones above the Salto, it shall navigate in them as far as the River San Antonio, *which is the second that enters it on the Southern side.*" (Fol. 31.)

b) *Spanish Diary, 1759:*

"... as far as the Salto Grande ... and the canoes being carried here overland over a space of one league, the passage is free even for large boats, then following *the Iguaçú which at three leagues from the Salto enters the Paraná* in Latitude 25° 31′ 51″ . . ." ("General description of the rivers," at the end of the Diary, Fol. 105 v.)

Jan. 6, 1760: " . . . although, besides the longitude and latitude which are known to few, the more visible and durable sign is found in the fact that *this river San Antonio is the second important river* that empties itself on the South bank of the Iguaçú above its Salto Grande, while the San Francisco, which is at a distance of one league and three quarters, is the first, though it is much smaller, as are also the rivulets that enter it lower down. . . ." (Fol. 95 v.)

2)
a) *Spanish Instruction, 1779:*
"This Party, taking to their boats at the port of the said Village of Corpus, will navigate as far as the mouth of the River Yguazú (in doing which *it will spend little more than twenty days), and, entering the same, will continue up four leagues as far as its Salto Grande (Great Falls)*." (Fol. 32 v.)

b) *Spanish Diary, 1759:*
The Commissioners *started, on June 20, 1759,* from Corpus *and reached the mouth of the Iguaçú on the 10th July.*

July 10, 1759: ". . . But its course being immediately interrupted by the interposition of its *Great Falls, four leagues from its mouth* . . ." (Fol. 55.)

3)
a) *Spanish Instruction, 1779:*
" . . . *and at 3½ leagues from its mouth a small sandy creek will be found, near a stream with a high*

Fall, which empties itself on the Southern side, where the boats can stop, and a camp can be pitched, until they go up and establish another, which will be necessary also above the Falls. . . ." (Fol. 33.)

b) *Spanish Diary, 1759:*

"*On the 12th at a distance of 3½ leagues from the mouth of the Iguazú, and a little more than one from its Falls (Salto), we found a little sandy creek near a stream presenting a very high fall, which stream empties itself on the Southern side,* and this place being less inconvenient for mooring the boats . . ." (Fol. 55 v.)

4)

a) *Spanish Instruction, 1779:*

"Before this creek, at a short distance, a place will be found in which to take above or over the Salto (Falls) all the canoes that are not very large, and in spite of the great labor, it can be accomplished *by hauling the canoes through these difficult places a distance of 3400 Toises until the upper waters of the same Salto are reached.* There trees will be found, which can be used for making canoes should they be necessary. . . ." (Fol. 33.)

b) *Spanish Diary, 1759:*

"Besides this it was necessary, in order that they might be hauled, to open in the wood a sufficiently wide track, cutting down trees, and in place levelling the ground, particularly in five rivulets they had to cross; all this was done successfully, *and having been carried a distance of 3400 Toises,* they were all placed on the waters above the Falls (Salto) on the 29th. This work having been completed, the building of the new canoes was commenced. . . ." (Fol. 57.)

5)

a) *Spanish Instruction, 1779:*

" *In the same place, on high ground, above the flood level, huts must be made in which to store a part of the provisions*, so that they may be preserved in good condition. . . ." (Fol. 33.)

b) *Spanish Diary, 1759:*

" While those were returning who had gone to survey the Northern bank, *storing huts were built upon high ground not exposed to inundations in which to deposit provisions the better to keep, preserve, and distribute them as might be necessary*. . . ." (Fol. 57.)

6)

a) *Spanish Instruction, 1779:*

" From this Salto (Falls) of the Yguazú the river will be navigated for a distance of *twenty leagues* as far as the mouth of the River San Antonio, *which will be reached after an eight days' journey, and which lies in latitude 25° 35' 04"*." (Fol. 33 v.)

b) *Spanish Diary, 1759:*

The Commissioners spent in the navigation from the Falls (Salto) to the mouth of the San Antonio *eight days* (16th to 24th November, 1759), *and reckoned about 19 leagues*.

From the 13th December, 1759 :

" Mean between all the observations : 25° 35' 04"." (Fol. 90.)

7)

a) *Spanish Instruction, 1779:*

" Entering this river, it will be found that *at a distance of a little more than a league and three quarters it divides into two branches, the smaller bearing the name of San Antonio-Miní,* and the Eastern branch, which is larger, must be followed." (Fol. 33.)

b) *Spanish Diary, 1759:*
November 24, 1759:

". . . and lastly taking another turn to the East, another reef is seen, and at a distance of *a little more than 1¾ league of its mouth a stream to which the name of San Antonio-Mini was given, enters it by its Southern bank*, forming with it a fork, where there were two huts made by our people before they removed to the encampment they occupy higher up. . . ." (Fol. 85.)

November 25, 1759:

"The Spanish Party led the advance, and taking the *Eastern branch, which is the larger*, and by which the other had gone, we continued the navigation. . . ." (Fol. 85 v.)

8)

a) *Spanish Instruction, 1779:*

"*The River San Antonio is not navigable, and can only be explored by following on foot the banks to its source*, which, nevertheless, presents a number of difficulties to overcome, and those who go on this exploration ought to be *on their guard against the wild Indians*, who dwell in this district. . . ." (Fol. 33 v.)

b) *Spanish Diary, 1759:*
November 26, 1759:

". . . with repeated reefs between which there are two rather extensive pools, especially the second, which is about ¾ of a league in length, and ends in a lofty fall, *which had prevented the Spanish Geographer from navigating farther*. . . ." (Fol. 86.)

December 9, 1759:

". . . and in the night of the 9th, being at a distance of 5 leagues from the encampment, in one of the numerous huts that were made all along that track to protect the provisions from the rain, *the wild Indians taking advantage of the deep sleep into which they had incautiously fallen, attacked them. . . ."* (Two Paraguayans were wounded, of whom one died.) (Fol. 87.)

December 13, 1759:

"On the 13th the Commissioners received a letter from the Spanish Geographer dated the 10th, in which he said that, *going down the river in the canoe, he found it so shallow on account of the very dry weather, that he had experienced great difficulty in travelling a little more than three quarters of a league in one day and a half;* and seeing that farther on were other reefs in the way, *he had determined to give up the navigation and to continue his track overland. . . .*" (Fol. 88).

". . . On the 16th (December), the men who had gone to build the canoes returned with the intelligence that the river which had been mentioned by the Spanish Geographer was very low, full of reefs, and absolutely innavigable. . . .

". . . and on its banks they had found very recent footprints of women and children, which proved that *the wild Indians* had a camp near at hand; and that they disturbed them on their march, following them with shouts and clamor. . . ." (Fol. 91.)

"And from here they began to see over a distance of half a league *recent traces of savages*, wide trodden tracks, and footprints of women and children which crossed the river: there were also to be seen the beds they had used, made of a large quantity of the broad leaves of the plant Achirá. . . ." (Fol. 93.)

It should be stated now that the Portuguese Government, in entire agreement with that of Spain regarding the number of the demarcating Parties and the task committed to each one of them, never approved as a whole the Spanish Instructions of 1778 and 1779. The Spanish Commissioners were governed by them, but not so the Portuguese.

The demarcation of the frontier comprised between the sea-coast and the Igurey, on the Paraná, concerned the First Portuguese-Spanish Division.

This Division, as has been said, was separated into two Subdivisions or Parties. The work of the First, beginning at the littoral, was to end in the North at the mouth of the Pepiry-Guaçú; that of the Second, commencing on the Paraná, was to comprise the demarcation of the boundary lines of the Iguaçú and the S. Antonio.

General VEIGA CABRAL was the first Portuguese Commissioner, and Captain VARELA Y ULLOA, Royal Navy, the Spanish Commissioner.

The Spanish Instructions of 1779 directed that the First Party should follow the course of the Uruguay-Pitá in order to reach the mouth of the Pepiry-Guaçú.

They said:

Mouth of the Pepiry-Guaçú. " In order that the Delimitation Commissioners of this Party may attain the end indicated to it at the mouth of the River Pepiri-Guazú, *they must guide themselves by the course of the River Uruguay-Puitá, as far as its confluence in the River Uruguay, because at the distance of two leagues and one third, following the bank of the River Uruguay in a Westerly direction, the mouth of the River Pepiri will be found on the side opposite.* The River Uruguay-Puitá is well known to the Indians of Misiones, principally to those of the village of S⁰ Angel, who are nearest to it, and its sources are crossed at the way leading to the Baqueria."

The River Uruguay-Pitã or Uruguay-Puitá, is not mentioned in any of the Articles of the Treaty of 1777. The Spanish Instructions advised the De- marcators to follow its course *solely because in view of the Map of OLMEDILLA, and of all preceding maps, it seemed that this would facilitate their arrival at the neighborhood of the mouth of the Pepiry-Guaçú.* {The 2d Uruguay-Pitã, 1759.}

The distance indicated of *two leagues and one third* between the mouth of the Uruguay-Pitã and that of the Pepiry-Guaçú, clearly shows that the Instructions referred to the Uruguay-Pitã, whose mouth was surveyed in 1759 by the first demarcators, that is to say, the second river to whose mouth the name of Uruguay-Pitã was given.[1]

The description of the Uruguay by LOZANO has already shown that along the left bank of that river large forests extended (page 141 in this Vol.). The Guaranys of the Missions were quite unacquainted with the courses of the affluents of the South bank of the Uruguay, because those forests were then inhabited, as they still were at the beginning of this century, by wild and fierce Indians.

MIGUEL LASTARRIA, who was the Secretary of Viceroy VERTIZ, wrote in 1804:

"The Wild Tupis wander through the large and dense forests of the Uruguay and other rivers which enter it by the East bank, spreading some 80 leagues forward towards the North and far into the interior of the Portuguese Dominions, from the headwaters of the Piratini towards the river Curitiva or Yguazú and the first headwaters of the Yacuy or Yguay. . ."[2]

Not having the slightest knowledge regarding the

[1] In Vol. V., Plans No. 29.
[2] LASTARRIA's Letter, dated from Madrid, December 1, 1804, in Vol. I. of the *Memoria sobre la linea divisoria*, Manuscript in the National Library of Paris.

course of those rivers, the Jesuits in their maps arbitrarily connected the headwaters of some
of them with the mouths of others known
on the Uruguay. OLMEDILLA, guided by
these maps, traced in the same manner the unknown
course of the Uruguay-Pitá, connecting the headwaters
of the old Trigoty, which the Guaranys of the Missions
supposed to be those of the Uruguay-Pitá, with the
mouth of the river, which on reaching the Uruguay
was thus named.[1]

The Trigoty, 3d Uruguay-Pitá of the Spaniards, 1788.

In this manner, supposing they had reached the
mouth of the Uruguay-Pitá surveyed in
the Uruguay, 1759, the Portuguese astronomer JOSÉ DE
SALDANHA and the Spanish geographer
GUNDIN, commissioned by VEIGA CABRAL and VARELA,
reached, in 1788, the mouth of the Trigoty, now Rio
da Varzea.

1st journey to the Uruguay, May, 1788.

Thence they went down the Uruguay to seek the
mouth of the Pepiry-Guaçú which, according to the
Instructions, should be two leagues and one third down
stream: but, as was natural, the starting-point being
different, they were unable to reach the true Pepiry-
Guaçú. They went down as far as the Apitereby, and,
returning up stream, they believed that the river now
called das Antas was the Pepiry-Guaçú. They left
upon a tree the following inscription:

Post facta resurgens, Pepiry-Guasú, Maio 9, 1788,

---

[1] The Spaniard OYÁRVIDE in his *Memoria* bears witness to the fact that many rivers which he surveyed have one name at their sources, and another at their mouths. He says:

" As among the Indians we have with us there is no special guide, it happens that they give the same name which they bear in the lower part of their course, and at their sources, to very few of the streams which we met on the march; but in spite of this want of accuracy in the information we have, these streams have been laid down on our plan with those surveyed along the way, as, from the nature of the ground and the density of the forests, which extend from both banks of the Uruguay, it seemed probable their course would run."

and the letters R. F. (Rei Fidelissimo,—Most Faithful King), on the Eastern side, and R. C. (Rei Catholico, —Catholic King) on the Western side.

Returning to the encampment of the First Commissioners, they found a Diary of the demarcation of 1759, and then they ascertained that *neither was the Uruguay-Pitá* the river upon which they were, nor the Pepiry-Guaçú the river at which they had left the inscription.

The Diary of SALDANHA says:

"Thursday, July 10 (1788). The whole month of June having been spent in accurate and careful investigations by the Principal Commissioners, as to whether or not the river we had now found was the Pepiri-Guassú of the previous demarcators, *a detailed and well-kept Diary of the demarcation of 1759, and upon the same subject of the Pepiry-Guaçú, at last came into the possession of the Spanish Commissioner, by the reading of which we were all undeceived. Neither was the Uruguay-Pitá the Rio da Picada, although the old Plans thus named its headwaters, nor was the Pepiri-Guassú the one we had recently marked*, although it had some appearances of it.

The error discovered as to the Uruguay-Pitá

"Such an error in so important a matter rendered a prompt remedy necessary; there was no other than to return a second time to the Uruguay, utilizing the good weather that still remained, and to hasten to the canoes which had been left in the Rio da Picada. ..."

VEIGA CABRAL and VARELA again sent the same SALDANHA and GUNDIN in search of the true Pepiry-Guaçú, giving them for this purpose, to guide them, an extract from the Diary of the First Demarcators.

2d Journey to the Uruguay, July, August, 1788.

SALDANHA went down by the Rio da Picada (the old

Discovery of the River of the Argentine pretension, 1788.

Trigoty and false Uruguay-Pitá), entered the Uruguay and followed it down-stream. GUNDIN, before going down the Uruguay, made an exploration up-stream, and discovered the mouth of a river at which he left the following inscription:

"*Te Deum laudamus. August 4, 1788.*"

SALDANHA had discovered on July 26th, the mouth of the true Uruguay-Pitá and, on the 28th, that of the Pepiry-Guaçú. Some days afterwards (August 13, 1788), the Spanish geographer GUNDIN arrived there and also recognized the river as the true Pepiry-Guaçú of the Treaty, nailing to a tree a plate of copper which VARELA had given him for this purpose and upon which were engraved the following words:

The Pepiry-Guaçú found.

"*Hucusque auxiliatus est nobis Deus. Pepiri-Guazú. 1788.*"

The inscription put up by SALDANHA on July 28th was this:

"*Sine auxilio tuo, Domine, nihil sumus. Pepiri-Guasú. 1788.*"

Thus, by common accord, was the mouth of the Pepiry-Guaçú of the Treaty recognized.

But the following year, the first Spanish Commissioner VARELA raised the question which is now about to be solved, by asserting that in the demarcation of 1759 there had been an error, and that the Pepiry or Pequiry of the Treaty of 1750 was the river discovered by GUNDIN on August 4, 1788, because that river was up-stream of the Uruguay-Pita.

Origin of the present controversy.

In this manner there came to be a third Uruguay-

Pitá more to the East than the second (of 1759) and it was claimed that the Pepiry-Guaçú should be displaced toward the East while the name Uruguay-Pitá should thus be transferred from one river to the other.

This pretension gave rise to a discussion, sometimes very heated, between the Second Commissioners Roscio (Portuguese) and DIEGO DE ALVEAR (Spanish). The latter, according to the Instructions of his chief VARELA, insisted upon a joint survey of the river discovered by GUNDIN, a river which the Portuguese called Caudaloso, and to which the Spaniards wanted to give the name of Pepiry-Guaçú.

The Principal Portuguese Commissioner allowed the exploration of that river, with the sole object of obtaining from the Spaniards their consent to survey as far as its principal source the true Pepiry-Guaçú. Exploration of the R. Caudaloso, Piquiri-Guazú of the Spanish Commissioners.

The exploration of the river of GUNDIN was carried out by CHAGAS SANTOS (Portuguese) and OYÁRVIDE (Spanish). The latter gave the river the name of Pequirí-Guazú, which was never recognized by the Portuguese.

The Instructions of ALVEAR to OYÁRVIDE, on November 17, 1789, contained these passages which are worthy of notice[1]:

"It being important to the service of His Majesty to explore and survey the river which we believe to be the true Pepiry-Guaçú, discovered by our geographer of the First Division D. JOAQUIN GUNDIN, and which enters the Uruguay about six leagues to the East of the Uruguay-pitá by the North bank, I have deter-

---

[1] In CALVO, IX., 200.

mined to put under your charge the execution of this work, trusting to your zeal and energy its most complete fulfilment. . . .

"In order to render here a service of greater importance, if the river running for many leagues should go through prairies, as can be expected from the great depth and breadth of its mouth, you will endeavor to ascertain with all care, now informed and assisted by the inhabitants of the country whom you may see, now guided by conjectures to which you may naturally be led, in view of the character and the configuration of the ground, whether there is in that immediate neighborhood another river whose headwaters lie opposite and can be connected with those of our Piquirí, and which, flowing towards the North, shall empty itself into the Iguazú.

"*The existence of such a river, which is very probable, may induce the Courts to choose it as a boundary instead of the San Antonio, which the Treaty designates merely as opposite to that which the former demarcators have erroneously called Pepirí, taking it for such, and which we can call Pepirí-Miní, in order to avoid a new error or misunderstanding. . . .*"

CHAGAS SANTOS only accompanied OYÁRVIDE as far

S. Antonio Guazú of Oyárvide, 1791.
as the source of the Rio Caudaloso or Pequirí-Guazú. OYÁRVIDE continuing, discovered on June 17, 1791, the sources of a river to which he gave the name of San Antonio Guazú.

The survey of the S. Antonio of the Treaty had been

R. S. Antonio.
made in 1788, from its mouth to the principal headwater by the same Sub-Commis-

sioners CHAGAS SANTOS and OYÁRVIDE, and that of the Pepiry-Guaçú by JOAQUIN FELIX DA FONSECA (Portuguese) and CABRER (Spanish), in 1789 and 1790, from the mouth to the source of an Eastern Branch.

<small>R. Pepiry-Guaçú.</small>

In the Diary of CABRER it is seen that, unable to find the mark placed at the principal source of the S. Antonio, he and FONSECA concluded that the Pepiry-Guaçú had improperly received that name, and they wrote upon the plate of copper which the Spanish geographer GUNDIN had set up there the following words: "*Pepiri prædato nomine cocor, 1790.*"

CABRER might have done this, but without the knowledge of FONSECA. The latter had positive orders not to touch the inscriptions placed there in 1788.[1] The letter of July 28, 1790, of VEIGA CABRAL to the Viceroy of Brazil gives a full account of the Survey made by FONSECA and does not mention that "*Pepiri prædator nomine cocor,*" which does not appear in the Report of CABRER, transcribed by OYÁRVIDE,[2] and was never quoted by ALVEAR in his discussion with ROSCIO. CABRER wrote his *Diary* many years after the conclusion of the survey.

All the arguments of the Spanish Commissioners of the second demarcation have been refuted in the first part of this Statement because they were based on the errors which they attributed to their predecessors of 1759.

The Spanish Government did not commit to them the task of correcting the errors of the preceding demarcation, but that of sur-

<small>The Spanish Instructions disregarded.</small>

---

[1] Order of February 8, 1789, of the 1st Portuguese Commissioner, VEIGA CABRAL.
[2] In CALVO, IX., 289.

veying and demarcating the rivers Pepiry-Guaçú and
S. Antonio defined in the Treaty, rivers which were
indisputably those surveyed in 1759, as was proved by
the examination of the official maps anterior to the
Spanish Instructions of 1778 and 1779.

The river Uruguay-Pitã mentioned in the Instructions
of 1779 (Plan of the Viceroy VERTIZ) was the river
known by that name at the time, and whose mouth,
according to the Diary of the demarcators of 1759,
was 2⅓ leagues to the East from the mouth of the
Pepiry-Guaçú.

The Commissioners, *starting from the mouth of this
Uruguay-Pitã, were to go down the Uruguay*, to find,
at that distance, the mouth of the Pepiry-Guaçú. *They
began by transferring to the Trigoty, whose mouth is
much more to the East, the name of the Uruguay-Pitã
of 1759*, the river to which the Instructions of 1779
referred, and *they went in search of the Pepiry above
the mouth of that false Uruguay-Pitã of 1788.*

The Spanish Government never took into consideration the change, proposed by its Commissioners, of the
border line defined by the Treaty of 1777.

In the *Memoria* of OYÁRVIDE the following occurs:

"The year 1796 having come without any solution
of the contention as to the drawing of the divisional
line from the Uruguay to the Iguazú ."[1]

And in the *Diary* of CABRER:

"The Court of Madrid never replied; why, we do
not know, but it is very easy to infer. Nor did they
ever acknowledge the receipt of the Plans and geographical Maps which were sent there even in triplicate
for information regarding the demarcation."[2]

[1] OYÁRVIDE, in CALVO, N., 67.
[2] CABRER, *Diario*, Manuscript, Vol. I., p. 617; edited by MILITON GONZA-
LEZ, II., 267.

IX.

In the River Plate the present controversy between Brazil and the Argentine Republic is always called the question of Misiones,— a designation which some Brazilian writers have adopted in recent times.

The contested territory was never a part of Misiones.

From the Argentine point of view, it is well applied, because the controversy turns upon the question as to what is to be the Eastern boundary of the Argentine territory called Misiones; but from the Brazilian point of view, and considering the Geographical History of South America, the designation is improper and inaccurate, because the Brazilian territory which the Argentine Republic wishes to acquire by substituting for the Pepiry-Guaçú and Santo Antonio of the Treaty of 1777 two rivers more to the East, found in 1788 and 1791, never formed part of the old Province of the Missionaries of the Society of Jesus in Paraguay, afterwards called by the Spaniards Province of Misiones.

In the XVIth century the Spaniards of Paraguay founded to the East of the Paraná and to the North of the Iguaçú, in the region which they called Province of Guayra, two small cities: Guayra, or Ciudad Real,

Missions of the Jesuits in the XVII century.

on the Pequiry, near the confluence of this river with the Paraná, and Villa Rica, on the left bank and near the mouth of the Quiribataí or Curumbatahy, an affluent of the Guibay, now the Ivahy. At the beginning of the XVIIth century, the Jesuits of Paraguay began to convert the Guarany Indians of that region and to collect them around the rude churches they were raising. The first missions founded by them were those of Loreto and Santo Ignacio Miní (1610) on the left bank of the Paranapané or Paranapanema, an affluent of the Paraná; afterwards they successively established those of San Xavier (1623) and San José (1624), on two affluents of the left bank of the Tibagiba, now Tibagy; Angeles (1624), on the left bank of the Curumbatahy; Encarnacion (1625), San Miguel (1628), and Jesus Maria (1630), on the left bank of the Tibagy, and San Pedro (1627), a few leagues to the East; San Pablo (1627) and San Antonio (1628), on the right bank of the Guibaí or Ivahy; Santo Thomé (1628) to the East of the Curumbatahy; and Concepcion de los Gualachos (1628) near the sources of this last river. On the right bank of the Iguaçú, near the Great Falls of this river, they founded the mission of Santa Maria Mayor (1626).[1]

The Map *Paraquaria vulgo Paraguay cum adjacentibus* presented to Father VINCENZO CARAFFA,[2] shows the places then occupied by the missions of the Jesuits, and the seats of those which were taken and destroyed, from 1630 to 1638, by the Paulistas.

The missions and cities of Guayra were bounded by the Iguaçú on the South, the Paranapanema on the

---

[1] In this statement the dates and positions of the missions are indicated according to the *Annual Report* signed at Cordova de Tucuman on the 12th November, 1628, and addressed by the Rev. F R NICOLAS DURAN, Provincial of the Province of Paraguay, to the Rev. F R MUTIO VITELESCI, VIth General of the Society of Jesus; and also from the *Historia Provinciæ Paraquariæ Societatis Jesu* by F. NICOLÁO DEL TECHO (Nicolas du Toict), printed at Lille in 1673.

The *Annual* of NICOLAS DURAN, giving the first account of these foundations, was printed in Latin and in French. Latin Edition: *Litteræ annuæ provinciæ Paraquariæ Soc^{tis} Jesu ad admodum R. P. MUTIUM VITTELESIUM ejusdem Soc^t. Præpositum Generalem, missæ a R. P. NICOLAS DURAN. . . . Antuerpiæ . . 1636.* French Edition: *Relation des insignes progrez de la Religion Chrestienne faits av Paraqvai Province de l'Amerique Meridionale, & dans les vastes régions de Gnair & d'Vruaig nouvellement découvertes par les Peres de la Compagnie de Iesvs, és années 1626 & 1627. Envoyée au R. P. MUTIO VITELESCI, General de la mesme Compagnie, par le R. P. NICOLAS DURAN, Provincial en la Province de Paraqvai. . . . Paris, 1638.*

[2] Map No. 1 A in Vol. VI. of this Statement.

North, the Paraná on the West and the Serra dos Agudos on the East. They were, therefore, situated to the North of the territory now contested.

Besides the missions of Guayra, the Jesuits had the following in 1630, the year of the first invasion of the Brazilians of S. Paulo:

To the West of the Paraná: Natividad del Acaraig (1619), Encarnacion de Itapúa (1615), and S. Ignacio Guazú (1610).

Between the Paraná and the Uruguay: on the left bank of the former of these rivers, Corpus (1622), and on the right bank of the second, beginning with the most Southerly, Reyes del Yapejú (1626), Concepcion (1620), S. Xavier (1629), and Assumpcion del Acaraguay or Acarana (1630). This last was the nearest mission to the Pepiry that the Jesuits had. It will be treated of later on.

To the East of the Uruguay: San Nicolas (1626) on the Piratiny; Candelaria de Caázapámini (1627), between the Ijuhy and the Piratiny: and Martyres de Cáaro (1628), on the Ijuhy-Mirim. *Conquest of Guayra and Rio Grande do Sul by the Paulistas.*

In 1630 and 1631 the Paulistas. led by ANTONIO RAPOSO TAVARES and by the sub-leaders FREDERICO DE MELLO, ANTONIO BICUDO, SIMÃO ALVARES. and MANOEL MORATO, attacked and destroyed in the Province of Guayra the missions of S. Miguel, S. Antonio, Jesus Maria, San Pablo, San Xavier, S. Pedro. and Concepcion de los Gualachos. "We have come," said they, "to drive you out of all this region, because these lands are ours and not those of the King of Spain."[1]

Collecting then at Loreto and S. Ignacio Miní the

---

[1] "Venimos a echarlos de toda esta region porque esta tierra es nuestra y no del Rey de España" (MONTOYA, *Conquista Espiritual*, Madrid, 1639. § 35).

fugitive Indians of the other missions, the Jesuits resolved to abandon the Province of Guayra and to settle those Indians on the territory lying between the Paraná and the Uruguay. The transmigration of the 12,000 remaining catechumens was effected in 1631, under the direction of F⁺ Montoya, and as the Caingang or Coroados Indians, masters of the banks of the Iguaçú and of the Uruguay above the Great Falls of those rivers, made a journey overland impossible, it was undertaken by water, down the Paranapanema and the Paraná on seven hundred rafts. With these Indians the missions of Loreto and S. Ignacio-Miní were founded near the left bank of the Paraná to the South of Corpus.

In the year 1632 the Paulistas took Villa Rica and Ciudad Real, and the following year, when they were marching to the mouth of the Iguaçú, the missions of Santa Maria Mayor, near the Great Falls of that river, and that of the Natividad of the Acaraig were hastily evacuated.

From that time (1633) the Paulistas remained masters of all the territory to the East of the Paraná and to the North of the Iguaçú. In the preceding year they had already crossed the Upper Paraná, dislodged the Jesuits from the positions they occupied to the West of the Rio Pardo, in Matto Grosso (missions of Itatines), and had destroyed the Spanish City of Santiago de Jerez, situated on a table-land of the Serra de Amambahy.[1]

---
[1] Map No. 1 A gives the ruins of the first city of Jerez, founded in 1579 on the right bank of the Mbotetey and evacuated shortly afterwards. The second Jerez was founded in 1593 on the right bank of the Mondego, and transferred in 1625 to a table-land of the Serra de Amambahy, then called Llanos de Vaguary. This was the Jerez attacked by the Paulistas in 1632.

In 1631, the Jesuits of Paraguay began to extend their settlements to the East of the Uruguay, where they had, as was said before, three missions. In 1636, there were already fifteen, bounded by the Uruguay on the West, the Ijuhy (then Iiuii) and the Serra Geral on the North, the Ibicuhy (then Ibicuity) and the Jacuhy (Igay) on the South, and the Taquary (at that time Tebicuary) on the East. To the Eastern part of this territory, North of the Jacuhy, the Jesuits gave the name of Province of Tape.

These were the missions, beginning with those most to the East:

On the right bank of the Rio Pardo (at that time Yequí or Rio Verde), San Christoval (1634) and Jesus Maria (1633); on the left bank and near the headwaters of the same river, S. Joaquin (1633). At the Passo (ford) of Jacuhy, left bank of the river of that name, Sant' Ana (1633). Natividad (1632) to the right of the Araricá. Santa Theresa (1633), near the sources of the Jacuhy, not far from the place of the present Brazilian town of Cruz Alta. San Carlos de Caápí (1631), at the headwaters of the Ijuhy Guaçú. Apostoles de Caázapáguaçú (1631), on the right bank of the Ijuhy Mirim. Martyres de Caáro (1628) and Candelaria de Caázapáminí (1627) between the Ijuhy and the Piratiny. San Nicolas (1626) on the left bank and near the mouth of the Piratiny on the Uruguay. Santo Thomé (1633) on the right bank of the Itú (then Tibiquaci), an affluent of the Ibicuhy. And S. José de Itaquatiá (1633), S. Miguel (1632) and SS. Cosme-y-Damian (1634), to the North of the Ibicuhy.

All these settlements were taken by the Paulistas,

under the command of Raposo Tavares, or abandoned by the Jesuits and their Indians, after stubborn fights which took place at Jesus Maria and S. Christoval in 1636, and at Caáro, Caázapáguaçú, Caázapáminí and S. Nicolas, in 1638. The Jesuits led to the West of the Uruguay the Indians who were able to escape from the disaster, incorporating them with those of the old missions they maintained there, or forming others which received the names of those that had just been destroyed. It was then that, between the Uruguay and the Paraná, the missions of Santo Thomé, Apostoles, San Carlos, S. José, Candelaria, Martyres, S. Cosme, Sant' Ana, S. Nicolas, and S. Miguel were established.

That of Assumpcion, founded in 1630 on the right bank of the Uruguay and of the Acaraguay or Acarana,[1] was transferred in 1637 to the mouth of the Mbororé,[2] because the former position seemed to the Jesuits much exposed to the attacks of the Paulistas, who freely crossed the territory now contested, then known as Ibituruna, according to the old ruttiers of the same Paulistas.

The Caingangs or Coronados Indians who inhabited that territory and the extensive forests South of the Uruguay, to the East of the Great Falls, were irreconcilable enemies of the Guaranys, and did not allow them or the Spanish Jesuits to approach, while they allowed the Paulistas a free passage and even aided them in their attacks against the missions.

The Guaranys of Paraguay and the Tupys of Brazil

---
[1] G 7 on Map No. 29 A (Vol. VI.).
[2] H 7 on same Map.

spoke, and all speak, the *Abañeenga* language ("the language of men"), named by the Portuguese—general language of the Brazilians,—but better known at the present day by the name of *guarany* given to it by the Jesuits of Paraguay. The Caingangs or Coroados, improperly named Tupys by the Jesuits of Paraguay and by the Spaniards, speak a very different language from the Abañeenga, and are included in the group of the Crens or Guerengs, according to the classification of MARTIUS, accepted by all anthropologists.[1] That accounts for the geographical names of the region to the East of the Pepiry-Guaçú and Santo Antonio from Campo Eré to the East of the Chopim and Chapecó.

From that territory, now contested, started, in March, 1641, going down the Uruguay in three hundred canoes, the expedition which, according to the chroniclers of the Society of Jesus, was composed of 400 Paulistas and 2700 Indian allies, and was routed in the attack on Mbororé, where the Jesuits awaited it with an army of 4000 Guaranys.[2] But, notwithstanding their real or supposed victory, the Indians of the mission of Assumption of Mbororé, immediately abandoned that place, as they had already abandoned the Acaraguay, and went to incorporate themselves with those of the mission of Yapejú, the most Southern of the missions of the Uruguay. In 1657 they left Yapejú to found the village of La Cruz, a little to the South of the mouth of the Aguapey.

The Brazilians of S. Paulo in the territory now contested.

---

[1] MARTIUS, *Beiträge zur Ethnographie und Sprachenkunde Amerika's zumal Brasiliens*, Leipzig, 1867, 2 vols. in 8°; and RIO-BRANCO and ZABOROWSKI, *L'Anthropologie*, in *Le Brésil*, by E. LEVASSEUR, *Membre de l'Institut*. . . . Extrait de la Grande Encyclopédie, Paris, 1889, 1 vol. in fol.
[2] SCHIRMBECK, *Messis Paraquariensis*, Munich, 1649, p. 4; TECHO, *Hist. Prov. Paraquariæ*, Lib. XIII., § 7.

In the same year as that of the fight of Mbororó, the Jesuits of the Missions between the Paraná and Uruguay went, with their Indians, to attack two forts occupied by the Paulistas, one on the Tabaty, the other on the Apitereby.

Intrenchment of the Paulistas on the Apitereby.

The Tabaty, upon which the mission of S. Xavier was formerly situated, is the affluent of the left bank of the Uruguay to which the Jesuits gave the name of Yaguarape in their maps of 1722 and 1732, and which, in 1759, according to the Portuguese and Spanish demarcators, was known as the Itapuã. It now bears the name of Camandahy.[1]

The river which the Jesuits then called Apitereby, as has already been shown, was the first above the Salto Grande (Great Falls), that is to say, the one the Paulistas knew as the Pequiry or Pepiry. The Jesuits applied this last name to the Mandiy-Guaçú of 1759, now Soberbio,[2] below the same Salto Grande.

But whether the entrenchment referred to was on the old and supposed Apitereby of the Jesuits, or on the small river to the East which retains that name to the present day,[3] the important fact is that in the territory now disputed the Brazilians occupied in 1641 a fortified position, according to Fʳ Lozano, the Chronicler of the Society of Jesus in the Province of Paraguay. He says that the Guaranys of the Missions, after taking the fort of the Tabatí, went to attack that of the Apitereby: "They passed on rapidly to another fort called Apiterebí, and, attacking it, obliged the Mame-

---

[1] H 7 in Map 29 A, Vol. VI.
[2] F 9 in Map 29 A.
[3] F 10 in Map 29 A.

lucos¹ to take to flight, leaving there all they had in the way of provisions, munitions, victuals, and prisoners, and they fled so filled with fear that never from that day to this did they dare to invade the province of Uruguay. . . ."²

In this last statement F^R. LOZANO made a mistake, since he himself relates, in another part of his work, that on March 9, 1652, the Paulistas, divided into four bodies, again attacked the Missions between the rivers Uruguay and Paraná,³ which is confirmed by several chroniclers and some as yet unpublished documents.

The chronicles and accounts, either printed or manuscript, of the Jesuits of Paraguay and those of S. Paulo, in Brazil, testify that shortly after the Spaniards and their missionaries were driven from the Province of Guayra (1630–1632), or,—to speak more precisely,—from 1636 and 1638, all the territory bounded on the East by the Paraná and on the South by the Uruguay, was under the sway of the Paulistas. After 1638 they freely overran all the lands stretching to the South and East of the Uruguay, where they were only twice attacked: the first time in 1639, at

¹ In Brazil the name of *mamelucos* is given to half castes, resulting from the crossing of the Caucasian and American races. The name is a corruption of *membyruca*, which means child of an Indian mother. These mamelucos were always very numerous in the expeditions from S. Paulo.

The expeditions had the name of *bandeira* (plural, *bandeiras*), and the men composing them, that of *bandeirantes* (singular, *bandeirante*).

² *Historia de la Conquista del Paraguay, Rio de la Plata y Tucuman*, *written by* FR. PEDRO LOZANO, of the Society of Jesus. Concluded in 1745, it was only printed at Buenos Aires in 1874 by D. ANDRÉS LAMAS, making 3 vols., large 8º. The passage quoted is from Chap. XVI., Lib. III., of Vol. III., p. 430.

³ LOZANO, Chap. XIII., Lib. III. of Vol. II., p.234 ; *Lettres Édifiantes*, Vol. XXI., year 1734, p. 368 ; CHARLEVOIX, *Histoire du Paraguay*, Paris, 1756, 3 vol. 4º, Vol. II., p. 127. It is unnecessary to make further quotations.

Caázapámini, between the Ijuhy and the Piratiny[1] and the second in 1641, in the fort of the Tabaty, as was stated already. Of the second of these fights the chronicles of S. Paulo made no mention. After the first (January 19, 1639), it is known that both sides declared themselves victorious. The Paulistas were led by ANTONIO BICUDO, and the Spaniards and Guaranys by the Governor of Paraguay, D. PEDRO LUGO, and by F^R ALFARO, who was killed in the conflict.

An old Paulista itinerary, preserved to this day and quoted by VARNHAGEN, VISCOUNT DE PORTO-SEGURO,[2] speaks of the mountain range of Bituruna, "which ends in the Uruguay," and of the plain that stretches there. VARNHAGEN says that this itinerary is an obvious proof that the ancient Paulistas knew the region called in modern times Campo de Palmas, but this proof, as has just been shown, is not the only one. Ibituruna was, in fact, the name given in the XVIIth century to the region between the Uruguay and the Iguaçú,[3] and the Bituruna mountains of the Paulista itinerary could only be those forming the watershed which slopes to those two rivers. Those elevations of the ground connect themselves to the West of the sources of the Pepiry-Guaçú with others trending from the Great Falls of the Iguaçú to the Great Falls of the Uruguay.

Having reconquered the territories which they believed belonged to them, the Paulistas next occupied themselves chiefly in the discovery and working of the

---

[1] "... in Caasapaminiensem agrum," says TECHO (Lib. XII., § 31). CHARLEVOIX wrote in error Caarupáguazú.

[2] VISCONDE DE PORTO-SEGURO (VARNHAGEN), *Historia Geral do Brazil*, 2 edição, p. 552.

[3] Map No. 1, Vol. V., and No. 1 A, Vol. VI.

gold mines of the interior of Brazil (Minas Geraes and Goyaz) and in the far West (Matto Grosso). The Jesuits were thus able to return to the East bank of the Uruguay, removing thither in 1687 the missions of S. Nicolas and S. Miguel, and creating five others: S. Luis Gonzaga (1687), S. Borja (1690), S. Lorenzo (1691), S. Juan Bautista (1698), and S. Angel (1706).

This last, to the North of the Ijuhy,[1] was the nearest to the territory now contested, but between them lay the extensive forests of the left bank of the Uruguay, inhabited by savages.

After 1706 the Eastern and Northern boundaries of the Spanish occupation in the territory named Misiones never varied. To the South, the forests occupied by the savages closed all communication with the territory now claimed. **Limits of the Spanish Missions, 1706.** To the West and North of that river, S. Xavier, on its right bank,[2] and Corpus, on the left of the river Paraná,[3] continued to be, as they had been since 1641, the most advanced Spanish positions and the nearest to the Brazilian frontier on the Pequiry or Pepiry, afterwards Pepiry-Guaçù. The affluent Mbororé[4] remained the boundary of the Spanish possessions on the Upper Uruguay. Thence, upwards, the Indians of Misiones did not venture overland. In 1759 they still went up in canoes as far as the Itacaray,[5] but in 1788 they no longer went so near the Brazilian frontier in the territory now contested.

All this is affirmed by the Spanish Commissioners

---

[1] I 9 in Map No. 29 A.
[2] H 6, in Map No. 29 A.
[3] F 5, in the same Map.
[4] H 7, *Ibidem*.
[5] F 10, *Ibidem*.

who made the two demarcations under the Treaties of 1750 and 1777.

Two passages of the Spanish *Diary* of the first demarcation, relating to the Mbororé and the Itacaray, have already been transcribed (pages 76 and 77 in this Vol.).

In the *Memoria* of OYÁRVIDE the following may be read in a note taken from the Spanish *Diary* of 1788:

"As far as the Itacaray stream, say the previous demarcators, the Indians came from the Villages for their supply of maté, which they stack and take down on rafts . . . . *Now they no longer go so far* since they make their supplies of the said maté herb nearer the village of San Javier."[1]

And in the *Diary* of 1789:

"At length we arrived at a sufficiently full-flowing river *which the guides called Cebollatí, and from here to the North they no longer know the country*, as it is only from this river to the South that the maté shrubs reach where they are accustomed to come to prepare their supplies. . . ."[2]

This river Cebollaty,[3] an affluent of the left bank of the Uruguay, is the one which at the time of the previous demarcation, in 1759, was known as the Paricay, and in the maps of 1722 and 1732 of the Jesuits, as well as in those of D'ANVILLE, and in the "Map of the the Courts," appears under the name Uruguay-Pitā, below the Great Falls, as already proved.

Until the middle of the XVIIIth century the Jesuits of Misiones maintained on the Uruguay, near the Yaboti or Pepiry-Mini,[4]—above the Itacaray, but to the West of the Great Falls of the Uruguay, and, there-

---
[1] *Memoria* de OYÁRVIDE, in CALVO, *Recueil Complet de Traités*, Vol. X., 74.
[2] Same *Memoria*, in CALVO, Vol. IX., 188.
[3] F 10, in Map No. 29 A.
[4] *Ibidem*.

fore, of the Pepiry or Pequiry,—a post of observation to give notice of the movements of the Brazilians of S. Paulo, or Paulistas.

The fact is confirmed in a passage already quoted from the Diary written by the Spanish Commissioners during the survey of 1759 (page 79 in this Vol.).

When the Spaniards of the second demarcation were unable to find a single guide who knew the Uruguay from the mouth of the Cebollaty, now the river Turvo, upwards—much less the territory now contested between the Uruguay and the Iguaçú,—the MARQUIS DE LORETO, Viceroy of the Spanish Provinces of Rio de la Plata, wrote under date of the 13th November, 1788:

" . . the Royal Instructions direct, that the Surveying Parties shall for this object take guides, if the Portuguese Commissioner has not any, we are to presume that on purpose and for some private end he did not seek them, since from that place he could have more skilful ones than we can, because their Paulistas have navigated the Yguazú as far as its confluence with the Paraná and even a part of the latter, down-stream, as far as Misiones; and by land they have made various explorations through all those regions, which is also confirmed by the existence of the path which you say was found for ascending as far as the Great Falls (Salto Grande) of the Paraná, opened through the woods, a few years ago, by the said Paulistas, who came down to reconnoitre these parts."[1]

---
[1] Letter of the MARQUIS DE LORETO to the Spanish Commissioner DIEGO DE ALVEAR, in CABRER, *Diario de la Segunda Subdivicion de Limites Española* (*Diary of the 2nd Spanish Subdivision of Limits*) Manuscript, Vol. I., p. 611; and in MILITON GONZALEZ, *El Limite Oriental del Territorio de Misiones* (*The Eastern Boundary of the Territory of Misiones*), Vol. II., p 262.

The Manuscript of CABRER, signed by the author, belongs to the Brazilian Foreign Office and is in the keeping of the Brazilian Special Mission at Washington.

The Portuguese and Spanish Commissioners, during the last century, and the Brazilians of the Joint Commission appointed under the Treaty of 1885, found at various points of the disputed territory evident signs of Brazilian domination in the XVIIth century.

In the *Diary* of the first demarcation, the following passage occurs under date of the 6th March, 1759:

"Not far from this second reef, on the bank, an old mortar was found which, from its make, the Paulistas recognized as having belonged to their people, who had probably left it behind in one of their former *maloeas*, *i. e.*, the inroads which they used to make against the Indians of these settlements; and there was also seen a small and very old clearing of trees, which was attributed to the same."

In the Spanish *Diary* of the second demarcation, this passage is found with reference to the encampment of the 11th December, 1789, between the rivulet of Corredeira Comprida to the West, and the mouth of the Chapecó (Pequiri-Guazú of the Argentines) to the East[1]:

". . . and here we slept, on the 11th of December, and we found various potsherds of well baked earthen pots with ornaments, which doubtless must have belonged to the Paulistas when they frequented this river to make their incursions into the settlements of Misiones . . ."[2]

Near the headwaters of the river Sandade, a Western affluent of the Chapecó, and in the longitude of the mouth of this river, are to be found even to this day, in Campo Eré, the so-called Muros, which are evidently the remains of an old fortification. On the summit

---

[1] F 4 in Map No. 25 A, and F 12, in No. 29 A.
[2] Oyárvide, *Memoria* in Calvo, IX., 213.

of a hill a truncated cone is to be seen whose upper part consists of a platform 36 metres in diameter, and whose slope now is 3 metres in height. The First Brazilian Commissioner personally explored the place in 1887, and ordered excavations to be made in the neighborhood, which revealed around that position an entrenchment formed of a double circular palisade covered with earth.

Thus, then, besides the fort of the Pepiry, which, at first, the Jesuits called Apiteriby, the Paulistas had in this territory another entrenched encampment.

The Indians of Brazil, Paraguay, and the River Plate did not construct buildings of earth or stone. Their villages were protected only by a circular palisade. Only at the mouth of the Amazonas and on the island of Marajó which, in pre-Columbian times, was inhabited by a people of more advanced civilization, some artificial mounds are found, which served as burying-places.

The ancient fortifications referred to cannot be attributed to the Spaniards or to the Jesuits of the Province of Paraguay. The latter never had missions or settlements in that territory, and always kept far away from it, only maintaining in its neighborhood the post which has been mentioned to watch the Paulistas. The way followed in the migration of 1631 shows the care with which the Missionaries avoided crossing this territory. Ten years later, when they went to attack the fort of the Paulistas on the Pepiry, the Guaranys of Misiones were momentarily on the frontier of Brazil. *The Spaniards, however, never trod the territory now contested or its neighborhood except on the*

> The Spaniards never trod the territory now contested.

two occasions when they went with the Portuguese to make the demarcation under the Treaties of 1750 and 1777.

There is no document whatever by which the presence of other Spaniards in this territory during the three centuries comprising the colonial period can be proved.

In some modern Spanish and Argentine maps, the course is erroneously marked along the river Iguaçú, of the famed Spanish expedition led by ALVAR NUÑEZ CABEZA DE VACA, "Adelantado" and Governor of the Rio de la Plata, which, setting out at the end of 1541 from the coast of Santa Catharina, continued by land as far as the city of Asuncion of Paraguay, and reached its destination in the following year.

Map VI. of the *Atlas de la Confédération Argentine* by MARTIN DE MOUSSY marks this course along the Northern bank of the Iguaçú; the *Carta Geographica de la Provincia de Corrientes*, dated 1865,[1] and the Map constructed in 1802 by CABRER,[2] represent it by the South bank, passing, therefore, through the disputed territory. But in the Map by CABRER itself there is a note of the author exactly describing the itinerary.

Lately, wishing to correct the error of a Brazilian writer who supposed that CABEZA DE VACA had passed along the old Pequiry or Pepiry, the affluent of the Uruguay, DR. ZEBALLOS endeavored to show that, according to the direction of the march, the Spanish expedition could only have crossed the Chapecó or Pequiri-Guazú to reach the river Iguaçú.

---

[1] Reproduced under No. 24 A, Vol. VI.

[2] The original manuscript belonging to the Brazilian Department of Foreign Affairs is in the keeping of the Brazilian Special Mission at Washington.

The distinguished Argentine writer said:
"If on the official Map of the disputed Misiones that route is traced in a W.N.W. direction it will take us to the Iguazú by cutting the Pepiry-Guazú (which the Argentines maintain); whilst drawing it from the Pequiry claimed by the Brazilians, below the Uruguay-Pitá, it leads perforce to the river Paraná, without reaching the Iguazú, unless the march of the expedition is changed to the North. Therefore the river Pequiry which ALVAR NUÑEZ crossed was that to the East, *i. e.*, that of the Argentines: and it is proved by the very quotation of that famous Adelantado, brought forward by the BARON DE CAPANEMA that, in 1541, the Spaniards and the Portuguese knew as the Pequiry the river which empties itself into the Uruguay above the Uruguay-Pitá. . . ."[1]

The contending parties in this discussion, both the Brazilian and the Argentine, made a mistake in confusing two rivers of the same name: one the Pequiry, an affluent of the left bank of the Paraná, which was the river crossed by CABEZA DE VACA, and the other the affluent of the right bank of the Uruguay, which bore that name, but of which nothing was known when the expedition in question took place.

It is easy to show that those Spaniards did not tread any part of the territory now disputed and, therefore, that they could not have seen either the Chapecó, as DR. ZEBALLOS asserts, or the Pepiry-Guaçú, formerly Pepiry or Pequiry, as was supposed by the Brazilian contestant. It is sufficient to peruse Chapters VI. to

---

[1] *Misiones*, § VI., articles written and signed by DR. ESTANISLAO S. ZEBALLOS, published in the *Prensa* of Buenos-Ayres (April, 1892), and afterwards in a pamphlet edited by PEUSER.

XI. of the *Comentarios*, written by Pero Hernandez, secretary to the Governor Cabeza de Vaca.[1] It is seen there that the expedition started from the river Ytabucú, now Itapucú, on the littoral of Santa Catharina, ascended the maritime range of mountains named Serra do Mar, went through the plains of the tableland of Curityba, crossed over from the left to the right bank of the Iguaçú, thence over the Tibagy (Tibagi, Chapter VII.) and followed on by the left bank of this affluent of the Paranapanema in the direction of N.N.W. Afterwards it crossed several rivers, among them *the Pequiry, an affluent of the Paraná*, and going in a Southerly direction, parallel to the course of the latter river, reached the right bank of the Iguaçú immediately above its Salto Grande (Great Falls). Then it came down the Iguaçú as far as its confluence with the Paraná, crossed this river and proceeded across the Paraguay.

All the Spanish historians who have spoken of this expedition have perfectly interpreted the *Comentarios* of Pero Hernandez. The most ancient chronicler of Paraguay and the River Plate, Rui Diaz de Guzman, also describes it exactly, by the Atibajiva (the *Comentarios* say Tibagí), Ubay (Ivahy), Pequiry, and afterwards along the Paraná, in a Southerly direction.[2] The

---

[1] *Comentarios de Alvar Nuñez cabeça de vaca adelantado y gouernador de la prouincia del Rio de la Plata. Scriptos por Pero Hernandez scriuano y secretario de la prouincia. . . . Valladolid, 1555 in 4º.*

The Congressional Library at Washington has this first edition and a later one. There is also a French translation published in 1837 by Ternaux Compans.

[2] *Historia Argentina del descubrimiento, poblacion y conquista de las Provincias del Rio de la Plata*, by Rui Diaz de Guzman (Lib. II., Cap. I.), written and concluded at Charcas in 1612, and printed by Angelis in his *Colleccion de Obras y Documentos relativos á la Historia antigua y moderna de las Provs. del Rio de la Plata*, Vol. I., Buenos-Aires, 1836.

Dutch and French cartographers of the XVIth and XVIIth centuries marked at once on their maps of Paraguay the rivers and settlements of Indians and the principal geographical and ethnographical names mentioned by PERO HERNANDEZ.[1]

The same may be said of all the modern historians who have treated of this expedition after reading the *Comentarios* written under the supervision of CABEZA DE VACA, which are the first and only incontestable source of information. Among these is DR LUIS DOMINGUEZ, now Envoy Extraordinary and Minister Plenipotentiary of the Argentine Republic in London.[2]

The illustrious author of the pamphlet *Misiones* was in error when he supposed he had met with a Spanish discoverer of the territory now contested, and when he asserted that in 1541 the Portuguese and Spanish knew under the name of river "Pequiry, the one which empties itself above the Uruguay-Pitá."

The Spanish expedition of 1541 never even saw that territory, and in the *Comentarios* themselves mention is made of the Portuguese who ten years before passed there on their way down the Iguaçú, when, by order of MARTIN AFFONSO DE SOUZA, commander of the Portuguese Squadron in Brazilian waters, they went to explore the interior.

LOZANO stated in 1745 that no Spaniards ever saw the Pepiry,[3] and the Pepiry of LOZANO and the

---

[1] Among others the maps of Paraguay by JODOCUS HONDIUS, J. JANSSONIUS, and G. BLAEU, in which these names are met, quoted for the first time in the *Comentarios*:—Ytabuca (Ytabucû in the *Comentarios*), Anniriri (Añiriri), Cipopay (Cipoyay), Tocanguazu (Tocanguaçú), Tibagí, Taquarí, Abangobí, Tocanguzir (Tocangucir), in latitude 24° 30' according to the *Comentarios*, Piquerí affluent of the Paraná, and the river Yguaçú (Iguaçú), with its Salto (Falls).

[2] *Historia Argentina* by LUIS L. DOMINGUEZ, 4th Edition, Buenos-Aires 1870, p. 58.

[3] *Hist. de la Conquista del Paraguay*, Lib. I., Cap. 2.

Jesuits was a river in the present Argentine territory of Misiones.

The territory now contested was indisputably discovered by Brazilians, and was always an integral part of Brazil. Evidence of its administrative occupation will be given further on.

X.

The Argentine claim to the Brazilian territory to the East of the Pepiry-Guaçú and the Santo Antonio is of very recent date.

First negotiation for a Treaty of Limits. In 1857, on the initiative of the Brazilian Government, the first negotiations for a Treaty of Limits between the two countries were opened at the City of Paraná (Entre Rios), which was the provisional capital of the Argentine Confederation.

The Conferences commenced at the end of October of that year, Councillor Paranhos, afterwards Viscount de Rio-Branco, being the Plenipotentiary of Brazil, while the Plenipotentiaries of the Argentine Confederation were the Minister of the Interior, D.ʀ Santiago Derqui, and the Minister for Foreign Affairs, D.ʀ Bernabé Lopez.

On the 26th November the Brazilian Minister presented a Memorandum, in which he stated briefly the principles defended by the Brazilian Government in the settlement of boundaries with States of Spanish origin, the divergence which had occurred between the Commissioners of Portugal and Spain in the demarcation made under the Treaty of 1777, and the right of Brazil to the line of the Pepiry-Guaçú and Santo Antonio located in 1759 and 1760.

On the 14th December of the same year, 1857, the Plenipotentiaries signed a Treaty, whose first articles described the frontier in the following manner: *Treaty of 1857.*

"ART. 1.—The two High Contracting Parties, having agreed in defining their respective limits, concur in declaring and recognizing as the frontier of Brazil and the Argentine Confederation between the Rivers Uruguay and Paraná, that which is specified below:

"The territory of the Empire of Brazil is separated from that of the Argentine Confederation by the river Uruguay, the whole of the right or Western bank belonging to the Confederation, and the left or Eastern bank to Brazil, from the mouth of the affluent Quarahim to that of the Pepiry-Guaçú where the Brazilian possessions occupy both banks of the river Uruguay.

"The boundary line follows along the waters of the Pepiry-Guaçú up to its principal source; from this it continues, along the highest ground, to the principal headwaters of the Santo Antonio, and, by this river, as far as its entry into the Iguaçú or Rio Grande de Curitiba, and by this as far as its confluence with the Paraná.

"The land which the rivers Pepiri-Guaçú, Santo Antonio, and Iguaçú separate belongs to Brazil on the Eastern side, and, on the Western side, to the Argentine Confederation, the waters of the two first mentioned rivers being the common property of the two nations, throughout their course, and those of the Iguaçú only from the confluence of the Santo Antonio to the Paraná.

"ART. 2.—The two High Contracting Parties declare, in order to avoid any doubt, although the designations of Article 1 are now well known, that the rivers Pepiri-

Guaçú and Santo Antonio mentioned in the said Article are the same which were surveyed in 1759 by the Delimitation Commissioners under the Treaty of the 13th of January, 1750, concluded between Portugal and Spain."

This Treaty was discussed and approved by the Argentine Senate at a secret sitting the 28th July, 1858, and by the Chamber of Deputies, at a secret sitting, also, on the 24th September of the same year.

The Treaty of 1857 approved by the Argentine Congress.

Two days later the Law of Approbation was promulgated in the following terms:

"The Senate and the Chamber of Deputies of the Argentine Confederation, assembled in Congress, grant their sanction and the force of Law to the following:

"Art. 1.—The provisions contained in the five Articles of the Treaty of Limits concluded between the National Executive Power and His Majesty the Emperor of Brazil, through their respective Plenipotentiaries, in this Capital on the 14th of December of the year last passed, one thousand eight hundred and fifty-seven, are approved.

"Art. 2.—It is understood that the rivers Pepirí Guazú and San Antonio, which are determined as the boundaries in Article 1 of the Treaty, are those lying more to the East, bearing those names, as shown by the operation referred to in Article 2 of the same.

"Art. 3.—This shall be communicated to the Executive Power.

"Hall of Sessions of the Congress at Paraná, the provisional Capital of the Argentine Nation, the twenty-fourth day of the month of September one thousand eight hundred and fifty-eight.

" PASCUAL ECHAGUE.—CARLOS M. SARAVIA, *Secretary*.
—MATEO LUQUE.—BENJAMIN DE IGARZABAL, *Secretary*.
" Department of Foreign Affairs.—Paraná, 26th September, 1858.
" The above shall be observed as a Law and published.
" URQUIZA.
" BERNABÉ LOPEZ."[1]

The Argentine Government allowed the second period, which it had asked by a Note of September 10, 1858, for the exchange of the ratifications of the Treaty, to expire. On the 14th of June of the following year, the Minister for Foreign Affairs, BEDOYA, informed the Brazilian Legation at Paraná that the Argentine Government had resolved to defer that formality until after the conclusion of the contest with the Province of Buenos-Aires:

Discussion relating to the exchange of ratifications.

" His Excellency the Vice-President[2] has directed me to communicate to Your Excellency that, in order that the ratification of the pending Treaties on Extradition and Limits may have the favorable termination which the Government of the Confederation earnestly desires, he thinks it expedient to abstain from opening now a new negotiation for the indispensable extension of the time in which this act is to take place, delaying it until the settlement of the Buenos-Aires question."

Another passage of the same Note explains the motive for this adjournment *sine die:*

---

[1] Transcribed in Vol. II. of this Statement (page 227) from the *Memoria del Ministerio de Relaciones Exteriores*, Buenos-Aires, 1892, p. 27 (" Report of the Department of Foreign Affairs, 1892 ").

[2] SALVADOR MARIA DEL CARRIL, in the absence of the President, General URQUIZA.

"This unfavorable result against which the Government desires to provide," said the Minister of Foreign Affairs, "will present itself to Your Excellency with a greater degree of probability, if you remember the serious opposition which the Government met with in the Chambers, notwithstanding the fact that the discussion was carried on under the impression that the sanction of those Treaties implied the condition that the Government of His Imperial Majesty would accord to that of the Confederation its moral and material support, in order to bring about the re-incorporation of Buenos-Aires into the bosom of the Nation."

<small>Why the Treaty of 1857 was not ratified.</small>

By this delay, it was hoped to bring about a Brazilian intervention into the internal affairs of the Confederation with the object of aiding General URQUIZA to subjugate the Province of Buenos-Aires by force of arms. The Brazilian Government, however, preferred to hold entirely aloof from this civil war.

Councillor J. M. DO AMARAL, the Brazilian Minister at Paraná, replied on the 1st August to the Argentine Note of 14th June, 1859.

"The Treaty of Limits," he said, "recognizes the boundary designated both by the *uti possidetis* of the two countries and by the former stipulations between Portugal and Spain.

"It is the same divisional line which is drawn on the chorographical map of the Confederation, lately published by order of the Argentine Government.

. . . .

"The Imperial Government, as well as the undersigned, deeply regret that agreements of such a nature, initiated so long since, and concluded when internal peace still subsisted in the Argentine Confederation, should seem to the Argentine Congress the preliminaries of stipulations which were entirely alien from the subject. This presumption, however, if perchance it may have influenced some persons, could not do so more completely than the justice of the very acts which it was sought to approve, the permanent interests they guaranteed, and the importance of good relations between Brazil and the Argentine Confederation.

" His Majesty's Government would therefore gladly believe that the vote of Congress was dictated by an accurate appreciation of those agreements, and that, if any external influence has been brought to bear upon its mind, it was the opinion of the Supreme Government of the Confederation, so amicably expressed in the following words of the Message of 1st May of last year:

" The Government of His Majesty the Emperor of
" Brazil have given us an unequivocal proof of their de-
" sire to draw closer the bonds which unite the Empire
" and the Argentine Confederation. Both Governments,
" sharing these enlightened and patriotic views, have
" agreed upon some conventions which frontier inter-
" course, reciprocal trade, and fluvial navigation required
" in their mutual interest and in that of other nations.

" To this end a Special Mission was sent to this City
" and, owing to the good disposition of both Govern-
" ments and to the merits of their worthy Plenipoten-
" tiaries, provision was made for the necessity both
" countries felt of Treaties finally determining their re-
" spective boundaries, assuring the extradition of crim-
" inals, and applying to the great affluents of the River
" Plate the principles by which fluvial navigation is
" regulated in Europe."

"Approved as these conventions have been by the Government and Congress of the Confederation, what is wanting to give them full effect? Only the exchange of ratifications by the Contracting Parties.

"The time fixed for this formality has expired, and this is the obstacle the Argentine Government sees to the conclusion of so solemn and necessary agreements.

"The undersigned begs, in the name of his Government, that the Government of the Confederation will be pleased to reconsider its decision.

"The time for the exchange of the ratifications of a Treaty is a transitory and eventual provision. Its strict observance, as well as its modification, is an act of mere execution which, however, does not depend on the Legislative Power. Since the two contracting Governments are agreed in this respect, nothing more is necessary, and neither of them can with justice refuse to carry out what was agreed upon and is approved by the competent Powers, merely because the time determined for the exchange of the instruments of that approbation has elapsed.

"As a rule, international acts do not begin to be effective before the exchange of ratifications, but the time determined for this formality is not a matter for legislation, it is an act which belongs by its nature and by universal custom to the Executive Power. . . ."

Notwithstanding the fact that the Treaty of 1857 remained of no effect for the want of the formality of the exchange of ratifications, it is never-

Importance of the Treaty of 1857, although it did not become effective.

theless a document of the greatest historical importance in the study of this case, inasmuch as it proves that the Argentine Government in concluding that agreement, and the Argentine Congress in approving it, expressly recognized, at that date, the right of Brazil to the boundary of Santo Antonio, Pepiry-Guaçú, and Uruguay, a right already recognized tacitly, seeing that from 1810 to 1858,—during 48 years,—the Argentine Government never formulated any claim or protest of any sort manifesting that it had any pretensions to more Easterly boundaries than those.

The debate in the two Chambers of the Argentine Congress cannot be known, because it was held in secret sittings at which stenographers were not present. A newspaper, *El Nacional Argentino*, of Paraná, published an abridged and incorrect report of the discussion in the Chamber of Deputies. Its discussion in the Argen- tine Congress.

What is known from that summary is that there was in the Chamber a Report of the Committee on Foreign Affairs recommending the rejection of the Treaty ; and that the Chamber, having heard the Minister for Foreign Affairs, rejected the Report and approved the proposal of the Senate sanctioning the same Treaty. Examination of the law of Congress ap- proving the Treaty of 1857. It is known, moreover, from the correspondence regarding the term for the exchange of ratifications, that both the Brazilian and the Argentine Governments considered the agreement as fully approved, although it is now sought to demonstrate that a clause of Article 2 of the Approbatory Law modified the agreed boundary, substituting for the rivers Pepiry-Guaçú and S. Antonio two others more to the East. If such a substitution of rivers could have resulted from the votes of the two Chambers, the Treaty would not have been approved. The Argentine Government would not have been able to say, in that case, as it said in the Note of September 10, 1858, that the Treaty of Limits had passed from the Senate to the Chamber of Representatives; nor would it, in another Note of June 14, 1859, have alluded to the approval of this Treaty and of the Treaty of Extradition by the two Houses of Congress, merely deferring the arrangement of a time for the exchange of ratifications till the close of the campaign against the Province of Buenos-Aires.

The *Memoria* (Report) presented in 1892 to the Argentine Congress by the Minister of Foreign Affairs, attached great importance to the clause contained in Article 2 of the Law of September 26, 1858. The Deputy GUTIERREZ, who opposed that Treaty, had said, in the meantime, and with much reason, during the sitting of the 24th September, that this Article was drawn up "in terms that meant nothing."

Reply to an explanation of 1892.

Art. 2 of the Approbatory Law says:

"It is understood that the rivers Pepiri-Guazú and San Antonio which are designated as boundaries in the 1st Article of the Treaty, *are those lying more to the East, bearing those names, as shown by the operation referred to in Article 2 of the same.*"

The operation referred to in Article 2 of the Treaty of 1857 is the survey of 1759, and the two rivers then surveyed and demarcated are indisputably the Pepiry-Guaçú and the Santó Antonio defended as its boundary by Brazil. This is admitted by the Argentine Government, and was acknowledged in their Diaries by the Spanish Commissioners of the Second Survey. In the Map by CABRER, and in other Spanish maps of the beginning of this century, the Pepiry-

Guaçú is designated as the "*Pepiry-Guazú of the previous surveyors.*"

To the East of the Pepiry-Guaçú and of the S. Antonio there are no rivers bearing those names. There are the two rivers discovered in 1788 and 1791. To the last the Spanish Commissioners never gave any other name than San Antonio Guazú, thus distinguishing it from the San Antonio of 1759. The river of 1788 they wished to call Pepirí-Guazú or Pepiry-Guazú (Pepiry-Guaçú), saying that the one which had borne that name since 1759 and 1760 was not the true river designated in the Treaty of 1750; but in the end they decided to adopt the name of Pequirí-Guazú, as may be seen in the *Memoria* of OYÁRVIDE, and in the three inscriptions that Spanish Commissioner left in different places when he surveyed its course.[1] The Argentine Government is perfectly acquainted with this distinction of names and does not dispute it, as an examination of the Treaties of 1885 and 1889 will show.

The Portuguese and Spanish Commissioners who, in 1759 and 1760, made the survey under the Treaty of 1750, did not reach as far as the rivers of the present Argentine pretension.

---
[1] "*Inveni quem diligit et Pequirí-Guazú, 12 Diciembre 1789*" (*Memoria* by OYÁRVIDE in C. CALVO, *Recueil Historique complet des Traités . . . de tous les États compris entre le Golfe du Mexique et le Cap de Horn*, Vol. IX., 215).

"*Tenui eum ; nec dimittam Pequirí-Guazú. 10 de Enero 1790*" (IX., 272).

"*Fundamenta ejus in montibus sanctis, Piquirí-Guazú, 14 Junii 1791*" (X., 11).

At the mouth of the Pepiry-Guaçú (not Pequirí-Guazú), the boundary of Brazil, the Spanish Geographer GUNDIN had left, on the 13th August, 1788, the following inscription on a plate of copper ordered by the Spanish Commissioner VARELA Y ULLOA :

"*Hucusque auxiliatus est nobis Deus. Pepirí-Guazú, 1788*" (Letters of the 1st Portuguese Commissioner VEIGA CABRAL, of the 22nd January, 1789, to the 1st Spanish Commissioner, and of the 20th July, 1790, to the Viceroy of Buenos-Aires.)

An examination of the cartographical documents anterior to 1750 showed that all of them, with the single exception of the manuscript Map of 1749 which the Plenipotentiaries then used for the tracing and description of the divisional line, represented the Pepiry below and to the West of the Salto Grande (Great Falls) of the Uruguay. In the Map of 1749, commonly called "Map of the Courts," the Pepiry or Pequiry occupies a more Easterly position, discharging itself at the right bank of the Uruguay, just above the Salto Grande.

If Article 2 of the Argentine Law of the 26th September, 1858, expressed anything, it can have no other interpretation than that which has just been given, the only one that is satisfactory and reconcilable with the survey of 1759, in which not the former Western Pepiry of the Jesuits, below the Salto, was demarcated, but the more Easterly, above the same Salto, and very near it.

It is not to be wondered, therefore, that the Brazilian Government should have insisted in 1859 on the exchange of ratifications, inasmuch as it considered, as also did the Argentine Government, that the Treaty of 1857 was fully approved by the representatives of the Argentine Nation assembled in Congress.

From 1859 to 1876 negotiations upon the subject were not renewed. The first three years of that period were marked by great political commotions in the River Plate. War broke out twice between the Confederation and the Province of Buenos-Aires; the Constitution of the Republic was amended; the Federalists were vanquished; the Government of Paraná disappeared; and

From 1859 to 1876.

the Argentine Nation could at length bring about its unification under the enlightened leadership of President MITRE.

The former Confederation then assumed the name of Argentine Republic, and the City of Buenos-Aires again became the capital of the Republic after its political reorganization.

Immediately afterwards grave disturbances arose in Uruguay, and a deplorable conflict took place between Brazil and the Government of Montevideo, which served as a pretext for the intervention of the Dictator of Paraguay, Marshal SOLANO LOPEZ. The Paraguayan armies invaded the Brazilian Province of Matto Grosso at the end of 1864, and, the following year, the Argentine Province of Corrientes.

War of Paraguay.

In consequence of that aggression, Brazil, the Argentine Republic, and that of Uruguay signed the Treaty of Alliance of May 1, 1865.

The war against the Dictator of Paraguay only came to an end in 1870.

During the war, the Paraguayans evacuated the positions they held South of the Paraná in the disputed territory of Misiones, and from 1865 to 1869 that territory was covered and protected solely by a division of the Brazilian National Guard.

It was also under the shadow of the Brazilian military occupation that, after 1866, the town which now bears the name of Posadas and has the rank of capital of the Argentine Territory of Misiones, began to be formed.

After the overthrow of the dictatorship of SOLANO LOPEZ, the Brazilian Government easily settled with the Republic of Paraguay, by the Treaty of January 9,

1872, the boundary question between the two countries, observing, as always, the rule of the colonial *uti possidetis*, which was much more advantageous to Paraguay than to Brazil.

The Argentine Republic, however, encountered great difficulties before it came to an agreement with the new Paraguayan Government upon the boundary question, because it claimed not only the territory of Misiones, but also the island of Atajo, at the confluence of the rivers Paraná and Paraguay, and all the vast region named Chaco, which stretches to the West of the river Paraguay. Only after strong resistance, and long and complicated negotiations, did the Paraguayan Government agree, by the Treaty of 3d February, 1876, to renounce all those territories; and it yielded only after obtaining a stipulation that its right to the Northern part of the Chaco should be submitted, as it was, to the Arbitration of the President of the United States of America.

Misiones and the Treaty of 1876 between the Argentine Republic and Paraguay.

Brazil can say that it contributed powerfully to the fact that the territory of Misiones, between the Paraná and the Uruguay, definitely belonged to the Argentine Republic. It contributed to this by occupying and protecting the territory during the war, by taking upon itself the greater part of the sacrifices in blood and money that the Triple Alliance had to bear, and by rendering to its Ally, after the peace, all the good offices it could in order that this boundary question should have a friendly and satisfactory solution.

It is not improper to say in this discussion that if Paraguay recognized as a boundary the line of the Paraná, renouncing the territory of Misiones, whose

Eastern boundary is the object of the present Arbitration, it did so in great part, yielding to the counsels of Brazil.

As soon as the boundary questions between the Argentine Republic and Paraguay were adjusted, the BARON DE AGUIAR DE ANDRADA, Envoy Extraordinary and Minister Plenipotentiary of Brazil, on a Special Mission, endeavored to reopen the negotiation that was interrupted in 1859, and, obeying the instructions he had received from the BARON DE COTEGIPE, President of the Council and Minister for Foreign Affairs, he showed the Argentine Government how desirable it was that Brazil and the Argentine Republic should define their boundaries by a Treaty, and suggested as a draft of the new Treaty that of 1857.

Negotiation between Brazil and the Argentine Republic in 1876.

On the 28th March, 1876, DR. IRIGOYEN, Minister for Foreign Affairs of the Argentine Republic, made the following proposal :

" I think that Article 1st of the Treaty of 1857 can be accepted in the new Treaty.

" Article 2 has reference to the survey of 1759 and, if am not mistaken, that survey had no definite result, because it was necessary to appoint new Commissions or Surveying Parties.

" In order to avoid every anticipated difficulty upon this point, I think that reference to the survey of 1759 should be omitted, and it should be provided that the rivers mentioned in Article 1 shall be defined in the light of the works, explorations, and surveys carried out last century by order of the Governments of Spain and Portugal.

" I also believe that in order to assure the definite

termination of the discussion on limits, we must agree that in the event of disagreement between the Commissioners, they shall refer to their Governments; and, if these do not come to an amicable compromise upon the controverted points, the disagreement shall be submitted to the arbitral award of a friendly Government.

"These are the suggestions I can offer to Your Excellency in compliance with your esteemed invitation. As they do not in any essential point modify the Treaty of 1857, I have considered that the instructions of Your Excellency would be sufficient."

This proposal not having been accepted, DR. IRIGOYEN proposed one of the three following forms for Article 2 of the new Treaty:

"*1st Form*.—Both Governments will appoint Commissioners who shall proceed to the survey of the boundary line laid down, for which operation they shall bear in mind all the works, explorations, and surveys previously carried out by order of the Governments of Spain and Portugal.

"*2nd Form*.—The Commissioners shall bear in mind the Instructions issued by the Governments of Spain and Portugal for the surveys carried out during last century.

"*3d Form*.—The Commissioners shall proceed to the survey of the boundaries defined at the end of . . . and keeping in view the historical precedents of this negotiation."

The Brazilian Minister opposed those proposals, which settled nothing, and insisted that the boundary line should be clearly defined, either with reference to the survey of 1759, or by determining the position of the rivers Pepiry-Guaçú and Santo Antonio.

"SR. IRIGOYEN informed me," the same Minister said,[1] "that he was not inclined to object to the divisional line of the Pepiry-Guaçú and Santo Antonio surveyed in the year 1759 . . . He suggested to me . . . an addition to either of the forms previously mentioned; for example: that the Commissioners should keep in view for the new survey especially the work done by *common accord* between the former Portuguese and Spanish surveyors, alluding in the expression—common accord—to the survey of 1759."

The Brazilian Government decided that its representative should make the following proposal:

"To eliminate Article 2 of the Treaty of December 14, 1857, and to draw up Article 3, which will become the 2d, in the following terms:

"After the ratification of the present Treaty, the two High Contracting Parties will each appoint a Commissioner to proceed by common accord, within the shortest possible term, to survey the said rivers Pepiry-Guaçú and Santo Antonio as provided by Article 1, which is based on the principle of *uti possidetis*."

In a letter of 21st August, DR. IRIGOYEN refused the proposal in the following terms:

"I accept the elimination of Article 2 of the Treaty of 1857. There would be no objection to the addition to Article 3, which will become the 2^d, of the phrase— 'which is based on the principle of *uti possidetis*'—if an easy application of it were found in treating of two nations whose rights are derived from others who previously defined their boundaries by clear and precise international treaties.

---

[1] Report of the 16th November, 1877, made by the Brazilian Plenipotentiary BARON DE AGUIAR DE ANDRADA, and sent on that date from Montevideo to the Minister for Foreign Affairs of Brazil.

" I consider that the *uti possidetis* is quite properly pleaded between American States which have been dependencies of one dominion and have undefined or confused boundaries. The territorial divisions in that case were dependent on one common jurisdiction and were defined by administrative acts which, having no permanent character, were modified at the will of the sovereign.

" But in treating of States whose titles are derived from international compacts in which the rivers and points to serve as divisions have been defined, a provision based on the *uti possidetis*, which is only accepted when, for the want of settled boundaries, possession is sanctioned provisionally or definitively, does not seem to me possible."

This doctrine of the Minister for Foreign Affairs of the Argentine Republic in 1876 is not in harmony with that of Dr. ELIAS BEDOYA, his predecessor, when, defending the Treaty of December 14, 1857, he asserted, at the sitting of the Chamber of Deputies of September 24, 1858, that " Brazil could not do otherwise than uphold that which it had upheld and possessed since 1801."

Dr. IRIGOYEN added in a letter of 21st August, 1876:

" Far from wishing to re-open the old controversies which divided the Governments of Spain and Portugal, we could conciliate common interests and principles by accepting the spirit of Articles 16 and 19 of the Treaty of 1777, giving them this form.

" The Commissioners appointed will bear in mind that the survey of the divisional line must aim, as agreed by the Governments of Spain and Portugal on the 1st October, 1777, to preserve that which each one possessed under the said Treaty.

"In the event of any divergence occurring between the Commissioners as to the carrying out of the present Treaty, they will endeavor to remove it provisionally without proceeding to violent measures to make any change, and they shall report it to their respective Governments in order that these may definitely decide the points which gave rise to the disagreement."

The Argentine counter-proposals meant a system of delay which was dangerous, inasmuch as its purpose was to entrust to Commissioners the localization of the rivers Pepiry-Guaçú and Santo Antonio, a subject it was expedient should be treated and decided by the direct action of the two Governments. It was probable that the discretion left to the Joint Commission would produce dissensions and, perhaps, a revival of the question raised in 1789 by the Spanish Commissioners, in flagrant violation of their Instructions; but the Argentine Government did not contest the point that the Pepiry-Guaçú and the Santo Antonio were to form the boundary, nor did it yet assert its subsequent pretension to the right bank of the Chapecó, or Pequiri-Guazú, and to the left bank of the river Chopim, then supposed to be the San Antonio Guazu of OYÁRVIDE. *The negotiation of 1876 without result.*

The Brazilian Government was unable to accept the counter-proposals of 1876, and thus put an end to the Mission entrusted to BARON DE AGUIAR DE ANDRADA.

In 1881, the pretension of the Argentine Government was, for the first time, clearly defined. *The Argentine pretension manifested in 1881.*

A Decree of the Imperial Government, No. 2052, of November 16, 1859, had ordered two military colonies to be erected in the Province of Paraná, near the rivers Chapecó and Chopim. In 1881, the Minister of

War took measures to give effect to this scheme. Having been informed of this by the newspapers, and believing that the two colonies were about to be established on the West of those rivers, the Argentine Minister at Rio de Janeiro, Dr. Luis Dominguez, in March of that year, made some verbal observations to the Minister for Foreign Affairs of Brazil, Councillor Pereira de Souza.

It was not difficult to relieve the mind of the Argentine Minister, nor was it necessary to give orders for the position of the colonies to be changed, inasmuch as it was already decided that they were to be established on the Eastern side of the Chapecó and Chopim.

This incident of 1881 did not give rise at the time to any Protocol or exchange of Notes. It had the effect of revealing, however, that the Argentine Republic no longer limited itself, as in 1876, to expressing doubts as to the exact position of the rivers, Pepiry-Guaçú and Santo Antonio. For the first time one of its official representatives, addressing the Brazilian Government, considered the territory to the East of those rivers contestable, and assigned as the Eastern boundary of the Argentine pretension the rivers Chapecó and Chopim. The Argentine Republic thus revived the question raised in 1789 by the Spanish Commissioners of the second demarcation.

The Brazilian Government from that time became fully aware of the pretension, but it took no step, nor did it make any declaration that could invalidate the rights of the Brazilian nation.

The military colonies were established to the East of the Chapecó and Chopim because that Easterly position had seemed more suitable to the Ministry of War. They would thus serve to protect the principal line of communication that had been open since 1845 between Rio Grande do Sul, Paraná, and S. Paulo.

If the Brazilian Government had found it preferable to establish them in 1881, or afterwards, to the West of the two rivers, it would have done so in the exercise of an indisputable right. The Argentine Republic has shown that it is permissible to occupy disputed territories militarily, seeing that, for some years, it maintained a body of troops at Villa Occidental, known as Villa Hayes, after it was restored to the dominion of the Republic of Paraguay, as was the Northern Chaco, by the award of President HAYES, of the United States of America.

Brazil did not need to found military colonies to the West of the Chapecó and Chopim in order to prove that it maintained then, as it does now, under its jurisdiction all the territory to the East of the Pepiry-Guaçú and Santo Antonio. There were the Town and Parish of Palmas, the Borough and Parish of Boa-Vista, and other less important nucleuses of population, besides numerous farms. The inhabitants were, and are, almost wholly Brazilians. Since 1836 and 1838, they have been in permanent occupation of Campo de Palmas.

Administrative occupation of the territory of Palmas.

The Argentine Government could not be ignorant of the settlement of the Brazilians in those regions, because it had a Legation at Rio de Janeiro, and official documents made the fact public as early as 1841. If it believed it had a right to the territory to the East of the Pepiry-Guaçú and Santo Antonio it should have protested against its administrative occupation as it protested against that of the Malouines or Falkland Islands by England.

In 1841 the President of the Province of S. Paulo, RAPHAEL TOBIAS DE AGUIAR, announced in his *Report* to the Provincial Legislative Assembly the occupation of Campo de Palmas by two expeditions from Curityba, then the chief town of a Comarca (Judicial Division) forming part of that Brazilian Province.

The expeditions referred to by the President of S. Paulo, and which were headed by Major JOAQUIM PINTO BANDEIRA, of the National Guard, and by MANOEL DE ALMEIDA LEIRIA, in 1838, had already been preceded by three others, namely: that which started from Palmeiras in 1836, under the leadership of Father PONCIANO JOSÉ DE ARAUJO, Rector of that Parish, and of JOSÉ JOAQUIM DE ALMEIDA, afterwards a Colonel in the National Guard; and two which came out of Guarapuava, having as leaders JOSÉ FERREIRA DOS SANTOS and PEDRO DE SIQUEIRA CÔRTES.

In 1840 a company of the military police of S. Paulo ("Municipaes Permanentes") was detached to Campo de Palmas under Captain HERMOGENES CARNEIRO LOBO. This company was created by an Act of March 16, 1837, of the Provincial Legislative Assembly of S. Paulo for the special purpose of occupying Campo de Palmas.[1] And the persons composing the different expeditions being in hot dispute concerning the division of the land,

---

[1] In the *Revista do Instituto Historico e Geographico do Brazil* (Review of the Historical and Geographical Institute of Brazil), Vol. XIV., year 1851, p. 425 to 438, is to be found an Account, the translation of whose title is: "An account of the discovery of Campo de Palmas in the Comarca of Coritiba, Province of S. Paulo, of its colonization, and of some events which occurred there to the present month of December, 1850, written and presented to the Historical Institute by Senhor JOAQUIM JOSÉ PINTO BANDEIRA."

At page 430 the following occurs: " . . . but as the Provincial Assembly, by a Law of 16th March, 1837, had created a company of Military Police (Municipaes Permanentes), in order that it might make on the part of the Government the discovery of these plains, the Government ordered it to be sent there to protect the farmers."

lawyer João da Silva Carrão, afterwards Minister of State and Senator of the Empire, and Major Pinto Bandeira were chosen as arbitrators to settle the difficulty. On the 4th April, 1840, they started from Curityba and arrived at Campo de Palmas on the 28th May, remaining there until August. In the same year Commander Carneiro Lobo founded on the banks of the stream Cachoeira the village called from that time Capella de Palmas.

The occupation of Campo Eré in 1840, while the arbitrators Carrão and Pinto Bandeira were making the division of the lands, is related in the following passage of the Account written by the latter in 1850, and printed the following year in the Review of the Historical and Geographical Institute of Brazil:

"For two months and a half which were spent in the division of the land, several explorations were made in the neighborhood, and from the information of the Indians other plains and tracts of coarse grass, to which they gave the name of Campo Eré, were discovered. . . ."[1]

This position, near the headwaters of the Pepiry-Guaçú and Santo Antonio, is the most advanced that the Brazilians occupy in the territory now disputed. In 1840, thirty-seven farms were established in Campo de Palmas which, in 1850, already had nearly 36,000 head of cattle.[2] In the same year, 1850, Campo Eré had five farms.[3] The lands owned by the farmers of this place were registered by the Collector of Palmas in 1855 and 1856.[4]

---

[1] Pinto Bandeira's cited Account, p. 430.

[2] *Ibidem*, p. 420: "As the number of associates, having reached sixty, had become excessive for the capacity of the plains, a few sold their shares, and only thirty-seven farms were established which now contain about 36,000 head of cattle."

[3] *Ibidem*, p. 431:—". . . Among others we will mention Campo Eré which already contains five farms. . . ."

[4] Information dated August 3, 1891, of the Assistant Judge "de Direito" of Palmas, in a telegram addressed to the Minister for Foreign Affairs of Brazil.

In the *Memoria del Ministerio de Rel. Est. de la Republica Argentina* (Report

On June 25, 1841, January 8, and August 27, 1844, General ANTERO DE BRITO, President of Santa Catharina, another Brazilian Province, protested against the jurisdiction of the authorities of S. Paulo, in Campo de Palmas, maintaining that all the territory to the East of the Pepiry-Guaçú and of the Santo Antonio belonged to the Province of Santa Catharina.

The protest of Santa Catharina became public and gave rise to discussions. The Report of 1841 of the President of S. Paulo was also a published document, of the Department of Foreign Affairs of the Argentine Republic) presented to Congress in 1892, it may be read at page 45 that in 1881 the Brazilian Government " returned with its troops to the frontier and, after encouraging the colonies of Chopim, Chapecó, and Palmas, which were advancing upon the contested region, entered resolutely to the heart of the territory, upon the heights which divide the basins of the Paraná and of the Iguaçú, throwing forward its outposts as far as Santa Ana and Campo Eré. *Such audacity* shows an error of the diplomacy of Rio de Janeiro. . . ." And at page 46 : " Moreover, *those recent usurpations* would not in any way benefit the claim of Brazil. . . "

There are several mistakes in the two passages quoted :

1st. The Brazilian Government did not send troops to the territory which the Argentine Republic has claimed since 1881, and it did not send them because it had no need to do so in order to prove that it is and always was in possession of the territory.

2d. The colony of the Chapecó was established in Xanxerê, a place outside the region claimed by the Argentine Republic.

3d. The colony of the Chopim was established in a territory which has only been contested since it was found, in 1888, that the river Jangada is the San Antonio Guazú of OYARVIDE, the decision arrived at by the Brazilian Government at that date having been thought worthy of praise of the present Minister for Foreign Affairs of the Argentine Republic, S! VALENTIN VIRASORO, in an interesting monograph published in 1892.

4th. The village, afterwards town of Palmas, was inaugurated in 1840, and appears under its name within the boundaries of Brazil in Map VI., engraved in 1865, in the *Atlas* of MOUSSY, published by order of the Argentine Government.

5th. Campo Eré, which is a more advanced position than S. Ana, was occupied in 1840 and, as has been said before, already had in 1850 five farms belonging to Brazilians. The lands owned by them were registered in the collectorship of Palmas in 1855 and 1856. In 1879 and 1880, the Judge " de Orphãos e Ausentes " (" of Orphans and Absents ") of the Termo (Judicial District) of Palmas proceeded to an inventory of the property left by VICENTE ANTONIO DE LARA, farmer of Campo Eré, a place which DR. ZEBALLOS supposes to have been occupied only since 1881.

printed and distributed, as are all documents of that nature.

In 1842, Captain PEDRO DE SIQUEIRA CÔRTES, the new Commander of the detachment of Military Police, began to open a road to the plains of Curityba, and the farmers another to Palmeira, and, in 1846, a third and shorter one, passing through Porto da União on the Iguaçú. The Provincial Legislative Assembly of S. Paulo had at different times voted funds for the opening of this last road.[1] In 1845, by order of the President of S. Paulo, General MANOEL DA FONSECA LIMA, afterwards BARON DE SURUHY, the opening of communications with Rio Grande do Sul was begun by the Passo (ford) of Goyo En, and by Nonohay. General CAXIAS, then President of Rio Grande do Sul (another Brazilian Province) encouraged and assisted these works.

Law No. 14, of 21st March, 1849, of the Provincial Legislative Assembly of S. Paulo, raising the old Parish of Guarapuava to a Town (Villa), provided that Palmas should form part of the new Township, (Municipio).[2]

The Law of 29th August, 1853, of the General Legislative Assembly of the Empire, detached from the Province of S. Paulo the Comarca (Judicial division) of Curityba, raising it to a Province with the name of Paraná. From that time, Palmas and its territory remained under the dependence of the Provincial Government of Paraná, and the Province of Santa Catharina claimed from Paraná the territory to

---

[1] *Review of the His. Institute of Brazil*, Vol. XIV. (1851), pp. 433 and 434.

[2] " Art. 1st.—The Parish of Bethlem, situated in the Comarca (Judicial division) of Curityba, is raised to the category of a Town (Villa) under the name of Guarapuava.

" Art. 2nd. The former boundaries including the Capella de Palmas shall continue."

the South of the Iguaçú and to the East of the Santo Antonio and the Pepiry-Guaçú, which it formerly claimed from S. Paulo.

This boundary question was after 1846 the subject of discussions in the press, in the Chamber of Deputies and in the Senate of Brazil. In 1846, a Committee of the Chamber of Deputies presented a Report on the claim of the Legislative Assembly of Santa Catharina against the occupation of the territory in question by authorities and expeditions from S. Paulo. In 1854 the subject was again discussed in the Chamber of Deputies, and, two years later, in the Senate.

By a Law of February 28, 1855, No. 22, of the Legislative Assembly of Paraná, the district of the settlement of Palmas came to form a Parish. Thenceforward the inhabitants of that territory, who, in the elections of the first degree for Senators and Deputies to the Brazilian Parliament, for Members of the Provincial Legislative Assembly, and in the Municipal elections, and those for Justices of the Peace, were put to the inconvenience of going to vote at Guarapuava, had as a point of meeting for these acts the parochial church of the Senhor Bom Jesus de Palmas.

Another Law of the Provincial Legislative Assembly of Paraná, dated October 9, 1878, raised Palmas to the position of a Town (Villa), forming of that territory a Township and a Termo (Judicial district) whose limits to the West continued to be those of the Parish, that is to say, the rivers Pepiry-Guaçú and Santo Antonio. Later, by other Laws of the Legislative Assembly of Paraná, the Termo of Palmas was raised to a Comarca (Judicial division)[1] and in this dis-

---

[1] *Termo*, a judicial district under a Judge called " Municipal." *Comarca*, a Judicial division under a Judge " de Direito " and generally comprising two or more Termos.

trict a second Parish was created whose seat was the village of Boa Vista.

All those public acts exercised during forty years, counted from the date of the Report of the President of S. Paulo (1841) until the first of the notice Argentine claim (1881), passed without the least protest or challenge from the Government of that Republic or from its Legation in Brazil.

From 1810, the date of the independence of the Provinces of the River Plate, until 1881, the long period of 70 years elapsed, to which, strictly, should be added the 19 years from 1791 to 1810, in which Spain took no notice of the recommendation of its Commissioners for the alteration of the divisional line defined in the Treaty of 1777.

During those 70 years, or 89 in the second case, first the Portuguese maps, then the Brazilian maps, and, generally, all the foreign maps, published in the United States of America[1] and in Europe,[2] gave as the boundary between Brazil and the Provinces of the River Plate, since then Argentine Confederation and Argentine Republic. the

Seventy years without a protest.

---

[1] For example, the one which has this title :
"*Map of the Basin of La Plata, based upon the results of the expedition under the command of* THO⁹ G. PAGE, *U. S. Navy, in the years 1853, 54, 55, and 56, and of the adjacent countries, compiled from the best authorities.*" This map occurs in the following work : "*La Plata, the Argentine Confederation, and Paraguay, being a narrative of the exploration of the tributaries of the River La Plata and adjacent countries during the years 1853, 54, 55, and 56, under the orders of the United States Government, by* Thomas G. Page, *U. S. N., Commander of the Expedition.*" New York, 1859.

[2] The maps published under the direction or according to the instructions of SIR WOODBINE PARISH, for many years Chargé d'Affaires and Consul-General of Great Britain at Buenos-Aires and author of an historical and geographical work upon the Provinces of the River Plate, a work which was translated into Spanish at Buenos-Aires and published (1853) a few years after the English edition.

Pepiry-Guaçú and the Santo Antonio, that is to say, the river that discharges itself on the right bank of the Uruguay, a little above the Salto Grande (Great Falls) and the tributary of the Iguaçú which flows in the opposite direction almost on the same meridian as the Pepiry-Guaçú.

The Argentine Government not only remained silent for 70 years without ever challenging the official Brazilian maps, but even authorized or assisted in the publication of others which represented the divisional line along those two rivers.

Argentine Maps.

The Brazilian Memorandum of the 26th November, 1857, and the Note of the 1st August, 1859, of the Brazilian Legation in the City of Paraná, quoted the *Mapa de la Republica Argentina* by the engineers ALLAN and CAMPBELL, dated 1855, "and printed by order of the Argentine Government." Many others can be cited and, among them, that of the *Confederacion Argentina*, of 1863 [1]; of the *Provincia de Corrientes*, of 1865, constructed from documents in the Typographical Department of Buenos-Aires [2]; those of the well-known *Atlas de la Confederation Argentine* by V. MARTIN DE MOUSSY, an indisputably official publication, and the Map of 1875, by the engineers A. DE SEELSTRANG and A. TOURMENTE, constructed

---

[1] Translation of the title: "*New Map of the Provinces forming the Argentine Confederation of the Oriental Republic of the Uruguay, and of those of Paraguay and Chile drawn and corrected from the most authentic and modern explorations made in these later years. 1863.*" (No. 23 A in the Appendix.)

[2] Translation of the title: "*Geographical Map of the Provinces of Corrientes and part of the Republic of the Uruguay constructed from the data in the archives of the Typographical Department of Buenos-Aires, and with relation to all the maps published to this day. Dedicated by the authors to His Excellency the President of the Argentine Republic, Brigadier General* D. BARTOLOMÉ MITRE. *1865.*" (No. 24 A in Vol. VI.)

specially at Buenos-Aires by order of the Argentine Central Commission for the Philadelphia Exhibition in 1876,[1] and appended to a book which was profusely distributed at the time, in the United States and in Europe, by the agents of the Argentine Government. The work, written by D. RICARDO NAPP, a federal official,[2] and by other Argentines in the civil or military service of the Republic, was translated into several languages, and has the following title in the English edition: "*The Argentine Republic, written in German by* RICHARD NAPP, *etc., for the Central Argentine Commission on the Centenary Exhibition at Philadelphia. Buenos-Aires. 1876.*"

In a Note of the 20th November, 1889, addressed by the Minister for Foreign Affairs of the Argentine Republic to his colleague the Minister of Public Instruction, the following may be read:

"The recognized want of officially authorized maps imposes on the various Departments of the administration the patriotic duty of selecting with the greatest care the maps that are to be used in training the minds of the Argentine youth in the knowledge of the territorial rights of the Republic.

"Criticism finds much to say upon the Atlases and maps which serve as text-books in the establishments I have mentioned, and with the object of preventing the evils with which Your Excellency is acquainted, and of avoiding by the repetition of acts of this nature the encouragement of foreign pretensions, I request

---

[1] Translation of the title: "*Map of the Argentine Republic, constructed by* A. SEELSTRANG *and* A. TOURMENTE, *Engineers, by order of the Central Argentine Committee for the Philadelphia Exhibition.* Buenos-Aires, 1875."

[2] "A national official, DON RICARDO NAPP . . . ." says the *Report* of 1892 of the Department of Foreign Affairs of the Argentine Republic, p. 59.

Your Excellency to *order a strict revision of the text-books of National Geography*, to which I have referred, so that new editions may be in accordance with the rights and propriety I have had the honor to indicate. . . .

"The Argentine Republic has no official maps, and if some claim that character, this Ministry does not recognize them in international questions, seeing that it has never authorized them. On the other hand, the fact that the editions are undertaken by public officials, subventioned by the State or bought by the Education Departments, does not make the Argentine Government responsible for their contents. . . ."[1]

This admonition from the Argentine Foreign Office was made because the Brazilian Government, in the Memorandum of 1882, and in the Counter-Memorandum of 1884, had quoted several maps as proving that the Argentine Government, in official publications, recognized until 1881 the frontier occupied and defended by Brazil.

In consequence of the representation of the 20th November, 1889, the Argentine Government promulgated a Decree denying the authority on questions of limits of all maps that were not approved by its Department of Foreign Affairs.

But the representation and the Decree cannot have a retroactive effect; and, instead of removing, they confirmed the fact that from 1810 to 1881 the maps published by order of the Argentine Government, scattered broadcast with its books of propaganda throughout Europe and America, and even School Books and

---

[1] Translated from the Report of D.ʳ ZEBALLOS, Minister for Foreign Affairs of the Argentine Republic, presented to Congress, 1892, § VIII., p. 60.

School-maps, as the Note of the 20th November, 1889, acknowledges, presented as boundaries of the Argentine Republic the rivers Pepiry-Guaçú and Santo Antonio, and not the Chapecó (Pequirí-Guazú) and Jangada (San Antonio Guazú).

The *Report* of 1892 of the Argentine Foreign Office, comprehending the force of this argument, seeks to destroy it but without attaining that object.

Regarding the Map distributed on the occasion of the Centennial Exhibition at Philadelphia, appended to the work of NAPP, the *Report* says that, in the text, the boundary is designated by the " Pepiry-Guazú and the San Antonio Guazú," and gives to understand that the Argentines only apply the adjective guaraní *guazú* to the rivers which the Republic claims as a boundary.[1]

This explanation has no foundation whatever, since the Pepiry-Guazú of the Map in question is the river whose mouth is immediately above the Salto Grande (Great Falls) of the Uruguay, and not the Pequirí-Guazú (Chapecó of the Brazilians) which empties itself very much farther to the East more than 149 kilometres (nearly 81 miles) distant from the Salto Grande counting the windings of the Uruguay. The question of the Guarany adjectives *guaçú* (guazú) and *mirim* (miní) was already discussed in this Statement (pages 109 and 110).

The explications given in the *Report* of 1892 about the *Atlas* of MARTIN DE MOUSSY are not more to the point than the one which has just been examined.

The *Report* asserts that Map V of that collection gives the boundary according to the present Argentine pretension because the Pepiry-Guazú and the San

---

[1] " It is not necessary to dwell upon what Argentine writers understand by great (guazú) rivers in this secular controversy " (*Report*, 1892).

Antonio Guazú are to the East of the two rivers there designated as Pepiry-Mini and San Antonio Mini, but it does not notice that, according to the Diary of the Brazilian-Argentine Joint Commission, there is in fact to the West of the true Pepiry-Guaçú a river, in the Argentine territory, known by the name of Pepiry-Mini [1]; it does not notice either that, much to the East of the two rivers Pepiry-Guazú and San Antonio Guazú by which, in this map, the divisional line passes, there is the river Magi, and that in Map VII of the *Atlas* it is seen that the same river, far outside the Argentine boundaries, has the names of " River Magi or Chopi" and passes to the North of the Brazilian town of Palmas, being, therefore, the river Chopim, claimed as a boundary by the Argentine Republic from 1881 to 1888.

The *Report* of 1892 alleges that Map VII was drawn after the death of the author of the *Atlas*, though the Map bears the date of 1865, and, in 1867 MARTIN DE MOUSSY was a Commissioner of the Argentine Republic and a member of the Jury at the Universal Exhibition of Paris. It states besides that the boundary is traced on Map VI along the rivers which the Argentine Republic now claims, and, as a matter of fact, what is seen on that Map is that the mouth of the " Pepiry-Guazú " is 9 kilometres (5 miles) above the Salto Grande (Great Falls) of the Uruguay, while the river the Argentine Republic wishes to have for its boundary (the Pequiri-Guazú, or Chapecó) is, as has been

---

[1] The Argentine *Diary* of the Joint Commission appointed under the Treaty of the 28th September, 1885, says:

"On the 13th day (July, 1887) the survey of the Uruguay was begun, the first station being situated on the right bank of the mouth of the river *which is known to the inhabitants of the place as the Pepiry-Mini, and to which others give the name of Jaboti,* which it has in the region of the village of San Pedro."

said before, 149.5 kilometres (80.7 miles) above the Great Falls. In this same Map No. VI may be seen, far to the East of the divisional line, the river Magi, the name Moussy gave to the Chopim.

In other maps of this official *Atlas* (XVIII and XXVIII) the boundary is seen to follow the Pepiry-Guaçú, the first river above the Great Falls of the Uruguay, as the Brazilians maintain, and not along the river proposed by the Spanish Commissioners as a boundary in 1789.

Brazil can, therefore, affirm that its right to the boundary of the Pepiry-Guaçú and Santo Antonio was recognized for more than seventy years by the Argentine Republic.

In 1881, the Law of the 22d December, passed by the Argentine Congress, established the Gobernacion de Misiones (Governorship of Misiones) forming it out of the territory included between the rivers Uruguay and Paraná.

By a Decree of the 16th March, 1882, the Argentine Government divided that territory into five Departments, designating their boundaries. The Departments received the names of San Martin (Corpus), Piray, San Javier (or S. Xavier), Monteagudo, and Iguazú. Later a sixth, that of Posadas, was created. Creation of the Gobernacion of Misiones, 1882.

Only five of those Departments border on Brazil: that of San Javier, which lies on the right bank of the Uruguay; that of Piray, on the bank of the Iguaçú, between the Salto Grande (Great Falls) of this river and its mouth in the Paraná; and those of Monteagudo and Iguazú, which are the most Easterly.

The boundaries of the last two were thus described in the Decree.

"Department of Monteagudo (Paggi).—Bounded on the North by the mountains; on the South by the river Uruguay; on the West by the river Acaraguay in its prolongation as far as the mountains of la Victoria; and on the East by the river *Pepiry-Guazú*.

"Department of the Iguazú.—Bounded on the North by the river Iguazú; on the West by the mountains of la Victoria; on the East by the river *San Antonio Guazú*; and on the South by the mountains."

The seat of the Government of Misiones, first established at Corpus (San Martin), was afterwards transferred to Posadas.

It has already been stated that the Argentine maps until 1881 always gave to the Pepiry-Guaçú of the Brazilians the name of Pepiry-Guazú, and to the Santo Antonio, or San Antonio, sometimes this name, and at others that of San Antonio Guazú.

As, however, this last name can be more particularly applied to the river whose sources were discovered in 1791 by the Spanish Commissioner OYARVIDE, and, on the other hand, as the Spanish Commissioners of the second demarcation asserted that the river named by them Pequiri-Guazú (the Chapecó of the Brazilians) was the true Pepiry of the Treaty of 1750, the Brazilian Government considered, in view of the Argentine pretension put forward in 1881, that the Eastern boundaries laid down in the Decree as those of the Departments of Iguazú and Monteagudo might give rise to the intrusion of foreign authorities into the territory which Brazil occupied and still occupies to the East of the Pepiry-Guaçú and of the Santo Antonio. It therefore resolved to safeguard its rights and to propose the opening of new negotiations, issuing instructions to that effect to the BARON DE ARAUJO GONDIM, Brazilian

Minister at Buenos-Aires, who carried them out by a Note of the 2d June, 1882.

The Argentine Government declared itself disposed to discuss the pending question, and, on the 29th July, BARON DE ARAUJO GONDIM proposed that for Article 2 of the Treaty of 1857 the following should be substituted:

"The rivers Pepiri-Guaçú and Santo Antonio, of which the preceding Article treats are: the first, an affluent which discharges itself into the Uruguay, on its right or Northern bank, a little more than a league above its Great Fall, and in latitude 27° 9' 23"; and the second, the one on the opposite slope of the watershed and the first important affluent which enters on the Southern or left bank of the Grande de Curityba or Iguaçú, above its confluence with the Paraná and in latitude 25° 35'. Both have their sources in the same locality on the summit of the mountain range which divides the waters of the rivers Uruguay and Iguaçú, and the two springs are only about five hundred paces one from the other, between 26° 10' and 26° 12' latitude: the Pepiri-Guaçú running in a direction of 15° S. W., and the Santo Antonio of 26° N.W."

This proposal was accompanied by a Memorandum.

The Minister for Foreign Affairs of the Argentine Republic, DR V. DE LA PLAZA, replied by a Note of 30th January, 1883, and a Memorandum of the same date, refusing the proposal and presenting that of his Government that the boundary should be traced along the Pequiri-Guazú (Chapecó) and by the river on the opposite slope of the watershed, whose sources were explored by OYÁRVIDE in the year 1791.

On the 30th December, 1884, the new Brazilian Minister at Buenos-Aires, Councillor ALENCAR, delivered to the Argentine Minister for Foreign Affairs the Counter-Memorandum of the Brazilian Government, written by the VISCOUNT DE CABO-FRIO, and, in a Note of that date, showed that the Argentine Government had attributed to the declarations made in 1881 by Councillor PEREIRA DE SOUZA a meaning they could not have had.

"The military colonies of the Chapecó and of the Chopim," says the Note, "exist, and it is certain that all possible development has been given them, but they are not the only ones. There are others, all belonging to a system formed long ago, without regard to foreign countries, nor to questions with them that may be pending. And it is to be remarked that the two mentioned colonies are not properly speaking on the border: as regards Brazil they are in the interior, because it has an indisputable right to all the territory situated to the East of the Rivers Pepiry-Guaçú and Santo Antonio.

"In the Department of Foreign Affairs, there does not exist any document, official, confidential, or private, showing circumstantially what passed between the late Councillor PEREIRA DE SOUZA and Dr. DOMINGUEZ. There is only a Note of that Minister, dated April 5, 1881, referring to the "important declarations" the former had made to him on the occasion "of the establishment of two military colonies which His Excellency the Minister of War proposed to found on the frontier which divides the Empire from the Argentine Republic between the rivers Iguaçú and Uruguay." This document does not enter into particulars, and the reply of Sr. PEREIRA DE SOUZA, given on the 12th of the same month, does not contain one word regarding the colonies, and only relates to the projected negotiations.

"Under these circumstances, without impugning the veracity of the statement made by Sr. DOMINGUEZ to his Government, the Imperial Government thinks that the declarations of the same Minister must be understood according to the occurrences of the moment and the nature of things. The news was then current here that the Imperial Government had ordered two military colonies to be founded in the disputed territory and, as the Brazilian Minister for Foreign Affairs was making arrangements at the time to bring about a new agreement, in order that his friendly effort might not fail, he declared that the withdrawal of the officers charged with the foundation of the colonies had been ordered. This was evidently a step suited to the occasion, aiming at a special end, which was not attained, had no permanent character, and did not deprive the Imperial Government of the right of carrying out its plan when the reason for the delay should cease; and it did carry it out without the least objection from the Argentine Government . . ."

After demonstrating that the Treaty of 1857 had been approved by the Argentine Congress, the Note of December 30, 1884, concludes as follows:

"As it appears from this extract, D.ʳ PLAZA said that the acceptance of the proposal made by my predecessor would be equal to a motiveless renunciation by the Argentine Government of the right which the Republic believes it has over the territory in question, and in his turn he proposed that taking the demarcation as made by the Chapecó, that is to say, by the Pequiry-Guaçú of the Spaniards, the latter should be continued by the nearest river having its source on the opposite slope of the watershed, that is to say, by the Chopim, which is the Santo Antonio of the same Spaniards.

"If, on its part, the Imperial Government accepted this proposal, it would also abandon its right to the boundary constituted by the true Pepiry-Guaçú and the true Santo Antonio. This it could not do.

"In the meantime, the Imperial Government, convinced of the right of Brazil to the boundary it is defending, conscious of the good faith with which, on its part, the Argentine Government disputes it, and certain also that both Powers entertain the most sincere and cordial desire to solve the question, in accordance with the principles of justice, safeguarding their respective rights, and:

"Considering that neither the rivers in question, nor the disputed zone comprised by them, were at any time explored by Brazilians and Argentines for the purpose of making on their own account the explorations effected by the Portuguese and Spanish in the last century;

"Considering that from this examination made by common accord and jointly, more light must be thrown upon the question, and desiring for its part to give one more proof of the sincerity of its sentiments and of the certainty of its right, it has resolved to propose to the Argentine Government, as it now proposes, that a Joint Commission of competent persons, in equal numbers, be appointed by the two Governments, to survey the four rivers Pequiry-Guaçú, Santo Antonio, Chapecó and Chopim, which the Argentine Government names Pepirí-Guazú and San Antonio Guazú, and the zone comprised between them, making an accurate plan of the rivers of the whole disputed zone, an idea, besides, suggested in substance to the Imperial Government by D.ᴿ Irigoyen in 1876."

The result of this negotiation was the Treaty of September 28, 1885, for the survey of the rivers Pepiry-Guaçú, Santo Antonio, Chapecó and Chopim, which was supposed to be the San Antonio-Guazú of Oyárvide. *Treaty of 1885.*

The Brazilian-Argentine Joint Commission entered upon its labors in 1887 and concluded them in 1890. *Survey by a Brazilian-Argentine Joint Commission.*

It was then ascertained that the S. Antonio Guazú of Oyárvide is the river Jangada.

The Argentine Commission proposed the survey of this river, and the Brazilian refused to consent to it, because the Treaty and the Instructions of 1885 designated the river Chopim.

The Brazilian Government settled the divergence by accepting the interpretation the Argentine Republic and its Commission gave to the Treaty.

The Report of the Minister for Foreign Affairs presented in 1888 to the Brazilian Parliament thus refers to this incident :

" The two Commissions, after carrying out in perfect harmony a great part of the survey, gradually separated in February and March of the current year, returning on account of the rains to this City and to Buenos-Aires, where they occupied themselves with office-work.

"There arose between them an important disagreement, which appears in a record appended to the present Report, and was submitted to the decision of the two Governments. It has reference to the survey of the river S. Antonio Guaçú, known as the Jangada in its lower course as far as that of the Iguaçú into which it empties itself.

"It was the opinion of the Argentine Commission that the said river was to be surveyed by both, and the Brazilian Commission refused to do so officially without the order of the Imperial Government, because, among other reasons, it understood that the Jangada was not mentioned in Article 2 of the Treaty, as one of the rivers that were to be surveyed.

"The Imperial Government duly appreciated the scruples of its Commissioners, but it did not have the satisfaction of agreeing with them, and this it declared to the Argentine Government.

"The Treaty determined that besides the Pepiry-Guaçú and the S. Antonio, a survey should be made of the rivers Chapecó and Chopim, named by the Argentines Pequiry-Guaçú and S. Antonio Guaçú, because, as to the Chopim, according to the information then available, the two names represented one and the same river. But from the survey now made the contrary was shown. The S. Antonio Guaçú is distinct from the Chopim and empties its waters into the Iguaçú about 200 kilometres East of the mouth of the same Chopim.

"The circumstance of the names Chopim and Santo Antonio designating two distinct rivers does not disturb what was agreed upon. The principal fact is the existence of a river which the Spaniards began to survey and which they named S. Antonio Guaçú. This and the Pequiry Guaçú are those which, as the Argentines think, form the boundary.

. . .

"The survey of the S. Antonio Guaçú is, therefore,

obligatory for Brazil, not only as far as the point reached by the survey of OYÁRVIDE, but over its whole extent, as far as its mouth, although this river is partly known under the name of Jangada.

"This does not invalidate the question of right. Whether the source of the S. Antonio Guaçú is on the opposite slope of the watershed on which is situated the source of the Chapecó or Pequiry-Guaçú, even though it may empty itself into the Iguaçú far above the mouth of the Chopim, it is still certain that those two rivers are not the ones mentioned in the Treaty of 1777. But, even though it were not so, the Santo Antonio Guaçú must be jointly surveyed, because the Treaty so determines and the Imperial Government must loyally fulfil what it agreed to.

"Besides the survey of this river, which must be made jointly if the two Governments do not accept the survey carried out separately, the exploration of a part of the intermediate territory still remains to be made. The Commissions must, therefore, return to the disputed territory."

The survey of the Jangada, or San Antonio Guazú, was made in consequence of this decision by a Joint Demarcating Party led by Engineer ODEBRECHT (Brazil) and by Lieutenant MONTES (Argentine Republic).

Señor VALENTIN VIRASORO, in a Report published in 1892,[1] recognized the loyalty of the action of Brazil.

"The river Chopim," he said, "disappeared as a boundary in dispute as soon as it was proved that it is not the San Antonio Guazú, and as the Brazilian Government, acting spontaneously in a spirit of truth

---

[1] *Misiones y Arbitraje* by VALENTIN VIRASORO in the pamphlet *La Cuestion de Misiones*, a collection of articles and monographs previously published in the *Boletin del Instituto Geografico Argentino*, Buenos-Aires, 1892, p. 110.

and justice, consented to the survey as far as the true San Antonio Guazú or Jangada."

At the beginning of 1889, long before the Joint Commission had ended its labors, the Argentine Minister at Rio de Janeiro proposed confidentially to Councillor Rodrigo Silva, then Minister for Foreign Affairs, the following draft for an agreement:

Argentine proposal for the division of the contested territory.

" The Empire of Brazil and the Argentine Republic etc., etc.

" Have agreed :

" 1st. To adopt as the definitive boundary-line the geometrical mean-line between the line claimed by the Empire of Brazil, and defined by the rivers Pepiry-Guassú and San Antonio-Guassú, and that claimed by the Argentine Republic, marked by the rivers San Antonio-guazú of Oyárvide and Chapecó.

" 2dly. It is to be understood that the geometical mean-line referred to in the preceding Article shall be established by a series of points occupying each one the centre of the lines parallel to the Equator which cut the boundary-lines claimed by the two contracting parties.

" 3dly. The expenses incurred in the fulfilment of this Treaty shall be borne in equal parts."[1]

Minister Rodrigo da Silva refused to accept that proposal and suggested that recourse should be had to arbitration in case it should not be possible to come to a direct agreement.

The negotiations were continued after June by Councillor Diana, the successor to that Minister, and, from them resulted the Treaty of Arbitration signed at Buenos-Aires, September 7, 1889.

Treaty of Arbitration. Sept. 7, 1889.

The original text of the Argentine proposal, in Spanish, is presented in Vol. II. of this Statement, page 263.

Some days after its ratification the Republic was proclaimed in Brazil, and, at the request of the Argentine Minister at Rio de Janeiro, the Provisional Government agreed to the division of the contested territory, an idea favored by the Government of Buenos-Aires since 1881.[1]

<small>The division of the contested territory an old idea of the Argentine Government.</small>

It has been asserted in Argentine documents that the initiative as to the projected division was taken in 1881 and 1889 by the Brazilian Government.

The project of 1881 will remove all doubts upon that point, inasmuch as it is written in Spanish, and the author of that of 1889, which was attributed to Minister DIANA, was an engineer who had no share in the Government. Minister DIANA subsequently affirmed that he had never thought of such a compromise, and that he was even convinced from what the Argentine Minister at Rio de Janeiro had said to him, that this point of disagreement was about to be removed by the final acceptance by the Argentine Republic of the line of the Pepiry-Guaçù and S. Antonio.

On January 25, 1890, a Treaty which divided the territory of Palmas between the two Contracting Parties was signed at Montevideo by the representatives of the Provisional Government of Brazil and those of the Argentine Republic.

<small>Treaty of Montevideo, 1890.</small>

In the Argentine Republic this solution was re-

---

[1] "Sr. DOMINGUEZ (1881) lost no time in recommending his Government to enter upon this new course, thinking it possible to divide the contested territory between the two Pepiris by the heights which separate the watersheds of the two rivers from those of the two S. Antonios." (*Report of 1892 of the Minister for Foreign Affairs of the Argentine Republic, presented to Congress*, page 47.)

Rejected by the Brazilian Congress. ceived with great enthusiasm. In Brazil, however, it produced a sentiment of the deepest grief and raised unanimous and vehement protests.

Thus, according to the phrase of an illustrious writer, the question of the territory of Palmas passed through the great test of the Judgment of Solomon.

The Special Committee elected by the Brazilian Congress to report upon the Treaty of Montevideo was of opinion that it should be rejected and that recourse should be had to Arbitration.[1] This Report was approved at the sitting of August 10, 1891, by 142 ayes against 5 noes.[2]

In fulfilment, therefore, of the provisions of the Treaty of September 7, 1889, Brazil and the Argentine Republic now have recourse to the President of the United States of America, in order that, as Arbitrator, he may give his award upon the subject of the existing controversy.

Washington, February 8, 1894.

---

[1] English translation, Vol. III., p. 204 ; original text, IV., 192.
[2] Vol. III., 211 ; IV., 199.

277

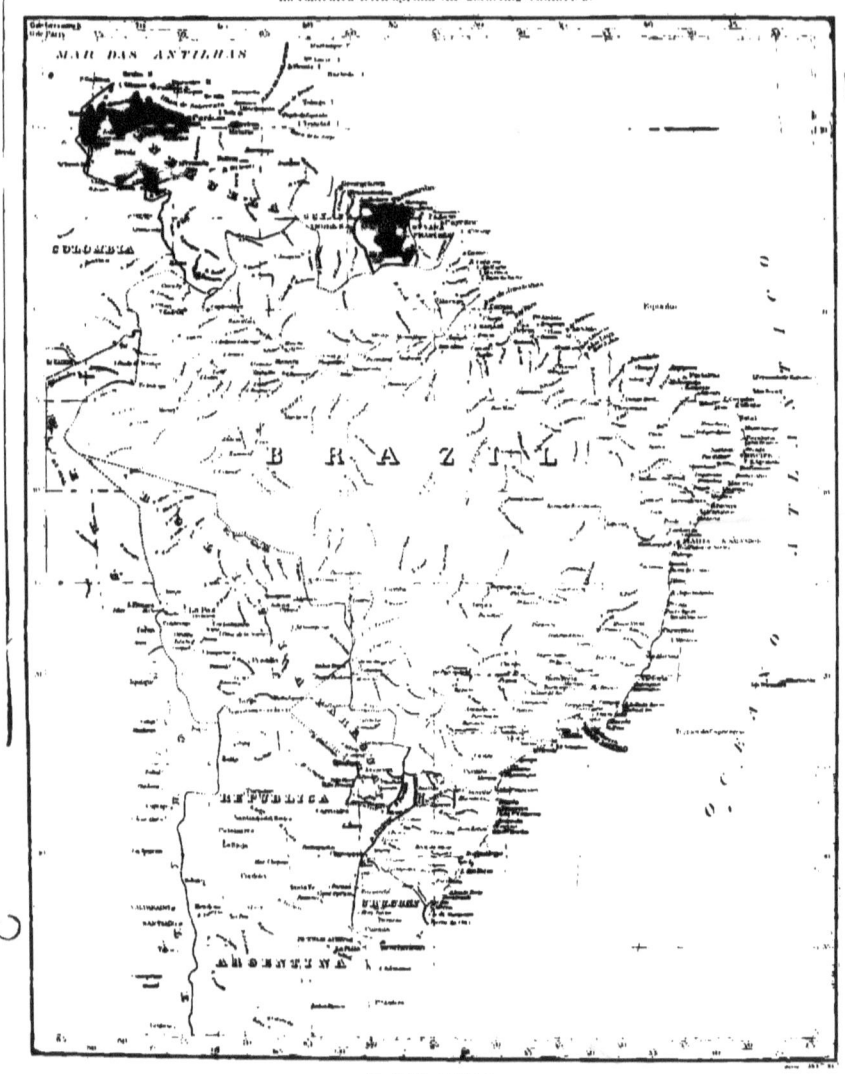

BRAZIL,
its contested territory, and the bordering countries.

O BRAZIL,
seo territorio contestado, e os paizes limitrophes.

MAP OF SOUTHERN BRAZIL,
showing that part of its contested territory claimed by the Argentine Republic.

MAPPA DO BRAZIL MERIDIONAL,
mostrando a parte do seo territorio reclamada pela Republica Argentina.

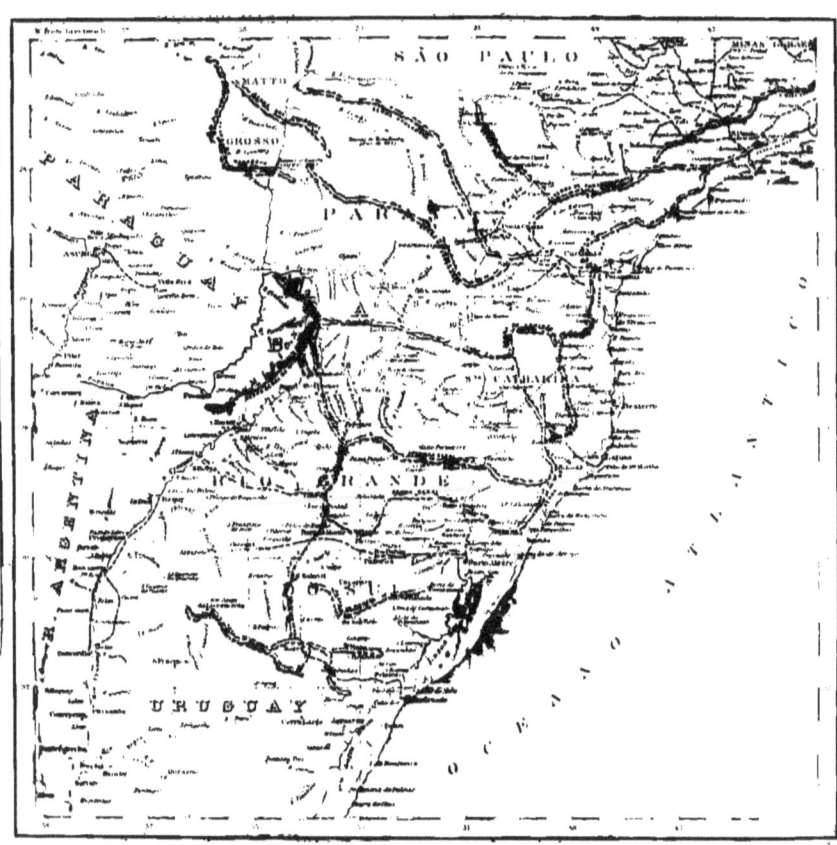

APPENDIX.

LIST OF DOCUMENTS.

	VOL.	PAGE.

Treaty of Madrid, January 13, 1750:

English translation . . . . . . III, 3-23
Portuguese text . . . . . . IV, 3-21

General Instructions to the Demarcating Commissioners (Treaties and Conventions Nº 1, 2, 3, 4, and 5, signed at Madrid, January 17, and April 17, 1751):

English translation . . . . III, 25-58
Portuguese text . . . . IV, 25-53

The Map of 1749, used by the Plenipotentiaries, commonly called "Map of the Courts," and the six authenticated copies thereof, made in 1751:

English translation . . . . III, 59-63
Portuguese text . . . . IV, 54-58

Special Instruction given on July 27, 1758, to the Commissioners of the 2d Demarcating Party:

Translation of the Spanish text . . . . III, 67-74
Spanish text . . . . . . IV, 61-67
Translation of the Portuguese text . . . I, 67-73
Portuguese text. . . . . . II, 64-69

Treaty of El Pardo, February 12, 1761:

English translation . . . III, 77-80
Portuguese text . . . IV, 71-74

279

280 APPENDIX.

	VOL.	PAGE.
Treaty of San Ildefonso, October 1, 1777:		
English translation	III,	83-104
Portuguese text	IV,	77-97
Royal Instruction dated Aranjuez, June 6, 1778, for the demarcation of boundaries, given to the Spanish Commissioners:		
English translation	III,	107-114
Spanish text	IV,	101-107
Special Instructions for the demarcation of boundaries in South America, proposed by General Vertiz, Viceroy of the provinces of the River Plate and approved by Carlos III., King of Spain, January 12, 1779:		
English translation	III,	115-134
Spanish text	IV,	108-126
Quotation of a Memorandum presented to Carlos III., of Spain, by Count de Floridablanca:		
English translation	III,	137-141
Spanish text	IV,	129-133
A few paragraphs of the Secret Instructions given by Carlos III., on July 8, 1787, to the Junta de Estado:		
English translation	III,	142-145
Spanish text	IV,	134-137
Brazilian Memorandum of November 26, 1857:		
English translation	III,	149-160
Original text	IV,	141-151
Treaty of Limits signed at Paraná, December 14, 1857 (not in force through the ratifications not having been exchanged):		
English translation	III,	161-165
Portuguese text	IV,	152-156

LIST OF DOCUMENTS. 281

	VOL. PAGE.
Approval of the Treaty of Limits of 1857 by the Argentine Congress and correspondence relating to the exchange of ratifications:	
English translation	III, 166-178
Original text	IV, 157-168
Treaty of Buenos-Aires, September 28, 1885, for the survey of the contested territory of Palmas:	
English translation	III, 181-189
Portuguese text	IV, 171-179
Treaty of Arbitration, September 7, 1889:	
English translation	III, 193-197
Portuguese text	IV, 183-186
Treaty of Montevideo, January 25, 1890 (rejected by the Brazilian Congress), for the division of the territory of Palmas:	
English translation	III, 201-203
Portuguese text	IV, 189-191
Report of the Special Committee of the Brazilian Chamber of Deputies upon the Treaty of Montevideo, January 25, 1890:	
English translation	III, 204-210
Portuguese text	IV, 192-198
Rejection of the Treaty of January 25, 1890, by the Brazilian Congress:	III, 211-212 IV, 199-200
Summary of the census of the Population in the Comarca (Judicial Division) of Palmas, December 31, 1891:	III, 215-220 IV, 203-208

LIST OF MAPS.

(All the Colored Maps are marked *.)

The Meridian Line of Demarcation agreed upon by Portugal and Spain at Tordesillas, June 7, 1494	Vol. I.	Page 16
Brazil, its contested territory, and the bordering countries* .	"	" 277
Map of Southern Brazil, showing that part of its territory claimed by the Argentine Republic* .	"	" 278
	Vol. V.	Vol. VI.
First Map of Paraguay by the Jesuits, XVIIth century . .	No. 1	No. 1 A
Paraguay by De l'Isle, 1703 .	No. 2	
Second Map of Paraguay by the Jesuits, 1722. Engraved at Rome, 1726	No. 3	No. 2 A
Augsburg edition . . .	No. 4	No. 3 A
Third Map of Paraguay by the Jesuits, 1732	No. 5	No. 4 A
Paraguay by d'Anville, 1733 .	No. 6	No. 5 A
Upper Uruguay by d'Anville, 1733	No. 7	
South America by d'Anville, 1748	No. 8	No. 6 A
Missions on the River Paraná and Uruguay by Quiroga, 1749. Engraved 1753 . . .	No. 9	

LIST OF MAPS. 283

	Vol. V.	Vol. VI.
The Map used by the Plenipotentiaries of Portugal and Spain in the negotiation of the Treaty of 1750, made at Lisbon, dated 1749, and commonly called "Map of the Courts" .		No. 7 A*
The above Map with several superpositions made under the direction of M. Emile Levasseur, of the Institut de France	No. 10	No. 8 A*
One of the copies of the Map dated 1749, made in 1751 at Lisbon		No. 9 A
Spanish Map drawn by Palomares (1750?)	No. 11*	
The same on a larger scale	No. 11bis	
Spanish Map of 1749 published by Borges de Castro . .	No. 11ter	
Paraguay by Bellin, 1756 . .	No. 12	No. 10 A
Spanish Map, probable date, 1760	No. 14	No. 11 A
Map of the frontier surveyed in 1759 and 1760, dated S. Nicolas, April 8, 1760	No. 13	No. 12 A*
Spanish Map by Millau, 1768 .	No. 15*	No. 13 A
Another by the same Millau, 1770		No. 14 A
South America by Sylveira Peixoto (Portuguese), 1768 . .		No. 15 A
South America by Captain Montanha (Portuguese), 1773 .		No. 16 A
South America by Olmedilla, 1775, the map used by the Spanish Plenipotentiary in the negotiation of the Treaty of 1777	No. 16	No. 17 A
Map of Paraguay, by Felix de Azara, dated 1787 . .	No. 17*	No. 18 A

APPENDIX.

	Vol. V.	Vol. VI.
Captainship of S. Paulo by Montezinho, 1791-1792 . .		No. 19 A
The contested territory. By the Spanish Commissioners after the second demarcation. Drawn by Cabrer . . .	No. 18	No. 20 A
The contested territory. By Miguel Lastarria (Spanish) 1804	No. 19	
Rio Grande do Sul and Montevideo, by Chagas Santos (Brazilian)		No. 21 A
Province of S. Pedro, by the Viscount de S. Leopoldo (Brazilian), 1839		No. 22 A
Argentine Map dated 1863 .		No. 23 A.
Argentine Map dated 1865 .		No. 24 A
Map of the contested territory surveyed by the Brazilian Argentine Joint Commission. Drawn by the Brazilian Commission	No. 20	No. 25 A*
The same Map, drawn by the Argentine Commission . .		No. 26 A
The official Map of 1749 (No. 10) compared with the Spanish Map of 1760 (No. 14) .	No. 21*	
The official Map of 1749 (No. 10) and the Map of the Brazilian-Argentine Joint Commission (No. 20)	No. 22*	
The Map of the 1st Portuguese and Spanish Joint Commission, dated 1760 (No. 13), and that of the Brazilian-Argentine Joint Commission (No. 20) .	No. 23*	
The Spanish Map of OLMEDÍLLA		

LIST OF MAPS.   285

	Vol. V.	Vol. VI.
(No. 16) compared with that of the Brazilian - Argentine Joint Commission (No. 20)	No. 24*	
The Map of 1749 (No. 10) compared with the Map by the Spanish Commissioners after the second Demarcation (No. 18)	No. 25*	
The Map of the Spanish Commissioners after the second Demarcation (No. 18) and that of the Brazilian - Argentine Joint Commission (No. 20)	No. 26*	
Fac-simile of several water-falls represented in Maps of the XVIIIth century	No. 27	
Mouth of the River Pepiry-Guaçû	No. 28	No. 27 A
Mouth of the Chapecó, called Pequirí-Guazú by the Spaniards after 1789		No. 28 A
Section of the Uruguay between the Guarita (the 2d Uruguay-Pita) and the Pepiry-Guaçû	No. 29	
River Iguaçû from the mouth of the S. Antonio to the Great Falls	No. 30	
Itinerary of Cabeza de Vaca	No. 31*	
Paraguay by W. J. Blaeuw (itinerary of Cabeza de Vaca)	No. 32	
Map of the Judicial Division (Comarca) of Palmas, in the Brazilian State of Paraná, of the Argentine Gobernacion of Misiones, and of a part of the Brazilian State of Rio Grande do Sul, showing the territory		

	Vol. V.	Vol. VI.
claimed by the Argentine Republic. Drawn up under the supervision of the Brazilian Special Mission at Washington by Rear-Admiral Guillobel .		No. 29 A*

www.ingramcontent.com/pod-product-compliance
Lightning Source LLC
Chambersburg PA
CBHW030747250426
43672CB00028B/1116